CONCRETE AND DUST

Concrete and Dust focuses on the performative nature of sexualized identity in Hollywood, the people that live in its underbelly and surrounding valleys, the sexual geographies of the place, and the ways in which sexual agency is mapped on the body and in consciousness. The cultural turn in ethnography has expanded the scope of ethnographic research methods, which now include innovative techniques that recognize and value sensuous scholarship (ethnographic works that incorporate visual, aural, and sensory texts). Hollywood has often been a focus in critical cultural theory; absent from the field is a provocative methodological perspective that collages visual image, arts-based ethnographic and autoethnographic narratives, experimental sound, poetry, and performative writing, in order to juxtapose the conflicting and complex performative nature of Hollywood, celebrity, glamour, and sexual agency.

Jeanine M. Mingé is Assistant Professor and Director of Performance Ensemble in the Department of Communication Studies at California State University, Northridge.

Amber Lynn Zimmerman is Assistant Professor in the Department of Drama and Speech Communication at the University of Waterloo.

INNOVATIVE ETHNOGRAPHIES
Editor: Phillip Vannini

The purpose of this series is to use the new digital technology to capture a richer, more multidimensional view of social life than was otherwise done in the classic, print tradition of ethnography, while maintaining the traditional strengths of classic, ethnographic analysis.

Available

Ferry Tales: Mobility, Place, and Time on Canada's West Coast
by Phillip Vannini

Digital Drama: Art Culture and Multimedia in Tanzania
by Paula Uimonen

Concrete, and Dust: Mapping the Sexual Terrains of Los Angeles
by Jeanine Mingé and Amber Lynn Zimmerman

Water in a Dry Land: Place-Learning through Art and Story
by Margaret Somerville

Forthcoming

Geographies of the Imagination: An Art Ethnography of Memories and Reflections on Exile
by Lydia Nakashima Deggarod

Beads, Bodies, and Transgressions: A Sensory Ethnography and Commodity Chain Analysis of Public Sex, Labor, and the Carnivalesque
by David Redmon

CONCRETE AND DUST
MAPPING THE SEXUAL TERRAINS OF LOS ANGELES

JEANINE M. MINGÉ AND
AMBER LYNN ZIMMERMAN

Routledge
Taylor & Francis Group

NEW YORK AND LONDON

First published 2013
by Routledge
711 Third Avenue, New York, NY 10017

Simultaneously published in the UK
by Routledge
2 Park Square, Milton Park, Abingdon, Oxon OX14 4RN

Routledge is an imprint of the Taylor & Francis Group, an informa business

Library of Congress Cataloging in Publication Data
Mingé, Jeanine.
  Concrete and dust: mapping the sexual terrains of Los Angeles/
  by Jeanine Mingé and Amber Lynn Zimmerman.
  p. cm.—(Innovative ethnographies)
  Includes bibliographical references and index.
  1. Sex in popular culture—California—Los Angeles—History.
  2. Sex—California—Los Angeles—History. I. Zimmerman, Amber
  Lynn. II. Title.
  HQ18.U5M56 2013
  306.70973—dc23   2012021430

ISBN: 978–0-415–80842–2 (hbk)
ISBN: 978–0-415–80843–9 (pbk)
ISBN: 978–0-203–07942–3 (ebk)

Typeset in Adobe Caslon and Copperplate
by Florence Production, Stoodleigh, Devon, UK

Printed and bound in the United States of America by
Walsworth Publishing Company, Marceline, MO.

FOR MILES AND ELLA

CONTENTS

MAPS

IMAGES

ACKNOWLEDGMENTS

By Jeanine M. Mingé

To Stacy Holman Jones for her encouragement, invaluable insight, dedicated mentorship, and forever friendship. Amira de la Garza for reading drafts, asking the difficult questions, and offering her higher wisdom. Patricia Geist Martin for believing in me, for encouraging me to write through the thick of it, and for teaching me how. I am forever grateful to these three wise women.

I would like to thank Michael Deragon for his artistic sensibility and collaboration on this project. He is a true artist. I am also grateful to my students and the Performance Ensemble at California State University, Northridge for guiding me through this difficult terrain. In difficult times, they offered me light on a dark trail. I am indebted to my colleagues in the Department of Communication Studies at California State University, Northridge for their personal and professional support. I would also like to thank the Mike Curb College of Arts, Media and Communication for their research support throughout this endeavor.

I would like to thank those closest to me for their sensuous consciousness and their generosities on this journey—Timothy Barrett, Nicole Embree, Stephanie Fugleberg, Bianca Smith, and Deborah Cloyed. To my Topanga family: Shari Geitzenauer, Richard Lee

Smith, Steven Smith, Megan Colvert, Phillip Boone, Zoei Alley, and Wil Sterner for community and grace. My father Ronald and mother Marilyn for their unwavering support, love, and faith in me and for always leading by example. To my siblings, Diana, Kristen, Marisa, and Steven for their laughter, their good will, honest reflection, and delicious hugs.

And to my love, John Burton Sterner, for arriving at just the right time.

By Amber Lynn Zimmerman

Many thanks to Diana Tigerlily, feminist performance scholar and friend, for the rich conversations we shared around this project. I am also appreciative of the scholars that have inspired me to witness and to create aesthetic experiences both critically and compassionately. Specifically, I pay homage to Craig Gingrich-Philbrook, Elyse Pineau, Ron Pelias, and Patricia Geist Martin. And to Sarah Lord for her capacity to listen, love, and offer critique when the pages weighed heavy on my mind.

From Both of Us

We are grateful to the editor of this series, Phillip Vannini, for making this project happen and for opening doors for artistic, creative, and innovative scholarship. And we are grateful to the reviewers, Brooke Wagner, University of Nevada, Las Vegas and Hunter Shobe, Portland State University for their time, energy, and insight.

Cover Image, Top of the World, courtesy of John Burton Sterner, Zoei Alley and Jeanine M. Mingé.

PREFACE

The Hollywood walk of fame attracts tourists who stand over a piece of concrete. They ogle the cemented names of stars, past and present.

The porn warehouses in Chatsworth, CA attract women and men trying to make it in Hollywood. Their lucky break happens while bent over chairs, on silk sheets, on kitchen floors, performing sexual acts for the camera.

My friends drag me, literally, into a Hollywood club and I am transported into a world I don't quite understand—women in stiletto heels and barely-there dresses, where bottles of alcohol are sold for thousands of dollars to those that can afford and so desire to sit in this space of privilege.

The stripper at Jennie's in Hollywood finds power in flaunting her body and makes double what I make as a college professor.

I lay huddled in a ball on some bed in Germany after he raped me.

Today, I run up the shifting trail and reach the top of the
mountain. I can see all of Los Angeles, a sprawling stretch of
landscape of concrete and dust.

* * *

This book focuses on the performative nature of sexualized identity
in Los Angeles, the people that live in its underbelly and valleys, the
sexual terrain of place, and the ways in which sexual agency is mapped
on the body and in consciousness. The cultural turn in ethnography
has expanded the scope of ethnographic research methods, which now
include innovative techniques that recognize and value sensuous
scholarship; ethnographic texts that incorporate the visual, aural, and
sensory writ large. The spatial turn in cultural studies and the cultural
turn in geography allow us to consider space and place as important
factors in determining the nature of our interactions, identities, and
experiences. Whereas Hollywood has often been a focus in critical
cultural theory, absent from the field is a holistic methodological
perspective that collages visual image, arts-based ethnographic and
autoethnographic narratives, experimental sound, poetry, and performative writing, in order to juxtapose the conflicting and complex performative nature of Los Angeles, celebrity, glamour, and sexual agency.

Our methodological approach is what we call arts-based autoethnography of place. We collected and storied field notes and informal
conversations as well as more arts-based ethnographic data, such as
photographs that mark everyday scenes and place-specific phenomena;
found sound recordings developed into compositions; collected cultural
objects that take collage form to evoke kinesthetic experience; and
sketches and paintings that reflect place-specific experiences. The
integration of these elements is the creation of this text. We use
performative writing, site-specific photography, artistic renderings of
place, and found sound recordings, and intend for this work to be a
model of the ways in which traditional ethnographic research methods
can collage and collide with visual, aural, and aesthetically driven texts
to create a holistic and embodied arts-based autoethnographic text.

This innovative arts-based ethnography, grounded within performance theory, critically examines the vulture-like or carnivorous nature

of Los Angeles. The city is in many ways ephemeral, difficult to pin down. There is a strange push and pull between objectification and power. We know the sexualized body as object holds power—but whose, how, and to what extent? How does a conceptualization of sexual agency shift in memory, embodied memory of sexual trauma, power, languaged violence masked as deep love, past personal experiences heavily materialized in the local acts of strained connections in Los Angeles? I navigate the empty promises made in this vulnerable city.

Examining Los Angeles, the hub of consumer culture, from a performative lens, as liminal space, exile, a multifaceted stage for performed identity, and glamorized image of celebrity, uncovers the unnerving dynamics of the sexualized body and power, memory and presence. The book introduces the reader to various characters that live in Los Angeles, and versions of the primary author, Jeanine, to whom "I" refers throughout these pages, who strives to find sexual agency in the mysterious echoes of memory, and the concrete and colorful LA. The book is a collage of personal narrative, participant observation, interviews, performance, found sound, photography, painting, poetry, and mediated imagery that holistically draws the reader into the painful underbelly of LA, celebrity culture, and sexual agency. This is an engagement of the senses that allows the reader to experience place. The intersection of linguistic, artistic, tactile, and visual texts creates a hybrid arts-based autoethnographic method, as well as a hybrid ontological position that represents an ecologically diverse range of discourses, ideologies, subject positions, and possibilities.

In contrast to books that use traditional ethnographic methods, or semiotic analyses of the advertisements, or solely theoretically driven texts, this book focuses on site-specific arts-based autoethnographic engagement with both the people and the terrain of various places within the county of Los Angeles. Each place-specific collage contends with the various negotiations of sexual agency—lost memory, re-memberings, sexualized interactions with men and women, mapping the way in which a body can get lost here, swimming in the sea of dust and trauma. How does a conceptualization of sexual agency shift in memory, embodied memory of sexual trauma, power, languaged violence masked as deep love, past personal experiences heavily materialized in the local acts of strained connections in Los Angeles? I navigate the empty promises made in this vulnerable city. The intersection of linguistic, artistic, tactile, and visual texts creates a hybrid arts-based autoethnographic method, as well as a hybrid ontological position that represents an ecologically diverse range of discourses, ideologies, subject positions, and possibilities.

The book is accompanied by collages uploaded on the Innovative Ethnographies website. The collage is made up of two parts, the visual and the aural. The first component of the collage is a visual juxtaposition of photographic text, poetry, and found object collage. The second component of the collage is site-specific found sound. The found sound is composed into five different original sound compositions that speak directly to the experience of each site and each chapter of the book. The sound composition is an original piece designed by multimedia artist Michael Deragon. Each sound composition is approximately four minutes in length and appears alongside the visually based component of the collage.

There are two audiences for this book. The first audience is comprised of current residents of Los Angeles and those interested in celebrity culture and the nature of Los Angeles from an insider perspective. It is also for those who are interested in the process of understanding and finding homeplace, both internally and in geographic space.

The book will also interest scholars and students of performance studies, queer studies, cultural studies, gender studies, sexuality studies, urban studies, American studies, cultural geography, and popular culture studies.

INTRODUCTION

LOS ANGELES RIVER[1]

Image 0.1 Los Angeles River

River.

> Grey space. Concrete. Flash of green.
> Grey Space. Concrete. Plastic Bag.
>
> Flash.
>
> Human body.
> Roar of truck. Exhaust puff. Silence.
>
> Grey Space. Plastic Bag. Blue tent.
>
> Flash.
>
> Human body.
> Lost sky.

The Pulse.

If you go looking for the pulse of New York in Los Angeles County, you will never find it. There is no city center. The pulse of place is scattered throughout LA's various locations.

River Theatre.

At a community-based theatre production set next to the river, the people talk about their losses, the deaths, the gang activity, and their love for the LA River. They are the river, the river is them. This place is their home.

An actor costumed as a turtle gasps for water.
He dies a dusty death.

> I hear him say, "It's a concrete river."
>
> I hear him say, "There is so much life there. It's just not what you might think about when you think river."
>
> I hear him say, "I just don't love you like that."
>
> I hear her say, "Rape really fucks with you."

Dry Bed.

> The dry bed of what was once contains the detritus of Los Angeles's fantasies. The river was there, then it wasn't. When

it wasn't there—when it was being diverted through tunnels and aqueducts and tunnels—and even when it was there, it was on its way to Los Angeles, but that was the fate of most rivers in the desert.[2]

Eyes.

I look at them, only in their eyes. I wait for the connection. For any spark.

We are all, after all, on this brink or the next. We are all here, together.

Mirage.

A layer of dust,
concrete slab after concrete slab
structures this desert terrain.

A thirsty newcomer.
I gasp.
Crawl towards then away from
Hollywood, an oasis.

I do not know if I will survive here.

Terminator.

An actor on a small motorcycle weaves through the puddles sparsely placed in the concrete wasteland. We hear the strain of the tiny motor, watch his face in pain, he quickly glances over his shoulder.

Then we see him, the robot from the future, the monster. The terminator flies over the overpass and lands onto the concrete river. Without emotion in his face and his eyes hidden behind black sunglasses grabs the boy off of his moving scooter onto the much more masculine Harley. He pulls out a shotgun and blows out the tire of the Mack truck that is following closely behind. The yellow wasteland now a wrecking yard is the perfect Hollywood backdrop for this violent destruction.

A few years after this film was shot, the actor was elected into State office. Most Californian's laugh and call him the "govinator."

Crumpled Bed Sheets

> the hotel attendant will straighten them
> after we've left our shadows of sex, and lust,
> and desire dancing on the wall.

To Travel.

One of Los Angeles' defining characteristics is the need to travel, to get from one location to the next. We sit in our cars or on a bus that moves along at a snail's pace. Los Angeles is a drive-by culture. Architecture, cityscapes, and city plans are based upon the automobile. Los Angeles' reliance on the automobile diverted people from the subway system. Downtown architects attempted to account for the automobile, erecting parking lots and ramps, eradicating the usable green space, the walkable spaces, the pulse of a city.

To get across the 4,000 square miles of Los Angeles we need to travel.

In this travel we become isolated, isolating, trapped in steel and rubber, and moving across concrete.

Disconnect.

In Los Angeles County, because the space is so vast and shifting, it is difficult to connect outside of your own community. People segregate based on social position, physicality, geographic location, and interest. "The average hyperindustrial modern city is a cluster—or more likely, sprawl—of diverse and unconnected interests, linked by phone lines and shared sewage systems but otherwise exclusive and mute."[3] One can exist without knowing what people are going through, what their struggles and successes are, what keeps them awake at night, and how they sleep, where they sleep, and with whom they sleep.

The River.

> A rubber, a duck, a weed.

> Compartmentalized
> rainwater stagnates in green pools.
> seemingly still.

A piece of plastic bag floats in the air,
in the hollow space where flowing water should be.

Flash.

Eagle Rock, Marina Del Ray.

Malibu. In and under light sky. Waves crash. We ate
lavishly. And laughed.
It is not my home.

Santa Monica
4th Street Promenade. We shopped. Caught a movie. Stared
at the ocean from above.
It is not my home.

Compton, Hawthorne, El Segundo, Pacoima
I've never entered these spaces.

Travel Time.

We are defined by how long it takes to get from place to place.
Anywhere and everywhere in Los Angeles takes 20 minutes. But this
timeframe inevitably turns into 40 minutes, an hour, two hours. All of
these projected times depend on traffic.

Geographically Desirable.

In Los Angeles saying that someone is "geographically desirable" means
that the prospective person you will date lives close enough to you to
sustain a relationship. There are so many bodies, and relationship
prospects, that Los Angeles traffic is a deciding factor on whether or
not to begin or sustain that relationship.

Access.

Traveling in Los Angeles takes time, miles, money, access, patience,
and sometimes a little bit of luck.

There are those who do not travel.

The way in which we are encouraged, permitted, and able, to
physically move about the world; the ways we are denied or allowed

to walk to school, or cross a street, or ride a bicycle; the literal signs, signs that tell us when to walk, where to turn, when to exit, and where— they are all politically charged and threaded with power and ideology.

Whose City.

Jane Jacobs once said, "Cities have the capability of providing something for everybody, only because, and only when, they are created by everybody."[4]

Materializations of Power.

Our every day performances, our actions of everyday living are materializations of structures of power, of choices made by other human beings to construct, to deconstruct, to create space. The specific configurations of space are manifested by choices made by human beings because their own experiences in the world are certainly tied to ideology. In Los Angeles, the water we drink is shuffled from some other location, taken from another community.

Cars.

Break lights. Horns.
I see the shadows of each lover, friend, and stranger come
alive, pass me on this highway.
Break lights. Horns.
Ani's Saab, Henry's restored Ford,
Mark's Rolls Royce, Scott's Chevy work truck.
Break lights. Horns.

I pass the man on the side of the freeway entrance holding his sign, begging for money. These shadows, encounters of a brief time, have shaped me, crafted a new version and knowing of a life lived in the places of Los Angeles.

Breakdown.

My hands shake. I can't catch my breath. I was his object, the object for sexual pleasure, his pleasure. I walk in the rain towards the cafeteria on campus. My knees want to buckle. I tell myself, "Keep walking." I hold my body tighter to keep my limbs from falling off one by one.

Tourist Snapshot.

San Pedro,

Long Beach.
Rehearsed here once. Drove onto campus. Through town.
This is not my home.

Culver City, Tarzana, Sherman Oaks.

Studio City.
Had a coffee. Watched a play. Stood on the concrete
sidewalk and congratulated him on a job well done. I hear
actors live there.
I do not live here.

Isolation.

Kingwell, through the lens of the postmodern condition frames urban center in the following light. "Always the city represents both hope and danger. There are many ways of being in the city, together and alone. Isolations can sometimes be a function of destiny, not sparseness."[5]

Isolation fueled my desire to write this book, to come to make sense of place in a city so vast and stretched. In each of the geographic terrains, I tried to make sense of my own personal subjectivities, sexual agency, place within community and body. And along the way, I met and engaged with other characters, people, as lives that intersect, even if only for a brief time. These intersections created both synergy and moments of discord in certain places. "The contact zones of the city are thus a constitutive feature of the simultaneous and iterative reshaping of place and identity. They become Goffmanesque stages of contestation, subversion, and disruption."[6]

These conundrums, moments of discord, have a lot to teach us about the ways we create pockets of communities, temporary places in which to thrive and grow.

Witness.

When I bear witness, I cannot turn my head in ignorance.[7]

The Tourist.

Los Angeles' geography creates the potential tourist body. Because there are over eighty-eight incorporated cities and far more subdivisions in Los Angeles County, there is the potentiality to become a tourist within your own city, your own county. As I move from Burbank into Malibu or from West Hollywood into Eagle Rock, Compton, Downtown LA, 20 minutes from the other, and worlds apart, I become a tourist. Watching, listening, engaging, all with a feeling of not belonging to the place.

Resuscitation.

The city is gasping.

Closing Gates.

> This desert, or vast plain of sand, called by some an extinct or dry lake, is locked in on all sides by rock-ribbed mountains whose peaks mount upward among the clouds. One could imagine oneself descending into the valley of death and having the gates closed after him.[8]

Sunrise.

When the sun rises, those sleeping on the street pick up their things in a grand chorus of fluttering sleeping bags, the breakdown of tents and movement of shopping carts. They begin walking . . . somewhere.

INTRODUCTION

LOS ANGELES RIVER, REVISITED

To most Angelinos, if they were aware of the Los Angeles River at all, any reference to it seemed like a joke; a smile or chuckle or jest followed. If it was a joke, it was a bad joke to laugh at—Los Angeles *is* the river and the river *is* Los Angeles.

—*Philip L. Fradkin*[9]

The Los Angeles River begins in the San Fernando Valley and weaves its way through Los Angeles County through channels on a concrete course. The Los Angeles Aqueduct, a constructed system channeling water from Owens River, also weaves its way through Los Angeles County. The Aqueduct was instrumental in post-World War Two development and industrialization. Following these two waterways through the county, we can see how the harnessing of the natural world provided life within rocky desert terrain, a world that is both lush and devastating. The allure and promise of Los Angeles is built on a concrete foundation that contains and directs water. If a community has enough water, it can create an intricate web of life that allows people to think beyond basic survival to aesthetic wants. The most influential areas in history were built around a steady flow of water.[10] The flow allows and accelerates human potential.

Within Los Angeles County there are over eighty-eight incorporated cities and far more subdivisions, each with their own striking characteristics. People choose to live in an area because of its character, personality, and its geographic charm. Some are forced into subdivisions, the gentrification process demarcated clearly in an ever-moving pattern.[11] Some have no home at all. Each of us is a part of the terrain, a part of the landscape. Identity is marked by and shaped by the map and the land. And the land is shaped by our subjectivities, and the material and embodied way we live, play, and work in that space.[12]

Another concrete channel in Los Angeles is the highway system. We sit in cars, trapped in the mobility of an automobile, that drives us from town to town, city to city.[13] Our cars keep us from one another. We move in patterns, like snails, or ants marching, one by one. The shadows of the bobbing head in the driver seat are mostly solo commuters on their way to work, to home, to another destination. On the journey through Los Angeles, we are all alone. Los Angeles is 4,083 square miles. The network of interstate freeways is immense, complex, congested. We move at crawling paces up Interstate 5, 105, 405, 605, 10, 110, 210, 710 and the US Route 101 that dumps cars into Hollywood.

In this book, we follow my journey to make sense of sexual identity within six marked locations within the greater Los Angeles County. I am a white, middle-class, privileged woman who is able to drive through and navigate certain areas with relative ease. I also carry the privilege of being blonde and physically fit, qualities that offer greater social access to certain areas in Los Angeles. These markers also make the navigation of certain areas more difficult. I am aware of the segmented and disjointed nature of Los Angeles, neighborhoods divided by race, nationality, and economic status. Movement in between these segregated neighborhoods is not as easily managed, each body a physical marker, each body categorized. Each body is also an individual person, moving through these cultural, social, and political expectations.

Place demands certain expectations of the body, expectations that have been cultivated through terrain, industry, and cultural values.[14] I come to understand my body through my own subjectivity, which has emerged through experiences of culture grounded in local, social, political, contextually based experiences and intersections of race, class, gender, and sexual orientation. When the expectations of Los Angeles exceed or conflict with my subjectivity, I feel a loss of agency. Within each place throughout Los Angeles there are differently marked expectations, all of which are connected to the sensory experiences of place as well as the social connections made with those that live, work, and play there. Place is also rooted in the geographic elements of the terrain. In Los Angeles, it is easy to question the terrain of the body, identity, and memory because the terrain seems to be slipping, rooted in nothing but the foundation of concrete and dust. Because of a past sexual trauma and my lack of connection with Los Angeles, I find myself disconnected from my body, my emotions, and subsequently my relationships. This is also a journey back to an empowered sense of self in sexual and emotional relationships.

The book is divided into eleven chapters crafted through use of a methodology that we call arts-based autoethnography of place.

Arts-based Research.

Arts-based research has carved a space in interpretive, qualitative methods in several disciplines.[15] For example, arts-based research is a methodology used in Education, Sociology, Communication, and Anthropology.[16] Like poststructural feminists, arts-based researchers believe that realities are multiple and complex. Arts-based researchers argue that there are many ways to know and represent the world. Within arts-based research, knowledge about this world is constructed into an artistic form of experience. Art is not a *representation* of the world or language but *is* itself world and language.[17] The intersection of linguistic, artistic, tactile, and visual elements creates what arts-based researchers call a hybrid method, as well as a hybrid ontological position. Carol A. Mullen[18] asks researchers to explore arts-based research as "an art gallery of conversational (and-ever-changing) montages, hybrid paradigms, mirrors of practice, doors to constructive change, spaces for open scripts, and synergistic circles."[19] As part of an interdisciplinary hybrid approach to inquiry, arts-based scholars are shifting the discussion from product to process. The question for many arts-based researchers is:

> But how do I *engage* in arts-based research? This displacement from *what does it look like*, which emphasizes a product driven representation of research, to an *active participation of doing and meaning-making* within research texts, is a rupture that opens up new ways of conceiving of research as an active space of living inquiry."[20]

This act of rendering[21] is a call back and forth between visual discourse and text. This document is not neat, but splattered.

Autoethnography.

According to Harry Wolcott the term autoethnography was first used to describe a method of ethnographically studying a group of which you are a part.[22] Today, autoethnography encompasses a multitude of terms and writing forms such as Crawford's personal ethnography,[23] Ellis and Bochner's reflexive ethnography,[24] Ellis's emotional sociology,[25] Wolcott's ethnographic autobiography,[26] Ronai-Rambo's layered account,[27] Denzin's experiential texts,[28] and Reed-Danahay's auto-biographical ethnography.[29] The autoethnographic method focuses on the self-narrative, or autobiographical voice, within social as well as spatial contexts. Tami Spry recognizes autoethnography as "the reflections and refractions of multiple selves in contexts that arguably transform the authorial 'I' to an existential 'we.'"[30] Our multiple layers of experience connect us all.

Knowledge is subjective and deeply connected to the knower. Norman K. Denzin states that autoethnography turns the "ethnographic gaze inward on the self (auto), while maintaining the outward gaze of ethnography, looking at the larger context where self experiences occur."[31] Carolyn Ellis states that this blending of forms and style highlights "the aesthetic sensibility and expressive forms of art."[32] One of the goals of autoethnography is to "practice an artful, poetic, and empathetic social science in which readers can keep in their minds and feel in their bodies the complexities of concrete moments of lived experience."[33]

Methodological Process.

I, Jeanine, the primary author, have lived and worked in Los Angeles for six years, engaging in the area as a participant observer. The place has mapped onto my identity, creating a rich ground for personal narrative, reflection, and analysis. And reciprocally, I have mapped and marked these different places, impacting people and terrain I encountered. Through the first five years, I collected and storied field notes and informal conversations. I also collected more arts-based ethnographic data: photographs that mark everyday scenes and place-specific phenomena; found sound recordings developed into composi-tions; collected cultural objects that take collage form to evoke kinesthetic experience; and sketches and paintings that reflect place-specific experiences. The integration of these elements is the creation of this text.

The authorial first-person voice in the text, 'I', marks the personal experience of the primary author while simultaneously standing in as a composite character from Los Angeles. The use of 'we' in the revisiting chapters marks both the primary and secondary authors' reflexive and theoretical unpacking of the narrative journey. The collective 'we' is a charge to the authors and readers to reflexively make sense of their own terrains.

The first person character, Jeanine, reflects the scholar as aesthete or an actor who turns life into art;[34] a performance of open subjectivity, where art and life are always a work in progress, commenting on each other to bring about change in both arenas.[35] Moreover, other characters that emerge in the text are inspired by real people but are ultimately composite characters. The use of characters participates in an arts-based aesthetic and focuses the autoethnographic narrative on textuality and communicability to reveal subjugated realities.[36]

While the narrative arc captures Jeanine's experiences within Los Angeles, the methodological process was collaborative. While auto-ethnographic research is primarily understood as a solo endeavor, we argue that autoethnographic inquiry is and can be collaborative. We found beauty in creating a collaborative autoethnography[37] as experi-ences are often best understood through sharing, discussing, and reflecting with a trusted friend. Jeanine wrote her autoethnographic stories and sent them to Amber who researched and uncovered the theoretical influences; grounding the experiences in the theoretical. We both collaborated in writing the sections on revisiting, offering multiple understandings of Jeanine's experiences within LA. In this way, the reflections and revisiting sections come from varying perspectives, broadening and deepening the experience of revisiting each place. The process for us was deeply interconnected, shifting and shipping pages back and forth. Over the past three years, we have stayed on the phone for hours across countries, asking questions, digging deeper, cutting, and rewriting. Our process is unique in its vulnerability, trust, and honor.

Place.

Analytic and reflexive writing collide in a collage of found sound, image, and narratives based on a specific place in Los Angeles. Scholars in various disciplines have long been crafting the definition and nature of space, place, and identity.[38] We understand place as the aesthetic qualities of the built environment that are inseparable from the natural environment and that impact identity, subjectivity, and the construction and reconstruction of memory.[39] The character of place is also determined by how people feel in space, how they experience space, tactilely, emotionally, and conceptually.[40] We hear stories from friends about home, their love for a certain place to which they once traveled.

We come to know place experientially, engaging with our senses. We also attach these places to specific memories and experiences.[41] "People make attachments to places that are critical to their well-being or distress. An individual's sense of place is both a biological response to the surrounding physical environment and a cultural creation, as geographer."[42] This book captures these senses, brings them alive for the reader using arts-based methodologies, crafting an experiential knowledge of Los Angeles, even if the reader is miles and years away. Within each place people create social relations that intersect and intertwine with perception. We draw out the aesthetic of experiencing place and the politics of place as contested territory. The character of a place is highly political, made of various subjectivities.[43] The various dimensions and materializations of race, class, gender, and sexual orientation impact my understanding and development of sexual agency as a character that navigates the places within Los Angeles.

Each chapter is driven by a specific location in Los Angeles and is listed in order of appearance in the book: Burbank, Chatsworth, The Hollywood Hills, West Hollywood, and Topanga Canyon. Each of these sites contributes to the overarching narrative of the book, and introduces us to several other characters that help to make sense of sexual trauma, sexual agency, and objectification in Los Angeles. After each narrative chapter, we revisit the stories of place to theoretically unpack the implications of experiencing the perceived expectations of place. We also hope to reconcile and chart the adversities and resolutions that I experience there.

Maps.

Between each chapter there is a map, a travel route that introduces the complex and isolating process of travel in Los Angeles. These maps are mixed media and digital collages that were created to mirror the essence of each chapter.

Additionally, the product of arts-based autoethnography is collages, which are a collision of personal narrative, participant observation, interviews, performance, found sound, photography, painting, poetry, and mediated imagery that holistically draws the reader into the painful underbelly of Hollywood, celebrity culture, and how the place influences sexual agency. These collages are accessible on our website. Please visit it to deepen and broaden your experience of each place covered in this book. A brief content overview follows.

When I first moved to Los Angeles County, my partner and I moved to *Burbank*. Most people that move to the greater Los Angeles area are shocked into the system of the entertainment industry. Many people feel a sense of displacement, which is the in-between or the liminal space; in Los Angeles, a city formed through frontier narrative, it is between commodity and consciousness, between purchase and desire, between lack and almost enough. Displacement is in excessive movement, never stillness, in this city of steel and concrete, stillness between the honk and the halt, the flutter of absences, the desire for more and for connection—any connection, or perhaps connection just long enough for you to remember my name—in the morning. Manifesting displacement, through the new concept of dis-memberment, my partner Ani and I move further away from one another and separate into different realities in Los Angeles.

I found a job as a bartender in *Chatsworth* and quickly discovered that this area of the San Fernando Valley is the Porn Capitol of the United States. After meeting, interviewing, and encountering porn actors and distributors, I became hyper aware of the overt sexuality of this part of Los Angeles. I write into the text an alter ego named Sophie and engage in imagined what-if scenarios, a hypersexual of my own body and the nature of my sexual encounters. Sophie is a version of Jeanine, an alter ego developed within the very real place of the valley. Sophie, the porn star, moves through Chatsworth to make sense of "agency" in sex. Sophie, the porn star, attempts to become what resides here in order to understand how a place shifts and materializes sexual identity and agency and yet grapples with the concept of disconnect. We are disconnected from the grotesque narrative. The grotesque narrative as a theoretical and practical reality often goes unexplored in academic texts. We don't often hear how the land is ravaged, mutilated as a form of cultivating place. Writing the grotesque narrative becomes a form of sexual, environmental, and academic agency. Agency is naming, reframing, and performing an identity that suits us, without the restrictions of essentialisms that both order and narrow our conceptualization of sexual possibility.

I begin to spend time in the *Hollywood Hills* with a group of old friends, all transplants, who relocated to LA from the east coast. Most people believe that if you live in the Hollywood Hills, you have made it. In these hills I reconnect with these women who have, in some ways, become the embodiment of LA plastique. No one is ever satisfied in the plastique. Plastique is not skin. I connect with the place, and begin to see my body as landscape, manipulate and stretch my own skin. This chapter connects performativity of sexual identity to the process of visual objectification and the layers of desire, lack, and privilege. The expectation of the place of the hills impacts me so much so that I continuously doubt my visual aesthetic. I feel both too large and powerless in a culture of manufactured beauty. In the hills, a plastique statue melts in the sun.

West Hollywood is a mapped and marked queer safe space that functions on a classist division. In this scene, queer bodies are commodified and ranked by sexuality and sexual preference. Ever since Ani and I split, I've not met a prospective female partner. Not purposely, I have only met prospective partners that are male. This renders me on the outside of the spaces in this place, as the most valuable bodies are those that have clear identity markers of gay or lesbian. Those that exceed these binary markers have less social access and are often ostracized. As a woman that identifies as queer, who loves and is attracted to people, no matter their gender identity or their biological sex, I do my best to hold on to my sexual agency and identity in this place, even as others try to deny my subjectivity. As I navigate these tensions I realize there is a demand for an aesthetic accuracy of identity to be marked as queer. I also find that West Hollywood exists within a performance of limited survivability because what it means to perform a queer sexual identity is limited.

Geographically, *Topanga Canyon* is nestled between the San Fernando Valley and Malibu. It is an exquisite landscape, with high peaks and jagged rocks. A creek runs through it. After years of living in Burbank, exploring the previous locations in Los Angeles, I move to the canyon for respite, retreat, and reflection. Topanga welcomes scavengers, squatters, and people searching through demons. I become a scavenger, living and learning about the pieces of her sexual identity. A sensuous consciousness is cultivated and developed as I become closer to understanding my body, the terrain, home, and community.

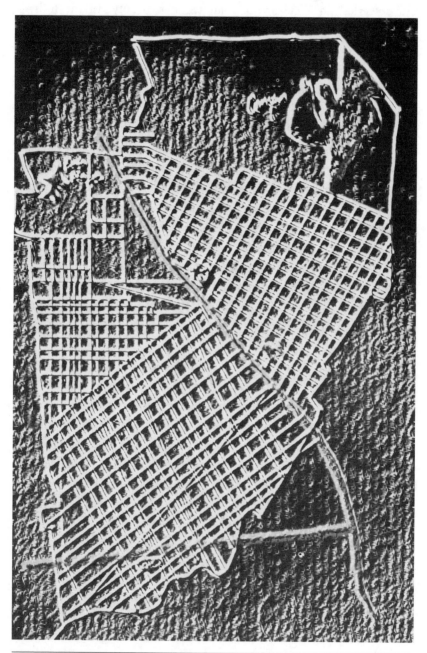

Map 1.1 Burbank[44]

1
BURBANK[45]

Image 1.1 Above Burbank

Main House.

> Behind a main house on a strip of concrete
> a woman laughs. The neighbor hears.
>
> Behind a front façade
> sit rows upon rows upon rows of apartment boxes.
> A Perfect City.
> The TV is always on.
>
> A man coughs. The neighbor hears.
> Murmurs in the main house.
> She sleeps
>
> with the TV on.

Never.

I never wanted to move to LA.

Fog.

A west coast mist covers the street this Sunday morning, the sky a cloud grey. No hint of rain, just fistfuls of fog batter in the air, in my lungs. The street at 7am is dark, blank except the yellow glow of a street lamp. I stand on a damp sidewalk waiting for something to move, someone to speak. One small black Toyota truck shifts into second gear and putters up the street.

Here.

"It's always been my dream," she says as we slip and snake naked legs. I move my fingers over her brown freckled shoulders.

"I know, babe. I know. And I think you should go. I *know* you should go. I will wait for you." My heart stutters then sinks as my words move smoothly from me.

"Would you come with me?"

"Yes," I say dreamily. I slip into her skin, wrap my arms around her body.

Place.

I moved to Los Angeles, Burbank specifically, in 2007, while writing my dissertation to follow my girlfriend who left three months earlier than I. She wanted to make it in Hollywood. I had to finish my semester.

I see jazz hands, the kick of the dancing foot and the wicked grin. I hear in singsong, "Hollywood. De de dena na na Hollywood."

I did not know it might destroy me, certainly destroy us, in the mean time.

A place seeps into the body—as you become a part of the landscape, through the rhythm of the surrounding cars, the jingle of keys, the stubble of grass against naked skin—the snap of a broken heart.

I am not a victim.

Phone Call.

She calls. "Hey Babe, I'm on set right now. You are never going to believe it. Yea, Kelly H. is a bitch. She is like walking around here as if she shat gold." I listen with an aching heart to her stories about her new job on set, the scandals, the insecurities, the falsities, and the promises of success. I have a few months until I join her. I don't know if I really want to go.

"Rolling!" She calls out and by default into my ear, then, she whispers, "I gotta go Babe. I'll call you in the morning. I love you."

I hang up and on this tan sofa in Florida. I look at our dogs curled at my feet. I hear the silence. I begin to cry.

From the east coast, I imagine the strange world she lives in. I can see her sleepy over the wheel, driving an hour from her Aunt and Uncle's home in Thousand Oaks into Los Feliz to cart stars from their trailers to the set. I see her getting coffee, kombucha, and water for their parched lips.

I hear her say, "You'll never believe who was doing blow in their trailer."

I hear her say, "Yea, they are all unbelievably skinny."

I hear her say, "Of course I'm attracted to her. She's an actress.

She is supposed to be beautiful."

I hear her say, "Craft services, yea, they get them whatever food they want. But D, she only eats salad and salmon. I don't think L eats at all."

I hear her say, "We've all been propositioned. Non-union members will do anything for a union card. Jack just got a blowjob in his car during lunch. The bastard didn't even give her a voucher."

I hear her say, "I love you."

She is "making it" in the entertainment industry, working as a production assistant. She has started at the bottom rung to move on up the ladder. It's a world I don't quite understand. Like Dungeons and Dragons, people in the entertainment industry maneuver unions and guilds, gain entry with time spent at the bottom. Pay their dues and yet, some don't make it quite like they thought they would. The rungs of this ladder seem oiled. At the top is a cloud that most fall thru.

Spool.

A large spool of rope just bounced off a truck and rolled past me into the oncoming traffic. I wait for the accident. Fear the swerve of the car that avoids it and jumps onto this sidewalk and smashes into my body.

Entertainment.

Much of the growth of Burbank echoes that of the entertainment industry. By 1940 Warners, Columbia Pictures and Walt Disney Studios all had locations in Burbank. In the next two decades they were joined by television's NBC, and the phrase, 'Beautiful Downtown Burbank' became a familiar refrain in TV-tied American households.[46]

And yet, Burbank is the hidden entertainment town in Los Angeles. At least to those on the outside, Burbank is not a recognized destination city. Tourists find the walk of fame first. They travel over the hill that separates Hollywood from the valley. And most are shocked to discover the rows upon rows of studio lots in Burbank. The clean city, the perfect city, hides behind the fantasy, glamour, and rot of Hollywood.

Airport.

The plane lands with a fickle jump.

Outside the airport, we embrace.

Kiss.

I feel overwhelmed, anxious.

I feel my fat jiggle.

I know my plastic sunglasses look quite silly.

Prada, Louis Vitton bags, teacup dogs. Fluffy boots.

Skinny jeans that fit emaciated bodies.

A wave of fear.

The browned roots show through my blonde hair.

A cacophony of insecurity.

I get in the car.

My yellowed teeth show behind this half-hearted smile.

The Frontier.

People migrated from the east, in search of gold, in search of the promise in change, to conquer the Western Frontier. In caravans, on foot, on horseback, one by one, two by two, town by town, homestead by homestead, California was a frontier of promise, or purpose and hope.

This frontier with the powerful Pacific and magnificent mountain range, green valleys, was on the surface magnificent. And yet, California, Los Angeles territory specifically was unabashedly painful, difficult to settle.

Blue Screen.

Standing on San Fernando Boulevard, the Verdugo Mountains a backdrop, like a canvas painted in perfect light, a blue screen. I wonder if at any moment, a cartoon bunny rabbit might break through the screen. Show me it is really an illusion.

Downtown Burbank.

Perpendicular to my street runs San Fernando road, which was once a trail that ran east to west. It now houses a revitalized Downtown Burbank. On the east end, the village district, red brick patches of road, break up the monotonous concrete. Quaint shops with bright signs, colorful banners, lettering, offer interesting consumer possibility —a gym, a tailor, another restaurant, a hair salon, a beauty school. Shop after shop, the one road village has a walk-able sense of community.

From the village, one block north is the civic center, an immense concrete structure, with floors of windows, a bronze statue of a Burbank police officer, a firefighter. Burbank, its own incorporated city in Los Angeles County, has its own fire station, its own city police. There are more police per capita than in other areas in Los Angeles. Some find this comforting. Others, with something to hide, notice that they are always patrolling, always watching.

Part of the revitalization boasts, on the west end, the Mall district with three different AMC movie theaters all right next to each another. Shop after shop after shop, then the mall, inside, shop after shop after shop. Then, on the north side of the mall, an IKEA, restaurants, all corporate restaurants lined next to double/triple parking. There are fourteen parking garages in a nine-block stretch of shops.

I don't like to shop.

I rarely have time to watch movies.

I do join the gym.

(Dis)placement: In (dis)memberment.

Since I've moved here, I've felt, no, created a sense of non-belonging,

I've purposively forgotten. Her. Him. The rape. The loss.

(Dis)memberment is comprised of forgetting, the detachment of limbs, and the disconnection of embodied memory from experience. (Dis)memberment, with organs on a steel slab, the heart's arrhythmia— a resentful rhythm that shapes cancerous cells as borders between her and me, borders between my past sexual trauma and who I am today. The body parts bleeding, in patches, in layers, creates a process of dehumanization, of othering someone so you can't feel them, feel the love or hate there anymore. (Dis)memberment creates an inability to articulate experience. You break the nerves, disconnect tendons, stretch skin until it snaps, and burn exposed skin so you can't feel. (Dis)memberment is a temporary solution, a survival tactic. (Dis)memberment is (dis)placement from our bodies, from our sense of identity, security, a sense of being somewhere safe.

Dead Flowers.

There are flowers rotting in the vase on top of my bookshelf.

On Saturdays I go to the Burbank farmers market in Downtown Burbank. There, I sniff peaches but never buy them. I don't like the way the peach juice grabs the insides of my cheeks and pulls them in tightly. I buy one jalapeño pepper, one green, one yellow, one red pepper. One bunch of broccoli for one dollar. I move in and out of the white erected tents with a brown cloth bag. I buy one clove of garlic. One head of lettuce. A tin of tofu from Dave the Korean man with cases of ginger and pickled seaweed. I pass the bread, loaves of fresh baked bread of all grains and flavors. I never buy a loaf knowing that it would only harden on top of my dusty refrigerator.

A boy sits in a stroller, reaches out past my legs towards the pumpkins piled high. It's almost Halloween and the air has not lost its summer tart. It's the dry snuff of pollution that makes its way in between palm fronds and burnt hills that sticks to the skin. The air here in Burbank is nothing like the muggy sweating heat of the east coast. The air here feels vapid, vacant, vast.

The boy cries at his empty hands as the stroller passes the pumpkins waiting to be carved.

The flowers, my flowers, hang in white plastic buckets, stripped of root and earth. Ken, the flower man, who asked me out, hugs me a bit too closely each time I arrive at the tent. I buy one bunch of lavender, one bunch of stargazers, and one handful of white lilies. One. For me. For the kitchen table. For the vase in the living room. For the vase in the foot-long hallway. For me. In solitude.

I leave the flowers in these vases for two weeks. After the first week, I watch them wilt. The smell moves from sweet and tender to must and rot. I leave them there. They hang, a slow death.

Perfect Teeth.

It was shortly after the War Between the States, in 1867, that Dr. David Burbank, a dentist from New Hampshire, bought parcels of both ranches in order to pursue a new future as a sheep rancher. Nearly twenty years later Dr. Burbank began selling portions of his property in a variety of land deals—first to the Southern Pacific Railroad and later to the Providencia Land, Water, and Development Company—both of which brought people and progress to the area. The new town of Burbank had its first lots for sale in the Spring of 1887. The City of Burbank was incorporated in 1911.[47]

Dr. Burbank, a dentist, helped to craft this place into a utopian community, houses, schools, fire department, and commerce, lined up like perfect teeth, straight, shiny, glowing white. He was one of the first to conquer this portion of the western frontier, to really wrangle the wildness out, to industrialize and modernize this space into a place of manufactured homes and lives.

Loathing.

I hated who she became, who everyone becomes here.

I didn't hate myself before I fucking moved here.

Run.

My legs push against pavement. I focus on the movement, the present moment. I push my limbs. Make it to Brand Park in Glendale and wind past the library to the trail that takes me up, to the top of a peak of the mountains. I move higher and higher, past rock and shrubs. I slow when the terrain is too steep, use my calf muscles and core balance to steady my body against this mountain. At the top, the very top, a steel tower is covered by barbed wire. A city sign bolted into steel warns me not to trespass. But past this fence, on the edge of this mountain, I can see the stretch of the valley.

I see the sketch of Downtown Los Angeles, the buildings like Lego blocks in the distance, to my right the ocean, the line of the horizon close to the cut of land. I see building upon building. The spaces of

Los Angeles separated by mountains, hills, in different pockets of built territories, sections of the city subdivided and sectioned. A map someone created.

Place upon place, there are worlds to discover here. People, ideas, moments that don't intersect yet are connected by the frame of this territory.

With fires at our doorstep, ash in the air, we hang in the liminal space, as transient culture. And I, atop this mountain on my thirty-first birthday, am an ant among many, working to carry weight on our backs, to survive, perhaps even, to thrive.

This Frontier

feels so unfamiliar to me. And it scares me. To know I have to be, feel as if I have to be, someone other than myself. The weight of this new territory, expectations, people, social norms, rites and rituals that are not my own, shifts into insecurity that feels heavy. Fear leads me from place to place, from task to task.

(Dis)placement: Carrying Memory.

I carry a history, the weight of my history like mountains of words on my back. Words such as 'unwanted,' 'penetration,' 'rape,' 'fear,' 'victim,' and now, 'survivor.' Words that I said such as 'no,' and 'stop.' This history comes back materially once in a while. Rears its head when I don't expect it to, in the bedroom, in a whisper from a stranger, a glance from a man that might look like him, in the realization that I am alone and I feel the hand over lips to mute my voice. The spine bones stick up in recoil from under thin skin, or maybe it is thick skin. I've had to train my skin to grow thicker, to take it.

These words, the weight of these words on this page, spoken in silent spaces, crush my esophagus, displace my breath. There is a really fucking breakable pattern trained in my skin, a barcode, a bruise that has formed on the inner layers, a bruise that leaks acid into marrow, and bone.

Carrying these words displaces my sense of self from my body, from a grounded present subjectivity. I carry this memory, this identity as survivor, with a Burbank smile, the perfectly timed television laughter. I mask the embodied memory, stifle the real pain, and push on.

The Burbank Studios.

From Downtown Burbank travel away from the Verdugo mountains over the 5 Freeway. Pass a funny strip of manicured lawns, close houses, strip malls, next to a coffee shop frequently closed for filming. Pass go. Collect $200. See the entertainment studios enclosed by concrete walls, gates, and numbered lots. Fancy cars move past the golf carts. Faux green slime hangs from the Nickelodeon building. Cartoon figures grin at the passing cars. A bank, then the Disney studio, orange-tinted concrete buildings hidden by gigantic posters promoting new television shows. Plastered posters of celebrities with goofy gigantic grins balance against the looming mountain. The NBC studio has tinted glass windows and sophisticated signage. People wait in lines to see The Jay Leno Show and others. The entrance to the Ellen Show stage is hidden on a side street.

Behind these barricades, the entertainment magic happens. I hear manufactured laughter, timed clapping. The audience dances on cue, like monkeys for a circus, for the camera. Guffaw.

In order to gain entry, as part of the studio audience, people wait in long lines, sit on metal benches, line up in numbers. They follow the rules and listen astutely. They laugh even if it isn't funny. They smile on cue. Some people are hand-picked for the closer seats, but this only happens if they look presentable. Jumping through these hoops, the studio audience holds on to the possibility that they too, might become a part of the magic.

Wrap Party.

In the sea of celebrity bodies, I move to follow her. I throw back a 15-dollar vodka soda to feel more 'secure' than I actually am.

I bump bodies with him. She introduces us. "Jeanine, this is Jeff. Jeff, this is my girlfriend Jeanine. Don't you dare hit on her, I know your type." I blush. He grins, the almost famous actor with the east coast flair grins . . . at me.

"Nice to meet you. Is she treating you well?" I ask and pull my lips into a flirty smile.

"Yea, she's great. A spitfire. I can't believe the way she talks sometimes though. She gets away with it," he pats her on the back and turns to look at his wife, a pale figure of a girl. She looks me up and down and turns with a scoff, a sneer.

"I'm going to the bar," she leans into his ear.

"That was Beth. My wife. I would introduce you but . . ."

"She's a bitch?" I think to myself but don't say anything.

Jeff touches my shoulder and I feel him. I feel him too close. And I like it. Maybe I can be a part of the magic.

Boxes.

After a long morning of writing, I walk my dog Miles up Magnolia Boulevard in Burbank. Well, really, he is walking me. Miles tugs on the leash hard and expends more energy than I. The sun soaks through my shirt and bakes my sweat. I let him lead and my eyes wander from small box house to small box house. The patterns change. A condominium looms taller than the trees. New construction is happening throughout these streets. I have counted seven different condos going up in my neighborhood. I pull back on the leash and order Miles to sit. I stare at the rafters and the hollowed shell of a plywood building. It is a skeleton of an apartment building. A blank face of quick construction stares backs at me. The bulldozer rumbles in my memory. It looks just like my father's old construction sites. I shake my head at this hurried fix of capital. I bet the owners of this land will make millions off of this investment. I turn the corner. A row of discarded toilets frames the sidewalk.

Hope.

I listen to the couple next to me at this coffee shop. Their conversation drowns in and out by the click of the traffic light, the hum of motors, a screech of tires, and the giddy punk rock band on the radio. Her blue bandana covers her bald scalp. Her blue sleeveless tee shirt sits on her broad shoulders. Her white pants cut off at the ankle revealing a small heart shaped tattoo. He sits facing me in unassuming brown slacks, his hair close cut to his slightly rounded face. Once and a while I see him glance past her, and assess me. My eyes shrouded by knock-off Ray-Ban sunglasses. He leans back in his chair, and nods in agreement at her searching words. He seems tired but in some way, postures as if he likes the authority he assumes over her.

"I feel so hopeless. I don't work. I just hate it here. I just don't find pleasure. I'm just bored all the time," she shakes her head and looks to the car-filled street. The pipe smoke from the man sitting behind me smells sweet to me, familiar.

"I hate the smell of cigar smoke. Ugh," she complains. Her complaints drive the conversation. This tires him. It tires me.

He moves one hand over the other then slides it in front of his lips and asks, "So do you want to leave this city? Go to San Francisco or something?"

"Well, yeah. I mean my rent is too high. God hasn't done much for me here. So many times I've experienced power outages. I thought when I moved here, ya know, things were going to be different. I came back here to work. And God is a liar. He hasn't made anything happen for me here." She doesn't move in her seat. Stubborn stillness.

"But it is God's love that brought you here and it is God's love that will help your plan work. You have to get yourself away from the situation you are in. Physical movement. So, where do you want to move? Will you stay here in Los Angeles?"

"No. I hate it here. I hate it here."

"What about Colorado? There are a lot of churches there."

I hear her timber, a struggling tenor moves through me when she says, "I'm surrounded by all this hate, ya know?"

I know the hate she feels in her body. I feel it surround me through her words. The hate she feels for this place is kinetic.

"I would like to pray for you—for you to find your way." They bow their heads together in the fading sunlight.

I feel it. I feel the strain of hate in this city where fear seems to guide us. The city is far too large to feel planted, rooted here. Perhaps the movies were right: we are a city of lost angels floating—in exile—to find connection. Floating above the terrain, transients cough into the smogged air.

Days.

She works 15-hour days.

I walk the dogs. shop. clean. take care.

of the home space.

I hear her say, "Rolling."
"Can't make it home on time."
"I'm sorry."

I hear her say, "Well, fuck you then. I can't apologize for my job anymore."

The Lock.

The lock of the urban masses, like iron plates that crank shut inside a bank vault—people sit inside houses that sit inches from the other. The urban masses locked inside cars that swarm up and down the highways. In Los Angeles two hours for 12 miles may seem like a reasonable commute time. We are locked inside the tin and steel of the commuter world and in the plastic and plaster of apartments and houses that seemingly protect us from sirens, from the mad man.

Monster.

I hear her say, "LA a city that builds you up just to watch you fall."

I hear her say, "It's the machine that makes the monster."

(Dis)placed: By the Machine.

We've both become monsters, versions of ourselves that seem as distant as television reality, frames and hours and days and rehearsals, and edits away from real life. We have become layers and versions and mediations of selves trying to fit inside a 32-inch screen. We are displaced by and into a mediated reality that impacts the day-to-day interactions between lovers, friends, and strangers. Los Angeles is the material version of the mediated imagery the rest of the television watching world believes in, except the materialized subjects are much more insecure, alone, escapist, tourists in their own right, searching for someone to hold them, to help them feel placed again.

Sunny CA.

It's sunny here in California. The grass is damp from one day of rain in three months. It's sunny here in California, always sunny. And when it isn't people drive like maniacs, unaware, not used to the puddles, the leaks of mud that shift over the concrete. They slow their cars to 20 miles an hour on a freeway that usually buzzes at 70. People hole up in their houses. Wait again for the sun. When it rains there are mudslides, houses shift with silt and soil, swallowed in earth.

The Pull Away.

The hallway is abuzz. People walk past each other quickly. They hardly look up. Voices and the tap tap tap of heels against concrete fill the space and bounce off the walls of Manzanita Hall. I feel her arm brush against mine and I position my body away from her.

"You used to love when we walked together," she says dropping her gaze to the floor.

"Well, I haven't told my students here yet. I just don't think our relationship needs to be public all the time," I say through my teeth as I wave to a student passing me.

"Hello Professor."

"Hi Leeanne. How are you today?"

"Good. See you in class!" She says with a bubbly lilt in her voice.

"Well, you used to be proud of me," she says as she stuffs her hands in her pockets.

She's right. I feel guilty. I used to be proud of her. But my drop of her hand and shrug away from her body is about falling out of love. Falling out of the factitious cradling arms, the whispers of "its ok. I am here for you." And then the brick smashed against my face. Falling out of the years of "its ok. I can make it better. for you. for us."

We just couldn't make it ok.

I just couldn't hold her hand anymore.

(Dis)placement: In Forgetting.

The act of forgetting buries pain inside the body. The mind may have temporarily calmed the tension, the anxiety, but the experience of abuse remains hidden there. The loss of presence is not a loss at all. The forgetting is only a temporary solution, like filling a cavity with food particles to protect the nerve from exposure. You don't feel intense pain, presently, but your gums are rotting, the enamel chipping and slipping away slowly, the root burning, waiting for the chance to remind you.

Duplex.

I pay $1,350 a month to rent my 570-square foot half of a duplex.

We used to split the rent.

People say I got lucky. After all I live in the city of Burbank and I have a backyard. Backyard spaces are few and far between in this city for this price. I get the most pleasure in the manufactured green and brown space, in the quiet, sitting on the metal chair with a glass of wine, a book, and the sun on my face. That pleasure disappears as I hear the neighbors over the fence scream about money or cheating. Because of the tall green fence, I only know them though their anger, or the pop fizz of a beer can. Sometimes, I hear my neighbor's cats scurry about. I know he can hear my dog bark, my coos of intimate moments, the creaking of the front door as I leave or come home. As neighbors, we know each other only through sounds. I physically saw my neighbor the other day.

The scruffy man across our paved alley tends to his potted plants. I wave.

"Hello," I say politely.

"Hello there." His gruff voice fits his scruffy appearance. "Sorry about the way the backyard looks. I was going to sell this house to condo developers but things have been happening a little slower than I thought." He offers his apologies and turns to carry the potted plants away from me. That was the last time I saw him. Even with our houses so close to one another, we are so far apart.

Numb.

The drinking got worse when we were together. First, it was fun. Drinking to lighten the mood. Festive. Exciting. It's hard to write about this. I drank almost one and a half bottles of wine a night. I tell people half of one. And they always seem really shocked. It got to the point where I was drinking ok, a bottle and a half a night, a shot here or there, and passing out. I wanted to numb her, to block out her voice, her telling me how to live my life, to do things her way. I wanted to numb him, the memory of him inside me. I wanted to numb my inner voice deconstructing my power, breaking myself down.

I hear her say, "to change. to stop crying. to clean the floors. to hurry up. to love. to be quiet. use wrinkle cream. stop pulling on my face. don't stay out too late."

After years of not being together, we talk. She says I need to take ownership over our failure. She is right. I shut down. I didn't stop the anger sooner. I became an active participant. I turned on my own anger, unleashed with bitter words and cynicism. I became a lonely, hateful person. I mirrored her behavior as a defense mechanism. And I drank more to hide from myself.

Free Horses.

Growing up we had sprawling hills and large expanses of land. One hill was our sledding hill, our slip-and-slide hill, and our tumble-and-roll down hill. This hill produced faces filled with grass, water, mud, and snow. Our bodies were always filled with excitement and laughter. I remember a barn with a row of empty stables. I always imagined them to be haunted by horses past. I would cautiously walk past the empty stalls. I would linger there with the stiff scent of hay and manure filling my lungs. I thought about the owners who loved or possibly hurt the horses. I wanted to set the horses, spirits, and memories of this space free.

Music.

There is a knock at the door at 2am. Jeff stops playing his piano. I jump. She enters. Drunk.

"You all sound really good," she stumbles over to the couch. Jeff looks at me with wide eyes. He can tell. He knows. She isn't here to compliment us. I start to shake. I need to sing. I need this friendship.

"How long have you been out there?" I ask, annoyed by her presence.

"About an hour. But you all sound really good. I didn't want to interrupt," her sincerity folded into her anger.

I look at Jeff, embarrassed. "I'm going to take her home."

"You sounded great tonight. We should do it again soon," Jeff says as he holds the large wooden door open so I can help her stumbling body out.

She listened on his patio not for the sound of music but the thump of bodies, the groan of intimacy, the thrust of passion.

We never played music together again.

Pills.

> I hear him say, "I don't love pills but people love to give them to me. Like little presents. Especially when I am working. Anything to keep me high, feeling good."

> I hear her say, "I was prescribed pain medication by my doctor. I trust her. I have a back problem."

> I hear her say, "The horse threw me off it. Now, I have constant pain. I need them. I have a million problems. This pill keeps me sane. This patch, even, this one helps me sleep. This one makes me feel good. This one makes me feel less antsy. This one, well, I forget."

(Dis)placement: Into Numbness.

We become displaced from sanity, from having to feel this loneliness. Celebrity culture, the machine of the entertainment industry capsizes a 'normal' life. Most people behind the scenes in the entertainment industry work 12–15 hour days. They arrive on set, on location, in Los Angeles and elsewhere. They work as a unit, a temporary family, a temporary community. After several months working alongside one another, finding a rhythm, the show wraps for the season or the movie is moved into post-production, and the community dissolves. People move to the next show, the next set, the next community. Some forget whom they worked with.

To understand (dis)placement is to assume that one has known a feeling of place. It also assumes this place is fixed, stable. But perhaps my sense of place in my body was taken years ago.

Some people chose to numb themselves, to forget, to ease the reality of the hours, of the lack of rootedness, the difficult familial relationships, the strain on loved ones, on themselves. Pop a pill. Shoot vodka. Chug that beer. And others in homes across this nation watch the celebrity demise on TMZ, or Perezhilton. They don't realize the very real materialization of this numbness. This exile impacts an actual person, a body, a place, or a family. Nerves dissolve, as memory fades, as presence moves towards absence. As place becomes (dis)placed.

Award Show.

Ani is invited to the Director's Guild Awards. I don't see her much anymore. She leaves the house at 6am and comes home at midnight. The hours are long. I don't know what or whom she does on set.

Countdown. It is five hours until the awards ceremony. She is nervous. She bites her nails—skin raw around the cuticles, almost no nail left on her pointer finger. She chews them down to the nub. She weaves the Saab in and out of traffic too quickly. I get nervous, anxious. I grip the handle on the side of the passenger door.

"Do you have to grip the side of the car like that? I think it's really rude," she says abruptly and cuts the car quickly to the right. I hear a honk and take a deep breath. I close my eyes.

"I'm sorry. I just get scared when you drive so fast. Can you slow down a little?" I take a deep breath.

"We only have a few hours to get ready. We both have to get our hair done and get dressed. And I know you are going to take forever." She steps on the gas pedal. The car lurches forward past the semi truck.

I stretch my body into a small black dress. Hair in ringlets, full, and bouncy. Make-up airbrushed and neat. I don't ever wear clothes like this. I feel small and large at the same time. I walk out of the house on wobbling heels.

"You look . . . ." and she doesn't finish. I hear the disdain in her voice. The disgust.

I look to my best friend Chris who is driving us to the show. She is angry at Ani, wants to rip her heart out for making me feel so small.

"Jeanine, you look amazing. Don't listen to her." We climb into the car.

I can't breathe.

We walk the red carpet. Photographers don't take pictures. We find our seats in a sea of famous bodies, important people in black tuxedos and flowing long gowns. My small black dress seems to shrink in size. Clint Eastwood is at the microphone. She does not talk to me. She looks around the room furtively. The woman to my right is friendly, engaging. I lift my glass of wine and gulp it down.

Ani wants to smoke so I follow her. Outside she sits on a padded bench and begins to talk to a man who works with "the names." He drops them like flies and she picks them up, excited about the possibility of being in his shoes.

"So, I think the way to make it is to be aggressive. I can tell you how to make it in Hollywood. I did. I work with . . ."

I join the conversation. "I think it may be a good idea to. . . ."

He cuts me off. "Oh really Blondie?"

A stomach smack. I look at his ugly suit, his smirked face. And I look to her for help.

She says nothing.

I walk back inside alone to the bathroom.

A monster in a small black dress and awkward heels waits in the stall for time to pass.

Eaten Alive.

I hear the smack of lips on ass.
the sick suck of entertainment industry cock.
the sniff of cocaine.
the pop of pills.

A few talented people make it because of their talent.
the others, make it any way they can.

the madness of the machine makes the monster.
but the machine is hidden/covered/behind the perfect smile.
behind hidden doors.
behind studio fortresses.

I hear her say, "This celebrity, that celebrity wanted this to eat today."

I hear her say, "You should have seen how slow this director, how impossible that director was."

I hear her say, "I won't be home until 3am. Can you take care of her?"

I hear myself say, "Fuck this. Fuck you."

We've been eaten alive
   by the impact of hungry, hollow Hollywood.

DreamJeffDream.

i found you just before break. "why find me at work? i'm working," you said. i followed you out the set doors with a swarm of people, the voices like trucks. "follow me," you said. winding path, turned dirt and gravel.

she, your wife, and her friend there now, they cut across the path towards us. I do not turn my head. you do not say hello to her, only to her friend. they will be on break with us.

i did not expect to see you in my dream last night. but you were there. with metallic dinnerware made by Duchamp. you had me hold up the yellow one so you could take a picture in your trailer on set that had the backdrop of damp trees and a yellow moon.

we avoided them or tried through endless hallways and bathrooms. i slid under the tub, ninja style, to turn off the shower, so she could enter, leave, and we could be alone. and you kissed me, like aloe on my lips, when I came back proud and sloppy from the water that flooded the tile.

Exploitation.

I hear her say, "If you're not getting exploited you're getting high.
   And nine times out of ten you are doing both."

I hear her say, "And they put coke up your nose until they don't need you anymore and then they turn around and ask, 'what's wrong with that guy?'"

Membering.

My first real love from years past is here, recording his album on Sunset strip. He calls and I come. His voice, a strong tenor, croons in a strange house in the middle of Hollywood, music that helped me sing. We sing together and in the middle of a verse that speaks about me, about us, about a past full of love and strength, I say it. "She broke me. I have to leave. It's time to leave. I can't. I just can't feel this way anymore." I fall in a heap on the carpet heaving out sobs of memory, heaves and huff of pain and passion. The horrible wail is a song to member my self, my body back together again. To gather the courage to walk away, to get away, to build my life back.

His brown eyes sink into mine. "I hate seeing you like this. This isn't you Jeanine" and he hands me my lungs. I inhale deep breaths to calm my stuttering chest.

"You need to come back," as he hands me my fingers. I refashion them to bone and watch as my fingertips grip into the palm and back out again. They still work. I pull at my hair and feel the root in the scalp. Pull harder to feel again.

"I know. It is time." I point to my heart on the carpet, pulsing, pulsing. I pick it up and look closely at the aorta, the veins, the blood barely wheezing through. I plug it back in behind my ribcage. I move my legs, kick and punch at air. I shift in place, from the heap to my knees, to my feet. I apply pressure. I feel these limbs. I hear. I see. I taste. I can move . . . again.

And Ocean.

The ocean. I don't see it enough. I live 12 miles from the ocean. And I won't drive there. I want to avoid the bumper-to-bumper crawl.

Like ants with wheels for legs we follow one by one, two by two, to the ocean. Past the mountain. Over the mountain. To the sand we go.

(Dis)placement to Placement: (Re)member.

I want to transform the forgetting into a chance to remember. I know I need to walk into those spaces, to recall to mind.

To (re)member my body, as a healthy, healing space, to fit the scraps
back together. But now, the limbs ripped off. I can pick them up one
by one, look at them, and re-engage in the possibility of agency in and
with my body. Perhaps I can fit them, stitch them back into layers of
memory, a memory that I may be able to live with.

The loss is an opportunity for a transformation, to (re)member.

How do I find my way home, into place, into presence with
subjectivity and body?

Present.

She came over last night. The excuse—to pick up clothes left in the
garage for over a year now. I am writing about this to get it down
before my brain erases her. That's what I've done so far. After the pain,
the stress, the constant verbal kicks in the stomach, the ugly adjectives
spit in my face, I've blocked her out almost completely.

"I brought you a chocolate frosting cupcake." She hands me a plastic
cup with a cupcake on the bottom. One sugar pumpkin pressed into
the chocolate top.

"Thanks." I take a bite of the pumpkin. She fills the frame of the
kitchen door. She used to live here. I wonder how it feels to be
back here. The house is a little different; the floors are dirtier now.
When I leave the floors unkempt, dusted with dog hair it is a passive
aggressive triumph. I know that if she were still here she would
hate the dog hair, the linoleum floors dull and spattered with coffee
and dirt.

"You want half?" I ask and hand her the half-eaten pumpkin.

"Yeah. Thanks. That was calling my name," she says and bites it
through the middle.

I walk her out to the garage. "So, how are you?"

"Good. Things are really good," her voice trembles a bit.

"How's work?" I ask. I can smell the whiskey or stale beer on her
body.

"Good. It's easy, like a nine-to-five job. Only ten hours a day. It's
pretty amazing," she says and flashes me her beautiful smile.

I think back to the months she worked from 6am to midnight for minimal pay and want to comment about the days I spent taking care of our dogs, the house, and bills, without a thank you. I want to point out that her only response to me was anger, critical remarks about my inability to use face cream or the detrimental effects of pulling on my skin. In a quick flash, I hear and feel long days and complaints about everything, anything.

I don't say a word. It isn't my place anymore.

"So here are the clothes," I say as I pull out each piece of fabric from the cardboard boxes in the seedy garage.

Garment by garment she responds, "Wow, I haven't seen that in a while. That jacket is really warm. That one isn't mine. Do you want this? Ewww. That is definitely not mine."

We hug. I smell her, familiar. She lingers pressure on my skin.

"I don't want to leave yet. Can you tell?" She mimes walking slowly to the door. She takes a deep breath and hugs me again. She whispers, "I'm sorry. I just want to say that." Her eyes fill and she chokes out the words, "I think about you everyday."

She lightens her tone, "If you are ever wondering if someone is missing you, they are. I am." She takes a step to the car and she trips over her feet.

"Are you drunk?" I ask, concerned.

She wobbles. "No."

She pulls on my arms, "Can I hug you again?"

I reluctantly take her body closer to me. We hug next to her open car door. I can feel her wanting to kiss me. To feel my skin. To draw me right back in.

I don't let her.

Main House.

> Behind a main house on a strip of concrete
> a woman laughs. The neighbor hears.
>
> Behind a front façade
> sit rows upon rows upon rows of apartment boxes.
> The TV is always on.

A man murmurs. The neighbor hears.
Murmurs in the main house.
She sleeps

with the TV on.

Never.

I never wanted to move to LA.
   But here I am.

2

BURBANK, REVISITED

ARTS-BASED AUTOETHNOGRAPHIC (RE)MEMBERING

If something inside you is real, we will probably find it interesting, and it will probably be universal. So you must risk placing real emotion at the center of your work. Write straight into the emotional center of things. Write toward vulnerability. Don't worry about being sentimental. Worry about being unavailable; worry about being absent or fraudulent. Risk being unliked. Tell the truth as you understand it. If you are a writer, you have a moral obligation to do this. And it is a revolutionary act—truth is always subversive.

—*Anne Lamott*[48]

Moving to Burbank, CA was a painful transition for me. I wasn't sure of who I was and would become in Los Angeles. I imagine myself a bohemian, an artist, writer, performer, and professor and I fancy myself a person that doesn't feel compelled to follow a crowd. I'm a feminist. I've fought and continue to fight for women's rights. In college I was the editor of a literary journal entitled, *Sister Speak*. I'm an activist, a lover of the outdoors, a hiker, in some ways a bit hippie, but mostly just eccentric. I never imagined myself living in Los Angeles. And I never imagined that Los Angeles could break open so many hidden facets of my identities, so many layers of who I was in the past and how this past manifests itself within me today. I never imagined the shifts and turns in my identities, the uprooting of my feeling of safety and placement. A place impacts an identity, just as a person can shift the feeling and politics of place. It's a reciprocal relationship, experiencing place as you become a part of it.[49] We approach Los Angeles as a new frontier and face the many promises and obstacles it takes to survive in this transitory culture. I am not in the entertainment business and do not aspire to be. But I am one of the many people who left lives and loved ones behind to become a part of the Los Angeles culture. And the shift in landscape, in terrain, in place was quite jarring.

We move in this chapter through four different places within Burbank to uncover the (dis)placement involved in wrestling with the realities of a new frontier and the memories of past trauma, to story an experiential text. We work through the layers of methodological choice and situate who I am in the present moment of experiencing the vast places of Los Angeles. I am still trying to write down the bones.[50] I have to be honest. I will unintentionally leave things out. My memory might fail me. This story is my own to write and I would prefer to disappoint you now, rather than later. Writing this story is prickly, sharp, and dangerous. It isn't an easy story.

In this re-visiting, we move through the streets of Downtown Burbank. These streets project the image of a village and yet, the purpose of navigating these streets feels absent. This frontier is not my place. I move into numbness, a (dis)memberment to protect myself. I work with my self-inflicted (dis)memberment, trying to escape my memories past, and the feelings that materialize within my body in this place. Next, we move into the movie and television studios, where the manufactured realities impact the expectations and demands my ex-partner and I make on each other; just as she made her first waves in the entertainment industry. (Dis)memberment materializes in our relationship. And I realize, in order to survive and to understand the very immense nature of this place, of these experiences, I need to write my way through it. I move into and through the story not away from it, to re-member using autoethnographic and ethnographic techniques.

Next, we move back through my neighborhood and watch as the house I share with my partner, and our sense of place together, collapse. Here, I make the conscious decision to create for you, the reader, an experience of Los Angeles with arts-based research to render the place of LA as it both impacts and is impacted by our presence within it.

Finally, we move to the top of the Verdugo Mountains. From this vantage point, I realize there are worlds upon worlds within the expanse of LA. There are stories to tell, memories to re-make and refashion. And as I move from place to place, my understanding shifts, my choices, my (re)membering of the body in relation to other bodies, as a sexual being, shifts. In a place as hyper-magnified and manufactured, and sexualized as Los Angeles, this (re)membering has been intense.

Downtown Burbank: A Frontier Story.

Imagine you take a stroll through the perfect street. You see the bright banners, the cobblestone patches at the cross sections of the streets. You see the movie theater, then another, then another, next to one another. The mall breaks the pattern of your stroll. Once through the mall, you reach IKEA, and a California Pizza Kitchen. Parking garage after parking garage. This once frontier land was crafted and shaped as the idyllic American community with spaces and stores in which to buy new things. The plethora of movie theaters offers you an escape into another world, many worlds. How do you feel at home here? What place is this? (Dis)placed from your once home, you find yourself transported into what many would call perfect. Do you hear the cash register ring and the pace of footsteps on super clean sidewalks? Can you smell the food from a corporate restaurant, any corporate restaurant waft out of glass doors into your nose? What do you remember about you, yourself, your once home?

The Frontier: (Dis)placement/(Dis)memberment

The frontier, according to Schneekloth, is embedded in an ever-evolving American, collective identity. The frontier identity is somewhere between wildness and civilization, a restless process of conquest and righteous violence "that supports developer 'cowboys' and fuels cultural industry." [51] The conquest of Los Angeles hinges upon colonial tactics of hegemony over the land, Aboriginal and Mexican people, and those that work for minimum wage to support capitalist development. In Burbank, the feeling of industry and development is palpable.

The studio boxes and well laid-out track homes are a constant reminder that settlement is undergoing. Yet, as Schneekloth points out, the idea that the frontier can ever be home is one of slippage: "home, as an imaginal place, is unchanging, safe, and comfortable, based on understandable rhythms and patterns. Frontier is the other, the alluring, desired, dangerous place, outside of civilized law and custom."[52] Within this slippage is where I feel displaced.

Frederick Turner, a nineteenth-century American historian wrote that the movement into the frontier helped to develop American values such as "coarseness and strength combined with acuteness and acquisitiveness; that practical inventive turn of mind, quick to find expedients; that masterful grasp of material things . . . that restless, nervous energy; that dominant individualism."[53] Burbank is the result of sprawl, an accident of city expansion that has produced specialized areas to contain people with specialized skills. The specialist here is the frontier individualist that is the best actor, director, videographer, or key grip. Each person plays his or her role "just right" to obtain the freedom of fame. Yet, this freedom is not glamorous. Rather, there are 18-hour days, intense competition, and the lure of drugs to live through it. Wendell Berry contends that specialization leads to displacement through lack of responsibility to one another, as to have a specialty means one is only responsible for an expert area—not to the whole experience of life.[54] Within this frame, human relationships suffer from an inability to connect beyond the performance of producing. This frontier feels so unfamiliar to me. And it scares me to know I have to be, feel as if I have to be, someone other than myself. The weight of this new territory, expectations, people, social norms, rites, and rituals that are not my own, is a shift into insecurity that feels heavy. Fear leads me from place to place, from task to task.

I am "betwixt and between," trying to move from displacement to integration.[55] This effort is complicated in Burbank as it is both a dual city and an altered space. A dual city is one that is characterized by social polarization where the gap is wide between rich and poor. An altered space is marked by the collapse of conventional communities with nothing stable having yet emerged to take their place.[56] I see the stratification and the lack of community and I wonder where can I take root? What can I hold on to when human relationships are relegated to the prestige of production? This liminal space is fertile with the need to grow and dramatic in the sense that there is no going back to pre-liminality and it is uncertain as to what may occur post-liminality. During this ambiguity of identity and expression, many avenues are explored—some that lead to pain and more questions. This liminal space frames and perpetuates a state of my own (dis)memberment.

(Dis)memberment: From the Body

(Dis)memberment is a state of numbness. Parts of the body function as separate units as the brain can't seem to bring them together because it would be too painful. To experience the body in its totality would necessitate the acknowledgement and processing of the body memory of living traumatic memory. To enter into a stage of (dis)memberment is to create a division between the mind and the body, which results in a schism between body and community.

I have yet to understand how my body re-members. How it carries this past with me, and materializes in my agency, my identity, my sexual relationships and understanding of sex. I am disconnected, disjointed from my sexual energy. "The memory of rape can thus make pleasurable erotic anticipation impossible: the past reaches into the present and throttles desire before it can become directed toward the future."[57] I feel (dis)membered, parts of my body disjointed, displaced, and certainly not in line with my mindful desires, or my hope for an intermingling of presence, mind, and body.

"One's ability to feel at home in the world is as much a physical as an epistemological accomplishment."[58] The physical accomplishment of my sexual body is complex. Most times, I have to remind myself to physically feel the touch, the skin, the hands, the penis, the fingers, the mouth, and the vagina. I have to tell my heart to sink back into the physicality of the sexual experience. When it comes to sex and love, fear really fucks with you. In Burbank, given the heightened displacement of human relationships, I have kept emotion and sex separate. I have not found a reason to feel sexual again. Moreover, placing sexual empowerment within the larger frontier of Los Angeles, how does this place play into my journey of (re)membering and placement?

Burbank Studios: Writing from the Liminal.

A wall of concrete, a fortress with uniformed guards at every entrance, every gate. The studios beckon visitors but keep unwanted guests out. It's alluring, this space of possible celebrity, of possible stardom. Hidden from the street, the sets once filled with people are an active space for creating entertainment magic, keeping us glued to a fantasy screen. And I fear its power and its possibility of demise. In Burbank, the studios are acres and acres of land surrounded by concrete and security cameras. The walls are lined with posters promoting television shows. A gigantic face grins at the passing cars. I can hear laughter that is not mine. Can you imagine the craft service trucks with mountains of food, choices lined out just for you? Can you hear the production assistant yell, "Quiet on the set?" Can you imagine the director behind a screen watching as the actors take their marks? Can you hear them yell, "Rolling, and Action!" You can't see them. They are hidden behind walls, entrances and exits that are not yours.

———————

Autoethnography: Writing from the Liminal Space

I am aware of the things that might be left out: I want to touch it all. Each exchange seems to have its own liminality, a welling space of ideas, feelings, and touch, seemingly ready to erupt in any direction, according to where fissures might be or where potential flows might offer passages to interpretation or discovery.
                                                                    —*Ken Gale and Jonathon Wyatt*[59]

Autoethnographic work creates the story of the self in culture. If I start with my vision, I may leave other visions out. I know this. But I have to begin this story where I think it begins, almost four years ago. Laurel Richardson states, "I write because I want to find something out. I write in order to learn something that I did not know before I wrote it.[60] I write these pages to find the storyline. Starting where I am implies that I am not sure where I am going, at least not completely. Eventually, I will uncover this narrative and craft it accordingly. For me, writing sits alongside creating tactile and kinesthetic elements.

Starting where you are implies an awareness of your own subjectivities. This is not to say that there is a sense of clarity to these positionalities, but rather that there is a jumble of knowing wrapped inside these texts. In order to sort through the intersections of thought, experience, and embodied memories, I use writing as one tool for discovery.

I might disappoint you with the openings, fissures, and the cracks within the story. While I do my best to incorporate the complications and the voices of those I encountered throughout this journey, it is my perception. Each person, reader, critic, enthusiast, comes to this text from different positions and personal attachments. I do as well. Knowledge is subjective and deeply connected to the knower. I have to own this authorship honestly, introspectively, reflexively, and without fear. In this way, this story can be considered autoethnographic. Laurel Richardson and Carolyn Ellis argue and demonstrate in their own works that autoethnography relates the personal to the cultural through intimate and embodied writing.[61] It gains access to the personal corners of interaction. I cannot tell this story from someone else's perspective. I am one person in Los Angeles, only a part, one person out of many. But I cannot separate myself from the research project. From the feminist autoethnographic points of view, realities become and are known through language. Knowledge is produced and reconstituted in and as language. I sketch these voices with both hesitance and great joy. Physically, I am now alone in this endeavor, scraping my memory, my notes, and the documentation of experiences past for a semblance of the story. But in my mind, in my memories, as I materialize the story for you in this text, I am with the voices of the people I encountered in Los Angeles.

According to Roland Barthes,

> Any text is a new tissue of past citations. Bits of code, formulae, rhythmic models, fragments of social languages, etc., pass into the text and are redistributed within it, for there is always language before and around the text. Intertextuality, the condition of any text whatsoever, cannot, of course, be reduced to a problem of sources or influences; the intertext is a general field of anonymous formulae whose origin can scarcely ever be

located; of unconscious or automatic quotations, given without quotation marks.[62]

Writing is always a rewriting. When I write and create I am creating intertexts of writings past, of theories, ideas, and structures of language that have influenced and contextualized my work. I am sketching these pages within a general field of formulae, even as I try to break out of it. The texts are only constituted once they are read, only in that moment of reading. You bring to these pages your previous readings, your standpoints, which also form intertexts. I am urged to find the plot, purpose, layers of contextualized experiences in LA, and the moments I might have forgotten. While I am aware of the possibility of losing moments, I have to accept that a "complete" text isn't possible. There will be memories that have lost their way. Losing memories does not compromise the survival of this text. If it is evocative, if you feel anything, gain anything from this document then it has survived, both in the text and in your interpretations.

The Duplex: Re-membering Home through Arts-based Research

I live in a one-bedroom duplex with hardwood floors. Sit in my kitchen with me, on the padded yellow chair. I'll pour you a steaming glass of tea. Miles, my dog will sleep lazily on the couch as we make our way across the hardwood floors, out the back door into the green fenced backyard. Look up above the fence. Do you see the apartment building that blocks us from the sky? Shhh. Listen. Can you hear the neighbor cough? Feels like he's right next to us. He is. Watch, you can see his baldhead move past the slits in the wood panels. Do you hear the pop fizz of the beer can opening? Can you taste it? Are you salivating? I am.

———

Home: In Re-membering

If I could do it, I'd do no writing here at all here. It would be photographs; the rest would be fragments of cloth, bits of cotton, lumps of earth, records of speech, pieces of wood and iron, phials of odors, plates of food and excrements. Booksellers would consider it quite a novelty; critics would murmur, yes, but is it art; and I could trust a majority of you to use it as a parlor game. A piece of body torn out by the roots might be more to the point.

—*James Agee*[63]

I was always told to start my work, my writing, where I am. I am here in my yellow vinyl 1950s kitchen chair with my dog, Miles. He whines at my feet. I pet Miles' soft head and stare at the stargazers on my kitchen table. They are opening. The petals are beginning to peel back, exposing a sensuous purple center. The deep brown of the stamen contrasts the white petals and offers a subtle explosion of color. Each day I gauge their movement and delight in their growth. I bought the flowers at Trader Joes for $4.99. I didn't pick them in a meadow or grow them in my own garden. They were perfectly packaged and convenient. Sometimes I regret making these purchases. Why can't I grow my own? Why haven't I already? The stargazers excite my interest in liveness, animation, color, and decay.

I want to give you the sounds, scents, voices, noises and kinesthetic moments of experiencing the place of Los Angeles, from the place of my body. Norman K. Denzin writes that autoethnography turns the "ethnographic gaze inward on the self (auto), while maintaining the outward gaze of ethnography, looking at the larger context where self experiences occur."[64] As the gaze turns inward and outward, the ethnographer questions the nature of ethnographic texts. How should they be written and what should they say? During this crisis of representation, the focus shifts to the way we should be writing—to bring the reader into the texts, into the experiences. Autoethnography emerged with texts that experimented with form and style. These different forms and styles attempt to wrestle with the sensory experience of place, of being there, of bringing others there, so they too can feel it, know it in their bones.

James H. Olthuis states, "Indeed, language or discourse is only one form of intercourse, only one of the great array of acoustic, olfactory, tactile, symbolic, and graphic ways of signification that we need to interpret in meeting the other."[65] The visual offers the reader a layer of knowing within the text. The visual and textual elements fuse to create embodied knowledge. Knowing through the intersection of textual and visual elements does not claim to be more truthful or encompassing than any other form of knowing. I argue here that it is another layer or approach to an account. Referring to the photograph in ethnographic research, Sarah Pink asserts:

> It does not claim to produce an objective or "truthful" account of reality but should offer versions of the ethnographer's experiences of reality that are as loyal as possible to the context, negotiations and intersubjectivities through which knowledge is produced.[66]

The photographs here are not meant to substitute for written experience but should enhance the lens we use to view the culture. Using a reflexive approach to photography within arts-based research, I am aware of the constraints and possibilities with my own photographic practice and choices. The photographs are records of my personal experiences. They identify to the viewer what grabbed our attention in that moment, from our particular viewpoints.

Choreographers and scholars Mary Beth Cancienne and Celeste Snowber combine dancing and writing to argue that the body is a site of knowledge. They state, "Combining dance, a kinesthetic form, and writing, a cognitive form, can forge relationships between body and mind, cognitive and affective knowing, and the intellect with physical vigor."[67] Like Cancienne and Snowber, I do not see the body and mind as separate entities. They play with each other. Their interrelationship allows for creative possibility, connection, really, the participation in the larger project of life and evolution. So when I walk around Los Angeles in a state of dismemberment, I don't have access to this larger pulse of life, leaving me flat and wanting. To re-member myself is the only way through this terrain.

Brand Park/Verdugo Mountains: Placement to Re-Member.
Deep breath.

From atop this mountain, your muscles ache from the climb. Inhale the fresh air, above the layer of smog that hovers over this stretch of land. You can see the San Fernando Valley below you. Rows upon rows of buildings packed into this valley. People upon people packed inside these buildings. Where do you reside? Which concrete building is yours? Can you see yourself here? In that building or another? Where is your place within this place?

———

Home is highly personal and political.

> What is home? The place I was born? Where I grew up? Where my parents live? Where I live and work as an adult? Where I locate my community, my people? Who are "my people"? Is home a geographical space, a historical space, an emotional, sensory space?[68]

Chandra Talpade Mohanty is convinced the answers are highly political. Biddy Martin and Mohanty state, "To the extent that identity is collapsed with home and community and based upon homogeneity and comfort, on skin, blood and heart, the giving up of home will necessarily mean the giving up of self and vice versa."[69] How do we configure home in actual experience?

I argue that surveying the terrain, as part of home, integrates the complex diversities of living and non-living, institutional, social, cultural, ecological, personal, and local elements that exist there. In her discussion of responsive design, which is one form of natural building, Susie Harrington situates my movements and organization in this book. She states, "Responsive design can be likened to a tree, in which roots, trunk and crown are seamlessly integrated."[70] The roots are the ecological and historical realities that I experience in the Los Angeles area. The trunk is the cultural and social network that exists here. The crown is how all of the factors come together to create the aesthetic complexity.

I experience Burbank as a place that has continuously disappearing marks. I begin to locate myself here through fragments of text, image, movement, and sound—all existing in a morphing panorama of possibility. Here, in this text, a studio of sorts, I create in order to remember myself within this displaced frontier. I collage and craft narrative as a way to bring you the liminal space, for your consideration and contemplation. For while this story takes place in Los Angeles, there are threads here that mirror many places.

Part of the journey through this text is getting comfortable with the fragments, getting comfortable with pain as an emotion and finding joy in the everyday. To reach compassion and connection we have to move through our pain. In Burbank, I have a fragmented sense of self, a whisper of wholeness, and I need to walk through the pain of this place and of my memories to realize fullness once again. To be an agent in a particular place, one needs to have wholeness, a sense of self and place, even if this sense of self and place is grotesque and full of unanswered questions. As of right now, I am searching for this wholeness and acceptance of self and place. This work is an effort in empowering myself to become an active, creative agent of change from a center of knowledge rooted in re-membering my body. These pages are an articulation of this journey.

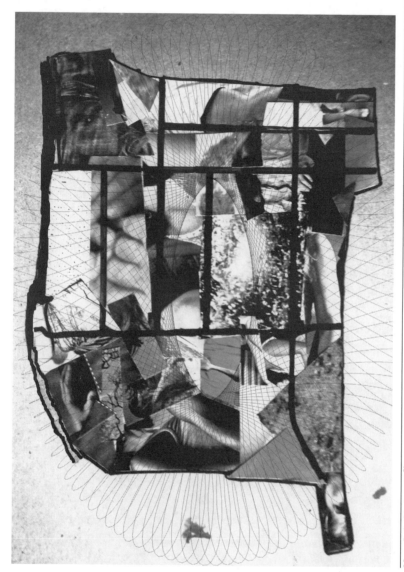

Map 3.1 Chatsworth[71]

3
CHATSWORTH[72]

Image 3.1 San Fernando Valley

Valley.

This valley is porn valley.
This valley is one big strip mall and suburban sprawl.
Buildings tick by in a pattern.

tick tick tick tick tick   tick tick tick tick tick
                    tick tick tick tick tick
One of these houses is rented to people in the adult
entertainment business.
tick tick tick tick tick   tick tick tick tick tick
                    tick tick tick tick tick
One of these women is a porn star.
tick tick tick tick tick   tick tick tick tick tick
                    tick tick tick tick tick
One of these women[73] is holding the camera.

Driving through the straight, flat grid of one of the thirty-six suburban
community plan areas, in the San Fernando Valley, I pass trash in
dumpsters, strip mall after strip mall. Lights blink. Traffic stops. Seven
cars wait at the lights. Then we go again. Pulsating in the grid of
unending condominiums in tan, light orange, and brown. The strip
strikes a quick red of a liquor store sign. The hum of a grocery store,
the silent park—all beat out a rhythm between thin rays of gray.
Concrete box after concrete box after concrete box, then a flash of
human, sitting with several bags at a bus stop. One, then two, they are
gone again.

This work buries me.

Access.

Chatsworth is home to a significant percentage, over 80 percent, of
the nation's adult production and distribution studios. Adult entertainment industry's top companies include Anabolic Video, Combat
Zone, KBeech, Red Light District Video, Third World Media, and
Wicked Pictures. Sex industry magazine and multimedia hub for the

entertainment industry AVN is also housed in Chatsworth. As much as I want to talk about going inside actual porn houses, I won't.[74] I access and make sense of the pornography industry in the San Fernando Valley on my own terms to reclaim empowerment in the sexual act. For the first time I will make sense of sex without emotional attachment, and perhaps, to discover agency. I will try to let go of emotion in sexual relationships and become Sophie. She moves through Chatsworth to make sense of agency in sex. She is another layer, a version of Jeanine, a character, an alter ego developed in very real terms within the spaces of the valley.

The San Fernando Valley.

> The San Fernando Valley is bounded roughly by the Santa Susana Mountains to the north and west, the Santa Monica Mountains to the south, and the San Gabriel Mountains to the east. It is a geographic area, not a political one, and lacks clearly demarcated political boundaries. It lies in Los Angeles County and includes all or portions of six cities: Burbank, Calabasas, Glendale, Hidden Hills, Los Angeles and San Fernando.[75]

> Forty-seven percent of the land and 36 percent of the population of the city of Los Angeles are in the San Fernando Valley. The Los Angeles portion of the Valley is nearly 20 miles across at its widest point (from Chatsworth to Tujunga) and 14 miles north to south (from Sylmar to Sherman Oaks). For planning purposes, Los Angeles is divided into 36 community plan areas. Fourteen are located in the San Fernando Valley.[76]

One of these community plan areas is Chatsworth, the adult entertainment capital of California.

Disconnect: Between Hollywood and the Valley.

"The valley" is over the hill from Hollywood. The valley is not the destination point for people who come to visit Los Angeles. Yet people in the valley travel into Hollywood.

I hear her ask, "Why would I want to go to the valley?"

I hear him say, "There is nothing there."

I hear him ask, "Oh, You live in the valley? Why?"

This is socio-geographical hierarchy.

This hierarchy creates a sense of disconnect. The valley is not part of Hollywood, yet yanks at Hollywood's skirt tails. Industry people do live in the valley, but not ones that want to been seen. Most people that grew up in the valley scoff at the ridiculous nature of the entertainment industry debauchery. Valley natives can tell who intimately knows their history and who doesn't. They see right through the façade of Hollywood.

The actors that perform here, besides the hospital location for a hit show about doctors, or the temporary shooting locations that are cheap, dirty, and quick, aren't "real" celebrities.

The disconnect lies in the fact that entertainment industry, Hollywood types do the exact same thing, only they give the illusion of it. They fuck the camera for a living. The hierarchy is shit. A lot of them, porn, film, daytime television, hit television shows, or reality television stars can't act. To make it in Hollywood it's about who you know—blow jobs, couch sessions, and all.

The porn stars fuck in the valley. Their bodies are torn and used—disconnected.

Their fame comes from cumming. Valley people have tasted Los Angeles for quite some time. They know her scent. They know that you, the transient, don't.

Arrangement.

Henry, my boxing instructor, and I make an arrangement that puts us on equal footing.

He doesn't want love. I don't want love, at least not with him. He doesn't want attachment. I don't want attachment. We just want sex.

Porn.

I live approximately 20 miles from Chatsworth. I teach at a university that is only five miles from this porn capital. I never knew it was such a lucrative and lubricated area.

I discovered the pervasiveness of the porn industry in Hollywood and the surrounding valley when I was with my colleague Doug, my ex-girlfriend, and another friend at a restaurant. It was late and we were all tipsy, actually, drunk as shit, eating sausages with a fork.

Ani, my ex-girlfriend, stands to go to the bathroom. She turns back to our table and gasps, "Holy shit. Ron Jeremy is right there. Ron Jeremy that infamous man with a huge schlong is standing right there! I mean, his penis is HUGE!"

She screams this a bit too loud and I look across the bar at this man who is getting a lot of attention from the surrounding tables. He is short, fat and really awkward looking.

I laugh.

Ani says, "I am going to get a picture with him."

My head shakes instinctively at the ridiculous nature of Los Angeles, the constant desire for celebrity sightings, the stories of running into so and so at the grocery store.

Sometimes we forget they are just human beings. I get annoyed at Ani's care to speak to him and sling my bag over my shoulder to leave. I hear a gasp and then a squeaky female voice say, "Professor?"

Doug says, "Oh. Hey, Cee Cee! How are you?" And then he laughs the most fantastic laugh.

This woman, no, young woman, our student, blushes and then turns to link arms with Ron Jeremy. She stands at least a foot taller than the porn star troll with a huge dick.

"See you in class," she says to Doug and shuffles out the door.

Classroom Flashes.

This is probably not the most appropriate thing to say but after seeing our student with a porn star, I can't help but wonder. I don't think about it all the time, I promise. But these musings will come in a quick flash. Which one of these women, an aspiring actress, was bent over a sofa making the face that says, "This is almost the perfect orgasm, keep trying big strong man." Which of these men takes Viagra to stay awake long enough to make it through hours of sexual intercourse? An enormous amount of aspiring Hollywood starlets end up in the warehouses in Chatsworth pounding away and rubbing naughty bits to make a living.

Dirty Pub.

I sling drinks at a dirty pub in the middle of the San Fernando Valley. When I was hired I was warned of knife fights, robbery, and cutthroat danger, literally. "Just don't give them the code," My boss says and hands me the golden key to the bar. He laughs, "Well, actually, you can't. I won't give it to you. It is for your own good."

The red cracked seats make their drunken bodies lean forward, so their moldy beer breath wafts in my direction. Gossip is gold here. Kate always comes in on unemployment payday. She follows the mailman on her bicycle to get her check. She plays keno and snorts lines in the bathroom. On payday she is a monster. She slurs insults my way and sips her vodka, soda, and splash of cranberry. On these strung out days, she calls me Justine.

Winston lost all of his money in Vegas. With his bruised face frozen with anger, he recounts his story of getting jumped by two Mexicans.

> They wanted this watch. My Rolex and I wouldn't give it to them so they hit me, kicked me. Those beaners wouldn't let up. But I held on to my watch. Give me a shot of Jack. A tall one. Don't short me. Ya hear?

This story is a lie. He was drunk and woke up in the bushes. He doesn't remember what actually happened.

Carl sips his Jaeger and then his MGD. "Ya know, I wanna warn you. Be careful around here. Sue was held up once. Gun to her temple, on her knees, beggin' for her life."

I see Sue there on the worn carpet that is stained with beer and puke. I can smell the urine that dripped down his right leg after he stumbled back from the bathroom—the tiny sweat-stained bathroom with bars on the window. I hear her pleading over and over, "I don't have the code. I swear. They don't give it to the bartenders."

Carl continues, "She was hit once on her temple with the barrel of the gun. She fell to the ground and the attackers fled with her 50 bucks in tips, cash from the drawer and a bottle of scotch. I suppose to celebrate with." Sue doesn't work here anymore. "You are so beautiful—a super model. I can't believe you work here," Manny says as I squeeze by his open palms, dodge the pat on my ass and make it into the bathroom. A small cockroach crawls up the wall with a hole in it that looks like the gap of a vagina and I stare at my skin beneath the florescent light. A dirty string hangs in front of the mirror and sections my reflection. The wrinkles around my eyes aren't laugh lines. Two faces look back at my empty eyes. One of me has a Ph.D. and is an Assistant Professor at a local university. They took 10 percent of my paycheck away and fed money into the jail system, so now the other half of me keeps the bar flies out of jail. I take their keys when they come in drunk. I cut them off, feed them popcorn and water, so they won't hit the grandmother crossing the street with their swerving car, and blame it on the blurry vision. Sometimes I can't stop them from stumbling out or stumbling in.

This version of me works in the bar in Chatsworth. I sell the image of Sophie to these patrons, smile when they ask me for another drink, call me sweetie, and check out my ass and breasts as I dust the bottles of alcohol. Sell me, a piece of my body, not just a beer, for a buck. Literally—one fucking dollar tip, for an hour of their time spent ogling the layers of skin. I take the pittance from Manny and my glossed lips stretch into a sweet smile, "Thank so much, darling. I hope to see you next week."

I rot in the middle of Chatsworth, CA, serving beers to sweaty patrons at 10am. Just to squeak by, to make do. A commodity but also a conscious woman, with an ass and breasts—yes, but also lips and lungs, and this mind that reminds me that this is not the way my life should be lived. Even if it is endearing when they call me Doc.

Disconnect: Between Commodity and Consciousness.

As a means of survival, to make do, I sling drinks in a local pub near Chatsworth. Each time I move past them, I can feel their eyes and I know my body is the commodity. I knowingly disconnect from my feminist positionality and allow my body to become objectified in order to make a living. While some commend me for my ability to move back and forth, to be humble enough, fun enough, enough of a woman to work for a meager wage, I know the cost I am paying for these Saturdays spent inside the walls. I know when Bill stares at my chest. I know he likes it when I bend over to scoop the ice into his glass. To be conscious, know, and understand objectification, to become the commodity, to scrape the barrel for money is both humiliating and humbling. There is a real strike of reality when I sit on the ripped black stool and talk to the locals about not having a boyfriend, about living alone, about teaching, about their pain, their divorces and drinking too much. When I know they come to see me because they think my body is attractive the consciousness and awareness of the objectification and loss of agency creates a complicated trap, a liminal space, the in-between commodity and consciousness, especially because I need the money. I understand the choices women in the sex industry make to make do.

To Justify.

I've never had sex just for the sake of having it. I've always connected with a sexual partner emotionally before engaging with them sexually.

I ask him if it is ok to write about us, about our sexual acts and our lack of an intimate relationship. He laughs and says, "I am sure there is a lot to write about. I'm funny." He is a more than willing participant.

Waste.

Toxic and radiological waste leaks from the Rocketdyne facility in the nearby Santa Susanna hills into the soil.

Tumbleweeds.

Driving into Chatsworth from the 118 Freeway, the sandstone boulders of larger than houses sit against the backdrop of the mountains. The basin of the valley is filled with rows upon rows of ranch houses lined by oak and sycamore trees. A tiny tumbleweed lazily skirts across the street.

Porn Chic.

Porn is chic again. Porn star Sahsa Grey is a known name in Hollywood circles. She likes to be fucked hard. At least she does in her movies. She says she likes her tits to be slapped. Her ass pounded. She, Jenna Jameson, and Ron Jeremy are infamous. They aren't laughed at, at least not publicly. They are branded.

> I hear him say, "Young girls are fucking. Anal sex is the new blowjob. That way, they can't get pregnant."

> I hear her say, "We don't need feminism. Fucking is our right. I'm going to do it cause I like it."

I lie on my back with my legs crossed as a pin-up model would. Hear the snap of the camera shutter. "Now, run your fingers through your hair. That's it. Perfect. You look great. Chic." I move from space to space, sweating in between frames. Uncomfortable, shifting, cautious. "K. Great. Let's try it this way," she grins.

Frank.

Frank, another bar regular with a beak-like nose, deep red hair, and thin frame, comes in to get shit-faced and stays until the bar is closed. He stays to help clean up. I think he just wants to linger for another round but without a bouncer in this rough town, his company is well received. I ask as he drunkenly lifts the stools from the floor and flips them to rest on the counter, "What do you do Frank? I mean, more than come here. What do you do for a living?"

He shrugs and turns to face me. "You really want to know, Sophie?"

"Yeah, I mean, why would I ask if I didn't?" I turn back to my bank and count the ones. I put a paper clip around the bills when I reach twenty-five. Shuffle the next set into neat piles on the tiny cockroach infested counter.

"Well don't tell anyone cause they don't know," he says slurring seriously.

"I won't. What? You in the mob?" I joke and pick up the quarters and put them in the moneybag.

"I do porn."

I stop and turn to face him. His face does not waiver.

"Really? Like what kind of porn?"

"I won't do gay but I fuck for a living."

"What's that like?" I ask waiting for a story about all the free pussy he gets.

"It's hard. And I don't mean that how you think I mean it. I mean it's hard work. You try to keep your dick up for hours on end and cum when they command."

I can see him slink into some form of frustration. "I mean, it's a job. It's fucking hard to keep my dick up and the women lubed. You ever have sex for eight hours straight?" He moves the last stool onto the counter. And I let it rest.

Burn Outs.

"Burn outs. Jumping Jacks. Let's go. Pick it up." We all move faster, want to be stronger.

I want to be stronger. I want my muscles to show, to pulsate out of my thin skin.

I swing another blow into the bag. Blow by intense blow, I get both weaker and stronger.

Tomorrow these torn muscles will repair themselves, and grow a bit. Today, they feel weak, pushed to a limit I don't quite understand. Boot camp feels like getting fucked.

I fight to wear myself out, to blow, to blow through the burnouts to expel air from my lungs and pull it back in, to push and push myself into oblivion. I've lost over twenty pounds since I've moved to Los Angeles and I still don't feel beautiful.

I worry that I need more muscle, less on my stomach, less to grab on to. In Los Angeles, I have been taught how to both shrink and expand. To drive further distances, move around the geographical space more, but also live in solitude. I've learned how to push myself into nothingness. To feel nothing when he blows on my skin.

I drive my glove into the bag and feel my shoulders expand and release, grow tighter and let go.

"Left hook. Straight right," he calls and my arms follow. "Left hook. Straight right."

"Left hook. Straight right." "Left hook. Straight right." "Left hook. Straight right."

"Left hook. Straight right." "Left hook. Straight right." "Left hook. Straight right."

I've learned to listen, to respond with force, to dig deeply. My arms move in a predictable pattern.

"Burnouts. Break."

Commodity Exchange.

After every class I pay him two to five dollars. I want to pay him more so he knows I am there. I wonder if this makes him the object. I feel like the man at the strip club throwing dollars, twenties, waving the money to get the women to dance for them. In their fantasy world, the commodity, the exchange is the power. I hand him a five and he says, "Good work today. Good work." I shuffle back to my bag and pack my things. So far, giving him more doesn't help him notice me.

Envy.

Sometimes I envy porn stars. I don't envy that they have sex for a living. It is not a sweet job. Bodies are pushed to limits. It is not easy to fuck for hours upon hours to get the right angle. In the performance of fucking for the camera there is more lubricant than you can imagine. There is pressure for the men to get it up, keep it up, but hold off on ejaculating. There is the pressure for the woman to moan and push her body into angles we might not think are possible. They rarely orgasm unless it is called for in the scene.

What I envy is the performed confidence, the ability for the woman to pretend she likes it that way. Her control is performed in the way she submits to the man's request. He flips her over. She takes it because she knows if she does she will orgasm.

This has never happened to me.

Vision.

Sophie sleeps with mascara on and when she wakes in the morning, the black smears down her cheeks in ridiculous patterns. It makes her look very dirty. She doesn't take care of herself, at least not like Sophie, the porn star, does.

You called Sophie, the porn star, gorgeous. Sexy. She pulled your groin muscles.

In Hollywood, it's easier to be noticed when you hike your skirt up. Pull eyelashes longer, and cake your face with oh so subtle makeup. The performance of an identity that is not me, maybe Sophie the porn star, but certainly a part of all of us, a part of our consciousness.

Between the Sheets.

Sunday. My friend Kelly and I stop after class and talk to Henry and his friend, Jay. They open up the back of the Ford Flex and sit there laughing.

"You wanna join our tailgate party?" Jay asks.

I saunter up with sarcasm and wit ready to go. "You have any beer? It isn't a tailgate party without beer," I say and sip the coffee I bought at the corner shop.

"Naw, it's a bit early for beer. Don't ya think?" I giggle. Kelly smiles. I look down and see a big jar of Vaseline in the bed of the trunk. Jay follows my gaze and starts to laugh.

"You boys having fun back here?" I ask with a half-grin. The joke breaks the ice and Henry laughs out loud. I got him. We banter about Vaseline and chicken wings, laugh about the way people stare at themselves in the mirror during burnouts. I think I may have him interested, at least a little bit.

I ask, "What are you guys doing tonight?"

Henry responds with a knowing grin and nod to Jay, "Nothing. Why?"

"You wanna go grab a beer?" I ask with a nervous flutter.
"Where?"

I make it up on the spot, "The Blue Room in Burbank. 9pm."

"Well, sure. Ok. 9 o'clock. We'll be there," he says and chuckles.

I'm nervous, all day nervous. Can't eat nervous. He gives me butterflies and a stomach ache and he is meeting me out.

They arrive at the Blue Room a half an hour late and a bit buzzed. I'm drunk. I tried to calm my nerves by drinking wine and I may have overdone it. Despite the occasional stumble, I'm on top of my game—

witty, punchy, strong. He wants to drink. He can't drink here. He is driving.

"You want to continue this?" I ask and lean up against his body outside of the bar. I look up to him and kiss him. I can tell he doesn't want to kiss me in public. His tongue moves too quickly, trying to fill my mouth with urgency, sexual anxiousness but his body doesn't pull me in. I want a gentle kiss but I push my tongue back, wrestling, pulling the passion out from somewhere. He glances over at Jay who just walked past us and I pull away.

"Yeah. But I gotta get out of here. What do we do with your friend?" he asks as he shoves his hands in his pants pockets and looks away from my desiring body.

"Um. I can't leave her here. Can we all fit in your car?" I look at his old tan Ford restored truck in the parking lot. It only fits three.

Jay ducks from around the corner and suggests, "Why don't you go with her and bring her friend home and then come back and get me."

"Yeah, alright. But let's go quick."

We pile into his truck. I notice that I don't really look at him, connect or make eye contact. It's too intimate.

Disconnect: Between Desensitization and Sensation.

The easier erotic story is the story we already know, the one told to us by images and romance novels, Disney films and fairy tales. The erotic story is the story we know the ending to. He cums on her face/breasts/in her mouth/on her ass after her sexualized mistreatment. The women are dressed-up dolls to be thrown around with holes surrounded by cutout lace or leather to be penetrated. Skin to be bruised. The more I watch porn made in the warehouses in Chatsworth, posted on Redtube, the more I feel desensitized to and turned on by this violence. During the actualization and materialization of this form of violent sex I never orgasm.

Stoney Point.

I climb out of my Toyota five-speed truck equipped with a scratched truck bed and ash on the exterior, making the black paint grime gray. I've driven past this large mass of boulders on the way to work at the bar in the bright tanned yellow morning, and from work, at dusk, when the rocks look golden orange. From the street the boulders are massive, overwhelming juxtaposed against the flat grid of Topanga Canyon road. The 118 freeway grinds rubber and cement, exhaust, silence.

I wind past horse stables on thin silt inhabited by fire ants. The frail trail winds me back behind the mass of boulders and chaparral. I decide to turn left on a path, seemingly visible but rarely taken. I sling the tripod before me up a rock face I wasn't expecting to maneuver with the gear on my back and flimsy flip-flops.

My fingers grip the stone and I position my body weight against the rock. I find a hold for my fingers, a step for my toes. Heave my body weight forward and upwards. I encounter boulder upon boulder. A rabbit shifts the brush to my left. A lizard skirts out of view to my right. I find another trail when I reach the top of this boulder, one wider, the one most take. I wind through and past another layer of sandstone. Almost to the top, I stop. Stunned.

They fucked Stoney Point.[77]

Earthquake.

On January 17, 1994 an earthquake hit Northridge, California. The earthquake registered 6.8 on the Richter scale. Fifty-seven people died. Twelve thousand people were injured. There were an estimated twelve billion dollars in damages to the buildings, roads, and structures in the San Fernando Valley.

Evangelical preachers such as Pat Robertson claim God has punished the San Fernando Valley because of the evil porn industry that resides there. They cited Isaiah,

> the foundations of the earth tremble. The earth is utterly broken, the earth is split apart, the earth is violently shaken. The earth staggers like a drunken man; it sways like a hut; its transgression lies heavy upon it, and it falls, and will not rise again.
>
> (24: 18–20 ESV)

The porn industry wasn't impacted by the quake. It never fell.

Its popularity only rises.

Disconnect: Between Knots and Memory.

I want to get the knots out of the back of my hair. Run my fingers through and rip out the bundles and bunches of him. Rip out the feeling of my head pounded against the back of the mattress. And the memory that feeds the intersection of fine threads of who I was before the rapist in Germany took over my body—before this pattern of self-destruction and self-loathing I always feel after a one-night stand. When I am fucked, when I allow the fucking to happen, when I fuck another, I feel the memory of my attacker. For a reasonable, no a lucky woman, no, a woman who is not one out of the three who has been raped, a woman who hasn't felt the weight of an undesired body on top of hers, a woman who hasn't felt the intense loss of body and emotional connection when being raped, she doesn't have these memories floating in. Or maybe she does, maybe we all have the violent cultural memory of "what if?" deep into our psyches.

Or perhaps there are some women that have reclaimed the violence and learned how to fuck for freedom. I do not know how it feels to be agentic in my sexual relationships—to feel power in between the sheets. I have not felt safe enough to not feel pressure, to be good enough, to be loved enough, to be on equal footing. To feel that I love myself, that I am enough to be loved. Rape really fucks with you.

> I hear him say, riding home at 5am in his brown antique Ford, "You shouldn't do this, Sophie. You really shouldn't have one-night stands."

> I hear myself say, "Don't tell me what to do."

As I write this, my face flushes. I look down at my scraped fingers. There is a massive bruise on my right breast from his hand cupping the flesh and pulling hard to the left.

I need to detangle the roots of this longing—this desire wrapped with guilt, pain, and anger. To learn how other women find empowerment between the sheets.

Contract.

Henry calls me weeks later. He talks about his parameters. "I don't want to feel trapped. I don't want to take someone out or make her feel special. I just want to have sex when I want it. I don't want her to stay in my bed after sex. I don't want to cuddle. I don't want to feel obligated. I don't want to have a family or children. OK, Sophie?"

He doesn't want. He doesn't want. He doesn't want.

I suggest, "You should print out a contract for women to sign before they get involved with you."

He laughs, "Yeah. I like that idea. No strings attached. No confusion."

Then I realize—we are talking our contract. I text him a few days later, "Let me know when you want me to sign the contract." He calls a second after I press send.

"Come over."

I buy sexy panties at Loehmann's. I take a shower. I shave my legs first then the area around my vagina, armpits. I want empty, clean skin. It's sexier. I think of the porn stars on Redtube, their bodies without a veil, unmasked vulnerable skin. I rub glittery lotion across the thin surface, and smudge perfume in all of the pressure points. I slide the panties on and push my legs into my jeans. I'm not going to dress up. That's too much. A light blue tank top hugs my breasts. I paint my face lightly with makeup. My heart beats fast—too fast. I grab my keys and leave to have sex with him. I reassure myself, "I am doing research on sexual agency. How can I be a sexual agent? It takes choice, desire, and a clear head. No manipulation and the ability to walk away unscathed."

I shift my truck into first gear and think, "Am I ready for this?"

Graffiti.

I navigate my way over piles of broken glass, bottle caps to reach the summit. I frown at the pizza box, the cigarette butts, and the volatile remnants of human devaluation of Stoney Point. The rock face is littered with scraping of words in reds, black, and blue. A sketch of a woman with enormous breasts and a phallic image next to her mouth, next to the sketch the word dildo clarifies the symbol for the reader.

On another rock, the words "GIVE ME HEAD" in white block print.

Another rock, etches of name, with deep intent scrapes scars into the rock face, a violent etching, with deep wounds and penetrative intent.

Another rock, the words "the drug den" and "Shroom" with a trip-intensified psychedelic feel.

Another rock, claims to the territory. A claiming, the desire to be named, remembered.

I sit behind a boulder and take in the view. I hear voices. A beer can flies past me, crashes to the ground with an empty tinny sound, the splash of the last of the liquid soaks into the stone to my left.

Disconnect between Nature and Culture: Fucking LA.

Los Angeles County, which includes the surrounding San Fernando Valley, is home to over nine million people.[78] As bodies in this space we disconnect through the traffic, the cars on freeways, the concrete shell that covers the dirt and soil, the commodity fetishism, the desire to have more, be more, want more. The larger cultural myth is that nature is female. "The hatred of women is the same as the hatred of nature" is one of the principle mechanisms governing the action of males and this patriarchal culture. The logic of domination naturalizes the idea that men have power over nature as they do over women.[79] This is embodied in practices such as rape, pillaging, and pollution.

We have fucked Stoney Point, which offers us the sunset panorama of the valley, the eagle-eye view of Chatsworth. It is home to rock climbers that work to counter the attack against this space and have annual clean-up efforts. Yet, on most days, the view here is not pristine, it's bruised and boiling with anger and fear, misogynist undertones and sexist slaps to the female body, both in and about nature.

We have fucked LA, disconnected from any emotional connection to this space. We use and abuse her. We fuck her as we have fucked women. And we inhale the aftermath.

Don't Do It.

I have to be careful not to get emotionally attached. We spend time together. Last night after a back massage, lotion over his back, intimate rubbing of skin, we fucked, and I put my clothes on to immediately leave. And he said, "No. You don't have to go just yet. I mean, if you want to stay, stay."

He may just be lonely. He did say as I entered his apartment and pet his aging bulldog Jack, "I'm sick of being alone. Ya know what I want, my girlfriend to buy me socks. I don't want to buy socks. It would just be nice to have her come home with a t-shirt and a pair of socks. That's all I want. Ya know split the duties. I mean, right now I have to do everything."

He shows me pictures of his ex-girlfriend—she is 19. He is 38. She is beautiful, tanned and toned skin, light freckles, thick lips, dark brown eyes. He loved her. She was the one.

Only the age difference keeps them apart. He let her go. She let him go. I ask him about her.

I hear him say, "Time is a brick wall bitch."

He hasn't called me in three days since then. I think he scared himself. He wants to set the record straight. He wants to show me I am not and will not be his girlfriend.

Disconnect: Between Fantasy and Reality.

It is not just the lack of rooted-ness but the encapsulated space of fantasy. In the valley, specifically Chatsworth, women and men perform sexual acts for the camera. On stages, much like low budget Hollywood stages, there are lights, tall trees with Fresnels and zooms. The action goes on for hours, and the lubrication, jump shots, and edits make the very act of sexual engagement solely for pleasure a farce. The mere fact that these warehouses are housed not only in Chatsworth but in any number of houses in the hills, points to the overwhelming number of porn actors and directors that reside in this city.

But, Los Angeles is so elusive. How can we tell one actor from the next? We rely on notoriety, imdb, paparazzi, and the Internet. We rely on media sources to ground us. I forget that I live in Burbank. I forget that the studios are less than a mile away from my house. I forget that the cultural myth of men and women engaged in sex acts in a sadomasochistic and masochistic state is perpetuated by these fantasy sets, the porn actors that make a living being fucked for show. I forget that (heterosexual) fucking isn't the only way in which a woman is penetrated. In Internet porn there are only a few positions that dominate the screen. Doggy style. Anal sex. The woman on top faces away from the man. The three-way. In most pornographic films, the woman is dominated. She doesn't dominate. She doesn't ask for certain positions. She only moans. In more horrific moments, the woman's neck is held tightly, her breasts never touched delicately, her ass pounded, slapped.

Watching porn helps many of us get off. This arousal marks an important distinction for me. I am turned on by these images. I am also angry, disgusted at my bodily reaction. I am uncomfortable, trying to reconcile my visceral reactions of the past with my current conversation with the computer screen. It's difficult to reconcile past wounds, sexually violent socio-cultural norms, and the need to express myself sexually. Dominating hyper-masculine imagery that has manifested in my sexual history, materialized, and has now become a part of my memory, the landscape of my body, the twists and terrain of my sexual desire and the sexual act. The pain, the sexual tension, and arousal connects these violent images to my sexual psyche without a balance of other forms of intimate relationships, I re-enact these scenes in our day-to-day sexual desires.

The Mirror.

She sits across from me with her braided pigtails that frame her striking face. We click when we begin to talk about research. I hear her anxiousness in her stories, the empowerment of proclaiming her abuse. She doesn't go into detail but lets us hear the many layers of repetitive abuse—the years of molestation, the multiple rapes, the bruised face, the implications of those traumas for her mother, not for herself. I listen to her acceptance, "It wasn't my fault but I am just one of those women that get abused over and over again. They just find me. I am sure it doesn't help that I drank myself into oblivion. But I never deserved it."

She eats a piece of egg roll and I listen to her coping mechanisms. I hear the pain, the falsity when she says, "I became the one that fucked because I liked it. Not because of any emotional attachment. I was one of the guys at my dorm. When I wanted it, I got it. I had sex because I liked it. And in this process I learned how to really accept me, my past."

She mirrors me. And I feel a knot rise in my gut. I'm triggered by this reflection. And I feel disgusting. The sickness I feel inside my skin is not about judgment but a realization.

Disassociating from sex, from relationships, from pain is the first gut reaction for survival. It's institutional. How do we survive? What devices do we use to cope? I read in her defensiveness over sushi and whiskey the need to shield her energy and protect her body, her heart, her ability to connect.

I hear in her blasé attitude towards him, the emotional hijacking. She is already attached to him but doesn't want to admit it. She fears abandonment so pretends she has already left. I listen to the process of healing from trauma.

I understand it.

It's my process.

Disconnect: Between Objectification and Agency.

I know what I am doing to my body—the sex without love, sex for the sake of making sense of trauma—is not healing. It's part of a spiral of destructive behavior that only continues to demean my body and my relationship to sexual desire and freedom.

I cannot free a body through careless and reckless aggressive sex.

When I, Sophie, fuck Henry, I disassociate, I don't allow myself to feel anything. I float above my bed, my body. I make excuses for the imprint of fingers on my skin. I pretend I like it rough. I don't.

There is a larger cycle of violence, of sexual abuse, that runs through subconscious desires. The images imprinted in our collective consciousness hurdled at us through Internet pornography, cultural myths of abuse and safety. We were told that men are supposed to colonize the body, to control and dominate women in bed. We are told that smog just exists in Los Angeles. We rape the land as we do women's bodies.

I see and feel this cultural myth in the slapping of my naked ass against his hips, the precarious positions, the grip of skin. I see the bruises on Sophie's body. I see the bruises in the landscape of the San Fernando Valley. The imprint of forms of desire created, not by and through a balanced relationship, but one of cooptation and fear. We are told the story of misogyny through the abuse of bodies in sexual relationships. We see this violent imprint on our disconnected consciousness.

I say abuse of bodies because in this type of sex, where I float above or out of my body, I am not present. I set it up. I set myself up. I entered into a form of sado-masochistic behavior and now it feels difficult to get out.

> I hear him say, "We are all animals. We need sex. There is nothing wrong with fulfilling desire."

> I hear her say, "He couldn't look at me the same. Once he saw the bruises."

> I hear him say, "It's just the valley. It's just the way it is."

·

This work buries me.

·

A Way Out.

He's bright as I enter the apartment. Welcoming. I put beer in the fridge and walk the concrete floors to the living room. We have started to hang out like old friends. He remembers what I said a week ago. He remembers parts of the conversation, the things I can't remember.

> I hear him say, "I don't want a relationship. Don't use that word."

We fuck again. I search in the dark for my pants and underwear.

> I hear myself say, "I don't think I can do this anymore. I feel like a whore with running mascara. And I'm not even cumming."

I move from his gaze and shroud in the darkness of the living room.

"Aw, you want love. You are one of those," he teases.

"Yeah, or at least a little emotional connection. Something," I smirk as I find the warm beer bottle from the old worn coffee table and take a sip.

"I don't kiss during sex. I get tired of kissing. I just want to hang out and fuck, if we want to. And I don't want a girlfriend. This is it. This is all you get. This is who I am, take it or leave it." I look at him sprawled out on the bed, in the light of the desk lamp, his bear-like body open, the sheets cover only his groin. He grins. I sigh. I'm beginning to hear him. Really listen to what he wants.

He continues, "I don't need sex. I just have sex with you because I think you want it. And I don't want to disappoint you after you drive all the way over here," he says and that smirk lingers.

"Can you just once say something nice?" I plead.

I turn from him and search blindly for my earring in the sofa cushions. Another lost casualty. First black socks now a turquoise gem that hangs from the gold casing. I stop in the darkness when his voice floats in from the bedroom. I don't move.

"Look. This is how I see it. When I first met you all I wanted to do was fuck you. That's it. Fuck and get out. But ya know, after time, I like who you are. I like smart conversations. I don't need sex, but it's fine if we want to have it."

"Uh huh," I shiver.

I hear him say, "We can be friends. That's fine. I like hanging out and drinking beers. No sex."

I hear myself say, "Perfect. Friends."

I'm beginning to hear me.

I hear myself say, "I have to go."

It's 4am.

Porn Valley.

The valley is porn valley. The valley is one big strip mall and suburban sprawl.

Buildings tick by in a pattern.

tick tick tick tick tick   tick tick tick tick tick
tick tick tick tick tick

One of these houses is rented to people in the adult entertainment business.
Let's hope they washed the sheets. I did.

tick tick tick tick tick   tick tick tick tick tick
tick tick tick tick tick

One of these women is a porn star. I wonder how she sleeps. I don't.

tick tick tick tick tick   tick tick tick tick tick
tick tick tick tick tick

One of these women is holding the camera. I can hear her say, "Fuck her harder."
He did.

Stop the car.
We've left the valley.

4

CHATSWORTH, REVISITED

THE COMMODIFICATION AND
PERFORMANCE
OF HETERONORMATIVE
MASCULINE DESIRE

As we revisit Chatsworth, we walk back into five spaces I navigated to unpack the way in which space and place impact my performance of sexual identity in my journey to find sexual agency. We revisit the aerial view of the San Fernando Valley to articulate the performative nature of space and place. We have a drink in the dirty pub to make sense of the commodification of intimate engagement. We put our gloves back on in the boxing studio to feel the impacting blow-by-blow of walking into a sexual arrangement that only rematerializes my memory of sexual trauma. We re-climb Stoney Point to align the perceived feminization of nature and parallel raping the female body and fucking nature, to rearticulate how the performance of nature and culture is a liminal space and re-readable, and constantly in flux. And finally, we step back into Henry's bedroom to discover how the performance of sexual identity is deeply connected to heteronormative ideology, our expectation and limitations, desire and lack that ultimately create the grotesque and abject body.

We use narrative snapshots of the story to make sense of these performative moments, moments with specific geographic location complicated by the emotional and colorful complexities of human narrative. From these narrative snapshots we seek to make sense of the performance of sexual identity. Performance of identity is not static; it is a constant process, a negotiation of identity, a fluid and ever-changing contextual experience. Space does not exist for us to fill it. We navigate space as we cultivate place. As we perform in the day to day, we continuously break down and erect borders. We both transgress and navigate what we have come to know as natural and normal. We follow rules. We break them. We create new rules. We come to understand spatiality in the process of doing. "The performativity of life describes the world as fluctuating, complex, improvised, and turbulent, and the relations between human and nature as continuous within it."[80]

Play in the spaces of the narratives, imagine new spaces opening and closing. Lines being erased and redrawn. We hope these snapshots offer a glance into the turning kaleidoscope of performative identity as played out in Chatsworth, CA. After and/or while you visit these narrative snapshots, navigate the spaces of embodied artwork, the collage images, the sound of the space on the website.

Performed Identity: Disconnections and Place-Based Hierarchy.

From Above: The San Fernando Valley

Imagine you are just below the clouds, about to land on the runway in Burbank, CA. You lean close to the window and capture this image. You can see the rows upon rows of houses, the smog that covers the land in a familiar layer. The mountains are far off in the distance. The grid. What you can't see are the layers upon layers past the rows upon rows of houses that go seem to go on forever, stretches and stretches of houses, apartment buildings packed on top of one another. What you can't see from this aerial view are the blocks of concrete, the light posts, the cars parked, moving or honking, the swish of wind as it moves through planted palm trees. What you can't hear is laughter.

Space and Place of the San Fernando Valley

Performance of identity within the valley is much different than the performance of identity in Hollywood, or the surrounding coast cities.

As people negotiate roads, freeways and the grid of the San Fernando Valley they are, through the local action and movement within that space, creating a kinesthetic, local understanding and ordering of space. The production of space in everyday life is tied to history, ideology, and desire. People create spaces from nature as manifestations of ideas. Spaces are created in order to fashion a reality, a way of being in the world, which dictates an individual's relationship to the space.[81] For example, in the San Fernando Valley, people have organized space to maximize flow of goods and people through major roadways and warehouse type buildings. We organize space to order the world around us. As we spend time within space we begin to cultivate a sense of place, which is a performed identity within space. Ultimately our identities are created and cultivated by the navigation of and relationship to space, in which in turn, after time spent within a space, we create a sense of place. Alexander states, "Maybe the major characters are 'space' and 'place,' each signaling how the nature of human engagement is contingent upon location and purpose. Space and place can have character: those combinations of qualities or features that distinguish and dictate doing."[82]

Performance of identity is intimately tied to spatiality.[83] Corey emphasizes, "Territories inform identities, identities inform the territories, and competing identities are defined in relation to each other."[84] Spatial practice structures the conditions of our social life, even as it isn't always obvious.

> A place is thus an instantaneous configuration of positions. It implies an indication of stability. A space exists when one takes into consideration vectors of direction, velocities, and time variables. Thus space is composed of intersections of mobile elements. It is in a sense actuated by the ensemble of movements deployed within it.[85]

Our spatial relationship to the space allows us to cultivate a sense of place. Place is also not static but in constant negotiation with our bodies, ideologies, ideas. But place is the cultivation of a patterned knowing, a performed identity within space. As we move through space we begin to cultivate body memory. We remember the curve in the road, the way in which to order a sandwich from the local restaurant. We find and revisit local haunts. Creating place is also creating a relationship to the environment, including the people that exist and perform within it. We gather with friends and family. The way we connect with strangers, make eye contact, touch skin. The way we have sex, the way we allow ourselves to connect to one another, to find and allow for intimacy, the way we see the rules of sexual engagement, the social, political, and the carnal rules of sexual engagement—all of these experiences are tied into and impact how we create a sense of place.

Chatsworth, an area within the valley, offers me an opportunity to explore my sexual agency. Chatsworth serves those working within the pornographic entertainment industry. The valley is porn valley, a different beast of celebrity culture in its own right. The space and cultivation of place within Chatsworth helps to guide and ground my performance of sexual identity.[86]

Disconnect from One Another: Space and Emotional Connection

The valley impacts me and materializes the ways in which I engage in sexual activity. In this period of time, I move away from emotionally driven sexual engagement into a state of disconnected fucking. The valley creates a sense of disconnectedness from each other, from the land, from the sexual act and emotion. Given that the human body is a product of the nation-state, city, and social drama through a process of rituals that reinforce social structures and expected boundaries,[87] it becomes important to ask, "What is it about Chatsworth that influences the experiences of place for the body and specifically, for me?"

The place of Chatsworth, the landscape of the body, the narrative, and the location of the author, all have an impact on the way in which sexual agency is understood in this context. I use my body differently in this space because of the specific and local knowledge that Chatsworth is the porn capital. There is also the awareness that porn is disconnected from reality, created specifically for the illusion, the fantasy, to create and stimulate desire. Often, this fantasy is directed by, and for, a heteronormative masculine desire that objectifies women's bodies as if they were raw materials to be exploited and consumed.

A seemingly transgressive act is not as grotesque in this context.[88] And as you read this text, you are situated within your own place. How does your context, place, influence how you read this chapter?

Looking around Chatsworth, one can see the ways in which the surroundings are manipulated in service of consumer desire. The artifice—the superficial and placement of strip malls, warehouses, shopping centers disconnect a sense of belonging to the land. Packed in tight spaces, there is an overwhelming sense of violence and hyper-masculinity, fear and loss, a fight or flight mentality. The knowledge that any of these houses may be porn studios, that each of the warehouses may house DVDs of pornographic entertainment, that any of the patrons at the bar may be involved in the pornography industry cultivates a sense of possibility, that I can be one of them, may be one of them. Desire in this landscape is fraught with expectations and limitations, which limits the possibility of intimate connection but opens the possibility of sexual relationships that in another place might be considered taboo.

The Dirty Pub: The Commodification of Intimate Engagement.

The image of the pub in Chatsworth is a partial view, a snapshot of the space. You can't see the cockroaches that move in and out of the glasses piled next to the napkins. You can't see the thick mats on the floor encrusted with grime from the years of spilled beer, vodka and gin. You can't see the browned ceiling caked with smoke and tar. You can't smell the rot, or hear the passing cars screech to a halt. You can't feel the air conditioning freeze your skin in the summertime or hear Johnny's voice when he orders his Miller light. You can see the neon glow of the tacky beer signs, the lines and rows of bottles that I dust every Saturday morning. You can see the broken coffee pot, the red surface of the bar, the sink and the soda gun. You can only through this image experience the product of a snapshot of the performance of bartending. Can you see me leaning over the bar to become more familiar with the patrons? Can you hear the lottery machine? The image of the space of the bar in Chatsworth is further removed from you.

————

Place of the Pub: Intimate Commodity

Yet, the space is not a thing, an empty medium or container that is distinct from its contents.[89] Space is produced, it is in constant motion which is counterintuitive to what the photograph seems to suggest, that space is made up of boundaries, lines, breaks in vision, boxes, maps that justify and align territories. Space is not finite. "Social spaces interpenetrate on another and/or superimpose them upon one another. They are not things, which have mutually limiting boundaries and which collide because of contours or as a result of inertia."[90] Rather, space is made up of movement, rhythm, and patterns of energy. Space is a performed process.

The place of the pub is created through the performances of the people that drink and interact there. The place of the pub in Chatsworth is created when the pub is experienced, physically, emotionally, intimately, and presently.[91] The place of the pub is created because of the collected performances that are performed within and on this stage.

There is something humbling, humiliating working in the pub. But I am grounded enough to know there are people within these walls, all of us are human enough to succumb to the weight of the environment—an unconscious reiteration of acts that characterize the performance of Chatsworth. Most of the patrons and the bartenders are alcoholics and don't have families anymore. Their families left them long ago. Most of them are on unemployment and gamble and drink their days away in several different local haunts. Some of them are accomplished and continue to be successful, stopping in for one drink on their way to or from work. I only work at this pub because the budget for education in Higher Education was slashed, as was my salary. But it is also because through education, we learn to identify and unpack the performances we are playing so we can hold the agency of choosing our identity performances.

Performance is the ideal space to address local culture, as kinetic subject (being) and a method (doing),[92] revealing the interdependence of the being and the doing as dynamic, and continuously evolving together. The interplay between being and doing offers us a space of reflection where we are aware of our performances. This is usually understood as a liminal space or state. Liminal states are places in-between boundaries, and it is in these places that we are able to shift social frames and imagine new possibilities.[93] Within this liminal space, we revisit the pub to make sense of the commodification of intimacy, the process of exchanging desire, the conscious choice to perform for the pub patrons, to allow them the space to formulate sexual fantasies and enact the scripts of emotional intimacy. How do these performances within the space of the dirty pub create a sense of place rooted in unfulfilled fantasy? How do these relationships enact the same hyper-masculine heteronormative forms of desire?

Being and Doing: Performance Consciousness of Commodification of Intimacy

The patrons also pay for the performance of familial connection. Being in the pub in Chatsworth makes them believe they have a home and an intimate and collective connection to people just like them. This collective identity rests entirely upon the cultivation of place within the space of the bar.

In terms of sexual identity, I feel power here. As a bartender, you are always seen. Respected, coddled, pushed to the limits, disrespected and respected at the same time, it's a constant negotiation of power but because you hold the alcohol, you are ultimately in control. Yet bartenders, especially female bartenders, are asked to look a certain way, to allow for momentary intimacy with the patrons so they want to come back. The commodity exchange is both sexually charged and driven by the intimate, yet brief, emotional connection a bartender can make with the patrons. One can embody the grotesque and abject body, and in doing so, call traditional forms of acceptable identity into question, while also enacting a body of desire.

Desire, as understood by Deleuze and Guattari, is "machined." In other words, according to Ingram and Protevi's analysis of this form of desire, "all production, 'natural' and 'social' alike, is patterned by processes of coding *and* decoding, reterritorializing and deterritorial-izing."[94] Desire is produced and reproduced across places and bodies in a dynamic interplay between organic nature and socially constructed beliefs, values, and actions. With such an open playground for desire, a "schizophrenizing" of desire emerges in which people can perform their identity in any way they choose, but this freedom is counterbalanced by the apparatus of capitalism which demands that the breaking of boundaries must turn a profit.[95]

Therefore, while I have the freedom to perform my sexuality as it feels good to me, I am influenced by what those around me desire and by how my performance can sustain me financially. But the performance of this identity, however empowering in the moment, is lost when the patrons say things such as, "Baby, get me a drink. Bartendress, hurry up. You know I would fuck you like you wouldn't believe. Just one time and you will be in love." Sexual agency is *not* objectification without choice. Sexual agency is *not* being made to be something you don't want to be. The trick is that we are all tricking one another. I will never see them outside of this space. I will, however, know them in memory. And in the constant re-membering that power and desire mediated by the commodity of fantasy, the commodity of intimate engagement is not satisfying for me.

The Boxing Studio: Physical Embodiment of Participant Observation.

In the space of the studio, you can see the lines of blue boxing bags, the room lined with mirrors, the carpet on the edge of the room, the wooden dance floor, the platform in the front of the room. You can see the steppers used for step aerobic classes, the hand weights locked away. You can see the spatial relationships embedded within the lines of the room. The platform exists for the instructor. The mirrors are there for detecting and correcting form. But most people stare at the form of their bodies, to make sure they are sculpting the right muscles, and by the squint of their eyes and the pull of their skin, you can see they feel less than beautiful.

You can't see the way bodies become broken and strong at the same time. You can't hear the pulsing music that helps to distract the mind from the physical pain. You can't hear the class self-elected captain saying, "Go Baby. You got this." You can't hear the grunts, the moans, the chatter, nor can you hear Henry's commands. You can't smell the rot of sweat mixed with deodorant and perfume. You can see and understand the space of the boxing studio. The space of the studio sets up the relationships that can connect and disconnect here.

———————

In the Studio: Space and Place of the Body

The place of the boxing studio is created though the performance of boxer, of aggression, of emotionless engagement, of focus and endurance, of the desire to become stronger, slimmer, *more* desirable. The materialization of perceived lack and desire sculpts the body in a particular form in the created space of the gym. The LA emphasis on the way bodies should look and the constant pressure to feel and look thin cultivates these ideologies. The pressure to live up to a certain standard of beauty helped to create the space of the gym. You may be tricked into believing that space is a container to fill with bodies. But rather the space of the gym is a materialization of the processes of cultivating a sense of place, identity, and the performance of achieving perceived beauty.

When we enter the space of the boxing studio we perform athlete, connecting to the body, the bag, the sweat and intensity of embodiment. The mind focuses on one spot on the bag, the way your fists curl inside the glove, you focus on form. The boxing studio becomes an outlet to explore the nature of creating relationships with the body, through the body, and allows the erasure of pain by diving straight inside one experience of it. In my agentic choice to sleep with a man without emotional connection I chose to re-script the narrative of sexual trauma in the attempt to erase the painful emotions that reside inside my body. Henry, the boxing instructor, taught me how to disconnect from emotion within the sexual act. The space of the boxing studio became the place to fight emotion, to try and knock out the expectation of emotional intimacy, to forego any expectation of romance.

The space of the body can be navigated, moved with and through from a distant perspective. The space of the body as landscape can be seen, objectified, outlined with vision. The objectification of the body is the process of understanding the body spatially. The objectifying gaze demands that the body account for all of its movements, most notably those that push past the expectation of the gaze, as is the case with the grotesque body. The body performing under this gaze operates more mechanically. But cultivating place with the body is connecting with another person's body emotionally, physically present, concerned, a mutual affection. Henry does not engage with the body as place but a space to fuck. For Henry, the female body, or more specifically my body is not a place but a space to navigate towards orgasm.

My sexuality, my sexual agency, my ability to feel empowered in a relationship is not based on commodity or exchange of the space of body. The choice to become an object complicates the idea of subjectivity and agency in sexual relationships. To make the decision to become an object for me only reaches deeper into the painful memory of sexual trauma. When I hit the bag in the boxing studio I feel the pain and ache inside my muscles. When I fuck without him seeing me, feeling me, loving me, I remember the unwanted finger, then dick, inside me. I see that man's face, feel his palm on my mouth. I feel trapped, frozen, a statue, a blow-up doll, the porn star on the screen. I moan for the performance of sexual pleasure. I thrust my hips to make him cum faster. And I get up now, right away, to shower, to change, to change the sheets.

Sometimes in order to make sense of the complexities and contradictions associated with identity, space and place, we have to make do. In the practical reality of making do within Chatsworth, I am faced with the very tactic of making do,[96] to disconnect my body and consciousness to survive a space while seemingly attempting to rein script the happenings of that space of my body, within a larger institutional truth that I exist within a capitalist system and within this system any extension of my body, the way I engage with others through and with my body can be considered an exchange, the commodification of intimate engagement.

Performed objectification allows me to make do in the moments of sexual engagement with Henry to see, for the first time, the space of my body as object. This distancing from my body allows me to reclaim my subjectivity. Was this decision to perform as object of masculine heteronormative desire ultimately fulfilling for me? We shift location and revisit Stoney Point to understand how my body became performed landscape. Perhaps we can make sense of the forest by revisiting the trees.

Stoney Point: Fuck Nature; Performed Intimate Engagement with the Land.

As you climb the mountain you may see the grain of the rock, the boulder that juts out into the horizon line. You may see the way the branches twist and turn in dark jagged lines. You can't see blossoms that aren't there. You can see the ground–dust minced with stone. You can see the graffiti. You can see the rows upon rows of buildings hidden within the green tops of trees. You can see the mountains in the distance, the pavement. You can't hear the flow of traffic, the buzz of metal and horns. But you see a car or two frozen. Imagine you reach the top of this mountain and see only decimation of the land, imprints of human anger and desire to conquer space, to leave a mark in the soft shale. Can you hear the wiz of the beer can that flies past your head and lands in a fizzing tinny clunk next to cigarette butts and broken glass? You stop and look at the boulder, the image of yourself extended into the mountain. Your silhouette frames the words "Give me Head" etched in the rock. You take a picture.

Performative Engagement with Nature and Culture

This space was carved by institutional and governmental decisions and human desire. It was originally marked as territory for hikers, rock climbers to enjoy the "natural landscape." Stoney Point is marked as state park land by the invisible governmental lines drawn on a map. When you enter the space of Stoney Point, you may think to yourself, "This is nature." Enjoy its natural beauty. Respect the line between nature and culture. Yet the space, carved out by the day-to-day performances of Chatsworth complicates my understanding of space, place, at the intersection of nature and culture. Graffiti lines mark the territory here and leave gross traces of a human's interaction with nature. Yet, understanding nature as a performance process, not as a material entity to be encountered but a part of the performance process, blurs the distinction between nature and culture. Stoney Point is a performed liminal space between nature and culture. For me, it is a disaster area, a poignant war zone. From an ecofeminist standpoint, those that fuck

Stoney Point articulate a much stronger desire, the desire to take over, to impede upon the landscape, to make a lasting effect on the land, to mark and scar the land. Encountering Stoney Point is a moment of performative engagement with nature and culture, with the ideological dualisms associated with men and women as culture and nature respectively.

In a moment of personal reflection, I desire to escape the concrete beat of Chatsworth and attempt to reconnect to nature at Stoney Point. Yet I was only reminded, sitting atop bottle caps and broken glass, of the misogynist, masculinist, heteronormative relationship most people have with the raw material of nature. I found myself contemplating, "If left to our own devices would we all continue to fuck the landscape? How does this image of nature in the hands of the disrespectful represent or point to the larger cultural implications of sexual identity and the performance of identity in Chatsworth? Am I the rock? Is my body this landscape? Where and how, then, do I retreat, find solace, connection?"

In 1974, Françoise d'Eaubonne first used the term ecofeminism to express the direct connection between oppression of women and oppression of nature.[97] Ecofeminism is rooted in the belief that there is a connection between feminism and ecological values. This connection has been shaped by what Karen J. Warren calls "an oppressive patriarchal conceptual framework."[98] This framework consists of value dualism, value-hierarchical thinking, and logic of domination. Value dualisms associate men with culture and women with nature. Women have been naturalized and nature feminized. Value-hierarchical thinking associates men with power because culture is said to dominate nature. The logic of domination naturalizes the idea that men have power over nature as they do over women.

Gillian Rose posits there is a strong relationship between the masculine gaze, man's relationship to nature, and woman as nature.

Following the work of Lacan, Freud, Mulvey, and Irigaray, Gillian Rose argues:

> The metaphor of land-as-woman affected men's attitudes towards the environment in complex ways. As the ownership

and exploitation of territory and for the raw materials of the new industries grew in the nineteenth century, this ambiguity led to increasing unease in North American male writers' relationship to their landscapes. Domination of the land began to be seen as both incest and rape, and the horror of this necessitated a psychological and emotional separation from the land and from woman."[99]

This male gaze is so ingrained without our unconscious that it has affected not only the actual material landscape but also my understanding, materializations, and interpretations of the landscape.

Performance, Possibilities in Nature, Breaking Boundaries

Nature is not an object or a thing to be manipulated. Like the body, space, and place, nature is something that happens in process with and within human interactions with it. Human beings are part of nature, not disconnected, above, or better than nature. If we come to see nature as a performance, a process, mutable and contingent upon these performances, we may begin to treat nature as part of us, and we a part of nature. A deep ecological approach, as developed by Aldo Leopold, portrays the land as an intricate system, an "intricately interwoven and interdependent intersection of elements that functions as a whole organism."[100] This branch of environmentalism looks for interconnections, diversity, and richness, and sees human beings as a part of a whole system. This approach rests on the holistic assumption that everything is linked and that all actions have an impact on all parts of the system.

A person's relationship to nature means different things to differently situated people. Subjectivities are grounded in local, social, political, contextually based experiences at the intersections of race, class, gender, and identity. Multiple subjectivities are grounded not in nature, nor in culture, but in the space between nature and culture. Anti-essentialist identity politics also opens up the space for differently situated political models, more specifically eco-conscious political models.

Donna Haraway's eco-conscious political model of civic practice includes responsibility with nature.[101] She understands nature as an active subject that can and should participate in civic culture. Rather than focus on oneness with nature, Haraway argues that people should focus on our relationality with nature. Human connectedness with nature is not stable or fixed but is rather fluid and constructed along the vectors of power that define civic life.

Braidotti argues that a nomadic subjectivity entails a constant state of becoming. Our subjectivities are always in process, in flux. The non-essentialized feminist subject is no longer grounded in feminine nature but is capable of ethic and moral agency. A nomadic subjectivity cultivates what Braidotti calls a feminist philosophy of 'as if.' The *as if* philosophy leaves room for a feminist imaginary, new metaphors, definitions, and new relationships between the body and technologies. The *as if* philosophy is a "technique of strategic re-location in order to rescue what we need of the past in order to trace paths of transformation of our lives here and now."[102]

The *as if* philosophy leaves room for me to help complicate distinctions within nature and culture, to re-envision my performed identity on top of Stoney Point, to re-envision the relationship between nature and culture, my body and sexual agency in Chatsworth. Similar to a performance perspective, Braidotti insists that a nomadic subjectivity is always grounded in real contexts and situations. Nomadic subjectivity is therefore not an essential act because subjective specificity is grounded in lived experiences, with multiple discourses, physicality, and contexts creating the flux of the *as if* philosophy.

If a nomadic subjectivity is always grounded in real situations, Braidotti posits the *body* is the mediator between nature and culture. Human beings originally extended the body "through tools, weapons and artifacts, then through language, the ultimate prosthesis."[103] Braidotti, like Haraway, proposes that there is no clear distinction between the natural and the cultural. What is important for this discussion is Braidotti's argument that the body mediates between nature and culture. The present subjectivity, the agentic person recognizes that the body is the tool through which we come to understand and mediate our understanding of sexual agency. Our body is both nature and culture, both feminine and masculine, non-essentializing the body also opens possibilities for the many forms that agency in sexual relationships may take. Agency is naming, reframing, and performing an identity that suits us, without the restrictions of essentialisms that both order and narrow our conceptualization of sexual possibility.

Porn Studio: The Hyper-masculine Fantasy and Performing the Grotesque Body.

You see the windows covered by curtains to block out the sunlight. You can see the height of his bed, the wooden bedposts, and the colorful quilt. You can see the desk fashioned out of broken parts. You can't hear the modem that normally buzzes into the night. Nor can you feel his skin against yours or listen to the way his dog breathes so heavily. The space of the bedroom is distant from you, visually stimulating yet your other senses engaged only in imagination. The vision of the bedroom, the spatial configuration of his bedroom, doesn't connect you to the layers upon layers of emotional and physical connection, the complex and confusing nature of sexual agency within this space. Can you hear her moan? Can you feel the thrust, the weight of urgency in desire, the moments of disconnect, and reconnection? The process of understanding sexual agency is embodied within the space of Henry's bedroom, with the intimate configuration of place with our two bodies, making sense of the terrain of our bodies, our emotional intimacy, together.

We enter Henry's bedroom, to revisit the materialized sexual acts that I perform as Sophie. How does this performance of object create an abject body? Is my decision to perform and fulfill the heteronormative masculine desire ultimately satisfying? For whom? And what, then, do we call my performance? How do I make sense of it now? How does Henry? And was this performed sexual act a reification of past sexual trauma? How can I order it all? How does Chatsworth at once free and confine me?

————

The Grotesque: Breaking Expectation

The connection between Henry and I is what some would call a grotesque connection, grotesque bodies performing in ways that question boundaries and ask what is proper and what is not; thereby redefining culture, knowledge, and pleasure.[104] The arrangement made of Henry and myself is not necessarily the accepted form of establishing sexual intimacy. In the United States, in white, heterosexual, middle to upper class, heteronormative groups the pattern of establishing sexual intimacy is as follows: first date, second date, third date. Establish that you are dating, a couple, before moving into bed. At least this is what I, as a girl growing up, was told. I was warned about the bad boys, and told to respect my body more than anything in the world and to fear the term slut, or whore. I was asked sexist questions such as, "Why would they want the cow if you give the milk away for free?" I was also told that the initial movement of desire usually came from the man's advances. The performance of sexual engagement is framed by certain rules of engagement and the cultivation of a relationship. Women are supposed to maintain purity and virginal qualities. Men, on the other hand, are allowed to have sex, as often as they want. We hear phrases such as, "Men want to spread their seed around. It's in their nature."

The sexual arrangement Henry and I made is seemingly grotesque because it breaks these expectations and patterns. The grotesque arrangement is a performance of a double standard. From a traditional heteronormative perspective, I may be seen as the grotesque body. I was supposed to be a lady, act like a good girl, maintain body integrity, find a man that loves me, and then get married. Can you see Cinderella? Imagine and see the impact of the cultural myth seeping in consciousness? The fairy tale story that pervades consciousness and is materialized in our day-to-day actions is that women have desire for emotional intimacy and connection and that men do not. I became grotesque because I did not want this fairy tale, nor did I perform the script of cultural expectation.

The Abject Body: Performing for You

My grotesque body also plays the role of abject body, or the body that society wants to push away.[105] In the act of pushing away, the performance of identity is troubled and with this trouble, we can begin to understand how social forces call upon us to perform through social expectations[106] and are maintained or disrupted by individual stylized acts of identity performance.[107] My performance of identity within Chatsworth is also for you, the reader. As you read these pages, do you want to push me away, as I did to the student that mirrored me? The abject body points to the boundaries, norms, and rules and regulations we put upon the body. My desire to become a sexual object may disgust and offend you and your sensibility. But it is also an honest portrayal of the acts of sexual engagement we all take part in and play out. As we push away and distance ourselves from the abject body, it is best to ask, how do we personally fulfill the roles we are so turned off and turned on by? How do we work to change the script, to identify with and not the possibility of different forms of sexual engagement? Who is your performance of pleasure and desire for?

An Exhale.

Without an origin, sexual identity is performative, constantly in flux, yet grounded in the institutionalized discourses and histories of sexual agency and empowerment.[108] The reiteration of my sexualized identity draws me closer to my trauma, the memory of rape frames the space of my body. Yet my performance of sexual identity and agency in Chatsworth and more specifically within the pub, the boxing studio, atop Stoney Point and in Henry's bedroom allowed me to make sense of the varying cultural expectations, materializations of these expectations. Using sex to disengage from these emotions did not offer a sense of empowerment. What I did learn is that using sex for only pleasure is not empowering for *me*. But without the materialization of the questions, vulnerability, and insecurity around the terrain of my body, of the space and performance of place in Chatsworth, I would not have the clarity I do now. Sexual agency exists in the performance of choice and the desire to allow for the fluid nature of sexual identity. Sexual agency for me exists in the feeling of safety; no matter what choice I make, a mutual trust must exist in the sexual act. This trust means creating a safe place in which to cultivate and explore sexual desire, without judgment, scorn, fear, or anger—to have safety in the possibility.

This new understanding will certainly shift and change as I navigate the terrain of Los Angeles. Each terrain allows for new consideration, to dig deeper into the cultural myths, to excavate the undercurrent of desire, agency and lack, and to discover how the space and lace of Hollywood scripts another fantasy upon the body. I wind into the Hollywood Hills to try to become . . . again.

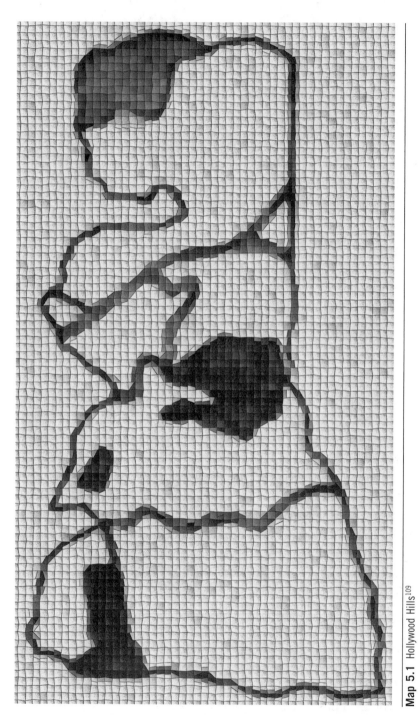

Map 5.1 Hollywood Hills[109]

5
THE HOLLYWOOD HILLS[110]

Image 5.1 Wax statue

.

A wax statue melts in the sun.

.

Cover.

The hills cover themselves. Winding up and through the Hollywood hills, the mountains provide both protection and then full exposure—once you hit the top.

green space, fence, yellow, fallen boulder, empty house, wall of clay.
She can't see how beautiful she is.
wind up.
green space, wall of concrete, yellow, fallen boulder, empty house, wall of clay.
He can't see that he doesn't need that too.
wind up.
green space, garage door, yellow, fallen boulder, empty house, wall of clay.
They can't see how lucky they are.

Satisfied.

She can't feel her nipples so she derives pleasure in his looking at me/her/woman as an object. Connection is made not in the touch—no nerves—but in our ability to look.

Nerves.

Delila walks out of her shared bathroom, the towel only draping her hips. Her breasts, pert and perky, and light nipples draw attention away from her raw face. It's rare to see Delila without make-up on. "So darling, how are you?" The other towel wrapped around her head pulls the skin on her tanned face back and her eyes look smaller than usual.

"I'm alright. Working. All the time." I look to the ground, embarrassed by her skin. Her tiny thin boned frame shames my big bones and undefined muscles. I change the subject.

"So, tell me about him. What is he like?" Delila glides through her bedroom grabbing clothes from the pile in the corner.

"He is a doll. Really. He is kind. He really listens to me. And it doesn't hurt that he pays for our trips to New Zealand, Cannes and Mexico," she says with a giggle. Delila's energy is chaotic. She moves to the mirror where she blots foundation underneath her eyes. She pulls her eyebrows up and points to the middle of her forehead, the space right between her brows. "Can you see the wrinkles? I just had botox a week ago. I can move my forehead again." She smiles and moves her fingers to her lips and slides across the delicate skin above the pink. "I'm going to have it here too. But the trick is to only have half of the vile. That way it doesn't ruin you. I just can't stand looking like a piece of rotting fruit."

"Dee, are you sure you need all of it? I mean, you're stunning," I say as I glance at my worn light cotton dress and dangling bracelets. I can see the fabric wearing thin on the sleeve. I haven't had time to shop. Delila slips a thin silk dress over her tiny frame and pulls mascara on her lashes.

In Hollywood, her thin frame and muscular arms are the envy of a party. Her blonde hair falls down her back. She grabs the hair curler and says, "I am not doing too much. I swear. I mean you should see what Tegan has done to herself. Another boob lift. But she is just gorgeous. Isn't she? She always says how beautiful you are. She thinks you are the prettiest one in our group." Delila smiles her warm smile.

I know why every man falls in love with her. She is beautiful, exciting, smart, witty, engaging, and that smile is so kind. She just goes for the wrong man, the billionaire that whisks her away, dines and wines her. Then leaves.

"Will you be a doll and pour us a glass of wine?"

I climb the spiral staircase that leads from her basement bedroom and pass the floor to ceiling windows. I pause to pull a cigarette out of my bag and walk out to the balcony.

The Stretch.

On the top of one of Hollywood's Hills, the basin of the city is filled with a million lights. The grid stretches to the ocean and back again, as if the land became the sky without clouds.

A Cry.

At the center of steel and stone in our modern cities stands the same individual that once stood in the shadows of an ancient desert. This individual yearns for the same spiritual rooted-ness to a universe larger than oneself. This cry for a glimpse of the ineffable is becoming increasingly audible as a public voice in the canyons of our urban environments.[111]

Santa Ana.

The Santa Ana winds pick up. The gum trees with peeling skin lean back and forth, and push into a back bend. I hear the breaking sound, a snapping branch, then, a rolling rock falls down this steep cliff. I'm standing on concrete held up by stilts, anchored in dust. And the winds carry me through the sky. The smoke from my lips soars towards the ocean. On the peak of Los Angeles, I feel like I'm flying.

"Jeanine, darling. Did you grab us that wine?" I turn from the railing. Delila has made her way from the bathroom. Her foundation is bronzed with a nice dust of glitter so that her face, arms, and legs reflect the lights from the valley below, like her skin belongs to the landscape. Her blonde hair, in ringlets, falls to her shoulders now. The wind blows the thin fabric against her skin. I am drawn to her flat stomach then up to her perky breasts.

"Sorry, I got distracted by the stars and the lights," I say realizing my eyes have lingered a bit too long. I wonder if she knows, can feel my jealousy, my insecurity. I draw my hands down the front of my dress, a cotton dress, from Target, feel the slight bulge in my belly and shift uncomfortably.

"Well, the guests will be here any minute. Let's get a glass before they get here. Did I tell you about the new guy Victoria is dating? He is just divine. A model. I know. Well, of course, right? Victoria can get just about anyone. And she can't decide between Mark, the model and Jim the Doctor. So she is fucking them both. I think she just met someone else again last night. Can I have a cigarette?"

I let her drag the cigarette from the pack I hold up and I look longingly at her manicured nails. I stuff the pack back into my bag, and look down at my own nails—stubby, dirt underneath the ridge, cuticles with sharp edges. "I'll go get the wine. I think I am going to need it," I say and leave her there on the balcony.

Slipping Hills.

The hills here are slipping—slowly.

Bogart.

The glass door leads into the foyer. The pattern on the floor reminds me of the yellow brick road in the Wizard of Oz. Humphrey Bogart lived in this house. I walk on the same marble he did. I think of his love affairs, the dashing Hollywood celebrity standing on the same balcony with a cigar and a snifter of brandy, looking out at the same lights, the same ocean. I wonder if he felt alone.

Typical.

I draw my legs up the steep stairs to the kitchen. The loose metal railing is low, so low that it runs parallel to my hips. I imagine: I lean the wrong way and crash to the marble floor. I hear cracking bone. My blood seeps against white marble.

The bell rings.

"Jeanine, will you be a doll and answer that?" Delila calls through the open balcony door.

I think, "Great. They are here. I'm not ready for this."

"Hiiiiiii Jeanine. Oh, you look . . . nice," Sara says with a snobby lilt in her voice. She speaks through her nose and it drives me insane. She takes off her designer jacket and pulls her scarf from her neck. She hands me her things and walks into the kitchen and puts her bottle of wine on the counter. "So, how are you?" she asks not really wanting to know the answer.

"I'm great, actually. I am just getting settled. Trying to make sense of it all. I am happy."

"Oh, yeah. That's good," She responds in her non-response so much so that there isn't a question mark at the end of her first phrase, her fickle backhanded slap.

I suck in my belly. I tense the abdominal muscles.

She moves quickly to talk about how she is. "I'm on top of the world," she says as she pours red into her glass and doesn't offer to top mine off. "I just got a raise and, get this, I am moving again but this time to Marina Del Rey, right next to the ocean. Can you believe it? I know. No more of that small cottage. I mean, who can really live comfortably in a one bedroom apartment?"

Jump cut to my one bedroom half of a duplex. I begin, "Well, I like my. . . ." She scoffs and begins her descent down the stairs.

Her three-inch heels click click click against the wood then marble. I hear her voice move into a muffled, "Hiiiiii. Oh my god, it's so good to see you. You look AMAZINGINGING."

Plastique: In the Desire to Be.

Women pull skin in the bathroom and feel incomplete. Here, beauty is a layer of skin, a tiny frame, pain and plastique. I use the term plastique because using it as a French term makes it sound more glamorous, elitist, but obviously manipulated–a snobbery with silicone, an air of fame and importance.

Behind the taut skin, and layers of gold, we are just down home girls that used to smoke cigarettes behind school buildings and steal earrings from the mall. Most of us would flirt with boys and cry to each other when they didn't flirt back. Some of us are the girls at slumber parties, on the soccer field, in the school band. Some of us ditched school and pretended to be older than we were by drinking booze. We fooled them with makeup and attitude. Perhaps nothing has changed except the context, the standards to live up to, the pressure to feel beautiful.

Surrounding Mountains.

The mountains here are what some would call rolling. They aren't exceptional like the height of the Andes or capped with snow, but the San Gabriels are majestic in their own right. Rolling expanse of mountain shifts in green and yellow, brown, backdrop for the image of Hollywood splendor. The white letters of the Hollywood sign starkly contrasted by the dust and shrubbery.

Above the Grid.

The streets in my city are a fraction of a larger grid, anchored to one in Los Angeles. That grid was laid out in September 1781. The Los Angeles grid is a copy of one carried from Mexico City to an anonymous stretch of river bank by Colonel Felipe de Neve, governor of California.[112]

I live in part of that grid. I am not alone in this. Waldie continues, "Three-quarters of the United States is platted on a grid that follows the lines of longitude and latitude across the continent."[113] In the hills you can see the grid, have a different view of the landscape, a different perception of who you are within it.

Roots.

I pour myself a glass of wine from her bottle just to spite her and wander into the unused dining room. The view on the top floor stuns me to pause. I see my reflection in between the pattern of light.

The roots of my hair are brown, almost two inches now. I can't afford to get my hair done as often as I would like.

Hills.

To get to the houses in the hills you wind up steep roadways. The dirt from the surrounding cliffs crumbles onto the broken concrete. Most of the houses are precariously resting on the cliff of the mountain. The view is best if your house is not below another.

Grant Cardone came to Los Angeles looking for a panoramic city vista, and he found it six years ago in a Tuscan villa-style home perched high in the Hollywood Hills. But it was impossible to enjoy the view with a row of olive trees and low shrubs running along the edge of the yard. "Literally, you couldn't see anything past the pool," he says. With the obscuring trees and shrubs long gone the 52-year-old motivational business speaker and author points to the swath of Southern California before him: Century City, the Pacific Ocean, Catalina Island. "Now this is what the house is all about," he says. "A view like this doesn't come cheap." From coast to coast, view homes are the most sought after and expensive properties on the market—and it's no wonder.[114]

Isolation.

Looking up at the hill, one light shines in the window of a house with fifty windows. The rest of the house, the floors, the surrounding trees and pavement are dark.

Freeze.

I move my fingers through my hair and draw my fingertips to the space between my eyebrows. I crinkle and unwrinkle my brow. I see lines, so many lines that play with my skin. I wonder what it might feel like to paralyze my nerves, fill these spaces with collagen, recreate my face.

"And this is Jeanine." I turn at the sound of my name.

Delila is there in the doorframe, a male figure behind her. "Jeanine is one of my oldest and dearest friends. We met in college and she just moved here. Jeanine, this is Matt. He is a prominent lawyer for ABC. Jeanine has her doctorate. She is the smartest one of the bunch."

I always hear that. I am the smart one. Growing up I was Simon of the three chipmunks—the nerd with glasses. I was never the pretty one, certainly not Alvin caliber, nor the "somebody" that moves through the same circles, the same clubs. I can't prance past the bouncers, the gatekeepers, the guards like Delila. My kind of nerdy and cute is not good enough for this slice of LA, for these hills.

I watch Matt turn back from me and follow her out of the dining room. He isn't interested in me.

I will make changes.

Scaffold.

As women age in Hollywood, we look for ways to strip the years, add scaffolding to faces, and pull out the plaster behind our skin. We freeze veins and nerves, and rarely check to see if the pipes are working. It's a fantasyland, a game to play, and a hollow desire. No one is ever satisfied.

Plastique: In the Desire to Be Desired.

The plastique of Hollywood creates a certain desire. A desire to be wanted. A desire that we are told can be achieved through attaining a certain form of beauty.[115] This idealistic image is solidified into our cultural conscious so much so that we desire the image of ourselves made beautiful by the dominating heteronormative male gaze. This desire manifests in the ways in which women and men make significant changes to their bodies, to their exterior. It manifests in the ways we make excuses for our decisions to purchase, to manicure, to make the house fit on the mountaintop, to alter the natural body to fit the perfect mold.

Filter.

There's a storm coming. I am grateful. It takes leagues of water, days of rain to cleanse this muck out of my lungs, to filter the sinew and bone.[116]

Prey.

"Motherfucker! You get back here. If you want me come and get me. I'm right here. Show yourself. I'm ready. I'm fucking ready for you," I scream into the air.

The street at 2am is empty. A flash of light bounds up behind me throwing shadows on the cars, spin and whirl around, mad eyes flash for a sign of him, any sign of his body.

I will rip him to shreds.

"Jeanine, get back inside. Don't be stupid." My best friend Chris calls breathlessly from behind the fence I just barreled thru after the man that has been watching me for weeks, watching all of us tonight play cranium, slug glasses of wine.

"Fuck him. Motherfucker, I will kill you," I call to the bushes. I know he is only feet away. I can feel him there and I need to protect my territory. A wolf, growling.

The Cost.

I search Trulia.com a real estate website for homes for sale near Delila's rented home in the hills.

1440 N Kings Rd, Los Angeles CA 90069
4 br | 4 ba | Single-Family Home
$3,170,000
*Price reduced by $200,000

Hip, slick architectural designed for those who want the best. Soaring gallery entry leads to huge open living space. New kitchen and dazzling living room, all with Terrazzo floors and high sleek walls. Two huge master suites plus large guest room with bath Attached guest house/media room with state-of-the-art projection. Sleek master, sparking pool, Zen waterfalls, high quality audio/video and stunning city views make this a rare find.[117]

602 Viewmont Dr, Los Angeles CA 90069
4 br | 4 ba | 5,878 sqft | Single-Family Home
$2,999,000

One of the best views in the Sunset Strip and the lowest price per sq. ft. Built in 1993, this is an opportunity to re-decorate this home to your own personal taste and style. Fantastic city and ocean views from almost every room. Beautiful wood floors, spacious rooms with great details. Numerous terraces and balconies, huge family room off the pool overlooking downtown Los Angeles. Don't miss this great opportunity to transform this home into a chic contemporary or an elegant traditional style.[118]

Three million dollars for a home that was sold for 700,000 in 1999. Three million dollars for a three bedroom two and a half bath single family home in the Hollywood hills.
Three million dollars for three thousand square feet.
One thousand dollars per square foot.
For the view.
1525 Blue Jay Way, Los Angeles CA 90069
4 br |5 ••• ba | 6,200 sqft | Single-Family Home
$13,900,000

An extraordinary offering of Art as Architecture. This property is a masterpiece, an unparalleled statement of vision and design. Located above the Sunset Strip in the prestigious "Bird" streets, the views are sensational. Walls of glass in every room open to patios and balconies throughout and out to sensational views from Downtown to the Ocean. Built to satisfy the senses, with the finest of today's technology and materials. Open spaces, high ceilings—the ideal floor plan for entertaining.[119]

Thirteen million for the bird's eye view.
$84,000 a month to pay the mortgage.

The 'In.'
Around the glass patio table, littered with candles, appetizer plates, and ashtrays for the smokers, we have a glass of wine, a bite of Brie and thin crisp crackers, another glass of wine. I listen to the voices float in and out. Some laughter. The wind seems to pick up.

I hear her say, "I know, her face is just such a disaster."

I stare off into the distance. The lights, the view, the pulse and still of the atmosphere distracts me from their words. Laughter again, the hollow sound of wine poured into another and another glass. I fade in and out of story and gossip. More laughter. I do distinctly hear, "Come on Jeanine. Time to go."

"Where?" I ask confused.

"I have an in at the new club. It's just down the street. It just reopened. It used to be called . . ." Delila puts her hand on my shoulder.

Matt breaks in, "They always do that. They change the name and get the same club popular again. I am sure it will close in a few months and open again as the new and hip club and the only thing changed will be the bouncer and a few lights." He waves his wine glass and nods emphatically at his own comment.

Sara laughs, "That's sooo true. That always happens."

I feel my heart stop. I can't breathe. I look down at my clothing. I pull closer to Delila and whisper, "I don't think I'm dressed to go to a club. I think I'm just going to stay here, or go home. I mean, my dog needs to go out and it's late." I can feel my skin start to warm, the redness peek out of my skin.

"Nonsense. You look beautiful, darling," Delila looks at me sweetly. "I really want you there. And besides, nobody is watching. You can go for a little bit and if you don't like it then you can go home. Deal?" She knows me. She knows the disdain I feel for the scene on the Sunset strip is part critical but mostly fueled by insecurity.

I feel the Brie bubble in my stomach.

Rent.

Delila and Victoria rent their house with three other people. In order to afford the location, the house is completely occupied. Vic and Dee share a bathroom with a broken bidet. The faucets drip, there is no space to store clothes or things, so their roommate has filled his glamorous marble bathtub, that shoots down into the ground eight feet, with boxes. The 1930's etched glass is half buried by clothes. I wonder how many people have been in this immense bathtub at once, back rubs and bubbles.

Plastique: In the Desire to Be Seen as.

The plastique perpetuates a desire to be seen as something different than we actually are. We hide behind ourselves. But just enough, to be seen, seen, desired, wanted, but not enough to show desperation.

There is a thin line in Hollywood. The plastique, if stretched too tightly, will show others, will show you, for who you are—insecure, the one that had to manipulate yourself in order to be beautiful. Don't pull too tightly or they will call you grotesque. Pull just enough so you aren't who you were before. Pull just enough so they will call you beautiful. Pull enough so you may desire and be desired. The exterior view, the landscape, the gestalt, needs to be manicured, kept together, framed just as they said it should be, a perfect balance of pesticides and plastic.

I hear him say, "I never noticed that you manicure your feet but not your fingernails. I think that's funny."

I hear her say, "I'm getting work done. I'll have to miss class."

God.

"View homes always, always, always increase in value because let's face it, God isn't making views no more," says Christine Lloyd of Rodeo Realty in Woodland Hills.[120]

Men.

Then there are the men in Dee's life.

Mark: Works in business acquisitions. He is a multimillionaire. He owns three homes in the hills. His ex-wife is paid over $100,000 a month in alimony.

Antonio: Hideously wealthy and prominent man in Mexico. He is constantly being watched, tracked, and followed.

Stan: CEO of one of the networks. I won't say which.

Air.

> It can be said that the mountains act as both hero and villain to the Southland's millions; they protect the coast plains from the desert's harshness and gather moisture from Pacific storms, but at the same time increase urban air pollution by lock in air masses.[121]

I can't breathe here.

Driving.

We find our coats and the chatter of buzzed breath echoes through the formal living room. I watch as they pair up:

- The television network executive and his date, the plastically enhanced fashion designer.
- The multimillion dollar real estate developer and his stunning and plastically enhanced wife, another fashion designer.
- Victoria, the photographer and her date, the stunningly handsome fashion model.
- Sara and her best friend, both exceedingly successful and wealthy women in LA. They don't have dates.

- Delila and her billionaire, a man that sweats too much in his suit, doesn't have much to say but treats her well.
- And me in my dress from Target.

I watch as they get in their cars and begin the long wind down the hill to meet at the club:

- The Range Rover.
- The Ranger Rover.
- The Nissan. (Victoria, as an artist, doesn't drive a fancy automobile.)
- The Lexus.
- The Range Rover.
- And me in my Toyota Truck.

Out that Way.

"He ran out that way. I was just sitting here on my couch watching TV and Miles was at my feet as always. And all of the sudden Miles just growls the most awful growl I've ever heard. He looked rabid." My neighbor says and lights a cigarette, shaking.

I say, "He's always been a great protector. He really knows if something is wrong. What a good boy Miles." Miles looks up from his bone, grinning.

"So yeah, anyway, I heard the growl and then Miles goes flying out the door and that asshole runs from your house through the backyard to this fence right here and opens it so fast I swear he was flying. Miles barking at his heels. It was so scary Jeanine. I went and got my gun."

"Was my backdoor open? Did he go in? Wait, what? You have a gun?" I definitely don't trust my neighbor with a gun.

"Yeah, don't worry I don't have bullets." Great. That's definitely a lie.

"I haven't told you all of it. I've seen him around before. I thought it was harmless. I thought he just had a crush on me. He lurks around our alley sometimes I catch him in the driveway looking in to my windows."

"So who is he after?"

"Me, definitely. Me, so you have nothing to worry about."

Wait. Is she proud of this? Is this a competition? He is her stalker.

"He watches me," she says pulling up her dress a bit.

"Is he dangerous?"

"He's schizophrenic," she says in a nonchalant tone.

"Marvelous," I say looking out the windows, searching for any sign of him.

"He just burnt down his mother's house so he has no place to stay," she ashes her cigarette and looks to Miles. "Good boy, Miles. I don't know what I would have done without him."

My heart crackles.

"I filed a police report. Here, check it out. They are looking for him right now. And when they find him he will be thrown in jail. He has an arrest warrant already. So there is nothing to worry about."

"Perfect," I think and look closely at the piece of paper, the officer's writing and see our names scribbled in cursive.

We are officially his prey.

Grass.

My landlord installed fake grass in her backyard. She ripped roots and layers of crab grass and pinned in artificial turf that is deceptively soft, bright green. It isn't obnoxiously green but deep healthy green. It isn't an obnoxious facelift that has stretched the idea of the lawn beyond repair. But you know immediately, it is plastique.

In Los Angeles, you see a lot of plastic surgery that has destroyed faces, lips, eyes stretched, or breasts that are too lifted, too large, and waists too awkwardly gaunt to support these breasts. I can't help but feel sorry for them but I also begin to question the terrain of my own body. The terrain that may be slipping, beauty shifting, rooted in nothing but the foundation of dust.

I hear her say, "They started leaking. I had to have them removed and now, I'm sick."

I hear him say, "I love fake titties. I think they are hot."

I look down and do not see mountains.

At the Door.

On the Sunset strip, between another hotel and another liquor store, hangs a giant billboard, a restaurant, between the lines of cars, feeding bodies through these velvet ropes, and hear a hum, an unending hum. Then a honk. Grab a ticket from the twenty-dollar valet.

Laughter. I turn and see the group pass under the hotel frame ahead of me. I move quickly. I can't stray from the pack. If I do, I won't be able to get past the bouncer. I notice the three inches of heel on each of them, the peek-a-boo thick straps that look like gladiator footwear. My "oh so last year" boots clunk. I pull my arms around myself, hugging into my chest.

It's not cold outside.

We move through the hotel lobby, pass people in stunning attire. It's the LA chic, the plastique, the "I am too cool to wear this so I will wear something that looks like I don't care too much" look. The men in blazers with tee shirts underneath and wool knit caps. The women float by in designer dresses, not ball gown dresses, barely there dresses, with hair extensions, or two hundred dollar jeans with thin silk tops. Skin, a flash of gold, and performed confidence.

> I hear him say, "I remember when the strip had the red trolley line. But my parents would never go there. It was too posh. We lived in Echo Park then. We would only go downtown to shop. This was before malls. The snobbery was too much for them. You know how high class people are highbrow? Well, us lower class people didn't like Hollywood very much. My parents turned their noses up at it. It just didn't feel right."

> I hear him say, "I never go there. I stay only in the valley. We're valley boys."

The Yard.

Their house sits on a small plot of land that slopes steeply down the mountain. The yard that surrounds the house is not kept, with weeds and patches of dirt that won't be used for planting. The old hot tub sits broken and molding on the far right side of the cracking concrete balcony. The view of the basin of Los Angeles distracts us from these realities.

Eye Contact.

Transients in this space, hoping to be seen as beautiful, plastique, glamorous, won't look you in the eyes. The nature of connection in Los Angeles is fleeting, eye contact while passing someone on the street or in a restaurant is a faux pas. It looks like you are trying to scout for celebrities. Most people on the strip keep their eyes down but everyone wants to be noticed.

> I hear her say, "Do you think he likes me?
>
> I hear him gloat, "She made all of these bags. She's the new up and coming designer. But don't tell her I told you that. I don't want her to get too cocky."
>
> I hear her ask, "Can you see my belly?"
>
> I hear them ask, "Was that John? Jack? Brad?"

Plastique: In the Desire to be Both Visible and Invisible.

The paradox of desired invisibility and visibility that has created the popular urge to know more, to be seen as, to be hidden. This gaze that taunts and titillates has also created the hyper-objectification of bodies, and people, and perceptions of Hollywood.

This hyper-objectification blurs the lines of desire and lack and the need for acknowledgment and connection. Connections, intimacy, sexual desires and drive are based on the image. People don't stay long enough to know you. They feel they know enough. They leave in the morning because in this sexualized intimacy, you have become too visible.

Strut.

On the strip, you strut. You strut like you are somebody, but somebody who doesn't want to be seen as anybody. If you don't strut with these precise calculations they see right through you. Yet the strut is not for anyone in particular.

The Payment.

Delila grabs my arm and walks confidently up to the bouncer. "Hey Steve, darling. Is Chris here? I told him we were all coming." Steve grins at her then looks me up and down. I think he just furrowed his eyebrows. I try to hide behind her. I shuffle uncomfortably but don't drop my gaze. I have to maintain the strut, even if it's only in my eyes.

I look down the side of the building. The line of people waiting to get in is growing. I can see them all looking at the front and thinking, "Will they get in? Won't they?" There is chatter and hubbub, a flash of a bulb, and Jack Osborne walks past us all, past the bouncers, past the doors, and into the abyss.

"I normally don't have to wait but because we have so many guys with us, I wanted to warn Chris ahead of time." I'm not sure if it was because of all of us or because of me, my non-Hollywood attire, my lack of sculpted hair, my minimal make-up, and damn boots. She adjusts the hem of her dress and fluffs the back of her hair. "Do I look ok?" She asks and I give her a warm smile.

"You look stunning," I say and I mean it.

Jim moves past Delila. I see a quick flash of money exchange hands. The others begin to move past him. The women float past his shoulder and say the scripted greeting with dancing eyes. The bouncer shakes the hands of the men and they nod with a smile.

"Come on, let's go," Delila grins. "We don't need to get Chris after all. Jim didn't want to wait the three minutes and just bought us a thousand dollar table."

"Huh? What does that mean?" I whisper and look around.

"It means the alcohol is paid for and we get to sit in the best area for free," Delila giggles.

"It's the only way to go to a club," Sara says as she comes up from behind us. "You shouldn't have to pay for anything. They get to look at you." She laughs.

I can't tell if she is joking or not.

Bear (Dream).

I step one foot out of the car then drag the next. I pass the metal fence that breaks up the road's path. I dart my eyes and pick up my pace. I can't breathe. I can't feel the movement. I stop walking after a minute or so. I can see it in my mind. The imaginings so clear, vivid. The bear one second at the river then next, in front of me on its hind legs. Growls into the air. Prompted by these terrifying imaginings, I think through my escape plan.

First escape plan, I lay on the ground—a flat dead weightless body. I still my breath and wait for the bear to leave—to think of me as nothing too important, nothing to fear or eat. I want to almost bury myself within the ground. But there is no time. So I lie as still as a rock or a stick or moss. The bear comes down off of its hind legs and walks closer to me curiously. I feel the snout warm against my neck. With my face planted in the earth, I inhale dirt and wet leaves. With one grand gesture the bear lifts his head, swings my rag doll body in the air and back down to the ground. Playing, toying, with me as my bones crunch against rock and branches.

The peaceful memory of this place shifts with the shale. My bloodied and bruised skin floats downstream in patches.

LA, the bear, breaks my body, cracks my skin, and rips my vision of beauty to shreds.

Up on the Ropes.

I grab Delila's arm and she moves through the space quickly. The club is full of mostly white people, packed from side to side, front to back. I notice the levels, the platforms. I can make out the bar in the sea of heads and lights and see arms calling in an upward gesture for the bartender. I feel the energy, the high hat of drunken splendor. As at the door, there is striking hierarchy here. The velvet ropes keep people that have not paid away from the tables. The purple curtains hang from floor to ceiling to shield the perceived elite from the public. Bouncers stand at every corner, we pass by them easily. People look, heads turn, we made it past them. We are somebody.

We make our way around bodies, sweaty bodies, slurring and blurred bodies to the table. I sit and I do not move the rest of the night. I watch, anxious, fearful. I watch as Delila, Victoria, Sara, and Tegan dance to the center then back again. I look across the U-shaped private room and only ten feet away is Jack Osborne. I think I looked too long. Shit. Strut. Jeanine. "Strut," I think. I inhale and exhale slowly, grab my vodka and soda and look around for someone to talk to. No one. I stand. Then sit. Stand and look at my dress, my cheap dress and ratty boots. I sit.

I hear her say, "He's not that great looking but he likes to travel."

I hear him say, "She's hot. That's all that matters. Did you see her ass?"

Opossum and Appearances.

I hear the scrape of thick fingernails against dirt. My dog whines loudly and scratches again and again and again. I open the back door, command Miles to back off, and turn on the porch light. I have to hit the sensor button a few times for it to actually click on. I crouch low and peek under the blue folding chair. A shaking baby opossum looks at me with its blind eyes. I watch as it senses Miles coming from around the other side of the vent to get it. The opossum lies on its side, its breathing slows, it looks as if it has just died. I order Miles away again and the opossum is on its belly again, looking, blindly, in my direction. I ask Miles to come back in and we leave it there a bit rattled but unharmed.

The opossum represents in the animal spirit world the ability to put on and off appearances, the ability to play a role in order to survive.[122] Much like the people that come to this strip in Hollywood, the opossum is nocturnal. This opossum is also young. It is also learning how to put on appearances, to perform for a crowd, to strut in the plastique.

Club Promotion.

She works as a club promoter. She says, "It really is messed up. I have a certain quota I am supposed to fill. I have to let more women in than men. And of course the women have to be beautiful. And if the men come in they have to be able to pay big bucks. The women draw the men in, who spend the money. I can't let too many people of color in. There is a certain percentage. And I'm half black."

She fidgets.

"But that's the job. I mean, they need to make money and I love it otherwise. And that's how it works out here."

I hear her say, "Do I really have to wait on this line?"

I hear her say, "Ok. You. You and You. Come in."

I hear him say, "Hey Baby. I have a table. Can I get you a drink?"

Air Hierarchy.

The air in LA, if polluted, is not equally polluted everywhere. The coastal and mountain areas, which tend to be the wealthiest, enjoy the cleanest air, on average. On the inland flats, the poorest, most heavily nonwhite and most industrial neighborhoods in LA suffer the worst air, along with alarming asthma and cancer rates.[123]

Grace.

I watch the fantastic way in which Delila enters and moves through the room. She glides. Men and women turn heads. A man offers her a drink. She declines. Another man smiles and she smiles back.

This is a perfect Hollywood strut. She knows how to politely talk to people, to engage in conversation, to really listen to what they are saying. She is the perfect debutant, without the accent. And the interesting thing about her is she is not faking it. She is what I want to be, what the others try to put on, what they try to be, but in their insecurity and fear, they become unkind. Delila is never unkind.

"Jeanine, you ever gonna get up from there?" Delila leans over to me. I pat the bench and she sits and pleads, "Come dance with me, silly."

I smile, "I think I'm just gonna go. I feel funny."

"Are you sure? I mean, look at all the free drinks."

"I just don't feel ok. I feel weird. I should have dressed up a bit more or something."

"Nonsense. You look great." As I said, Delila is never unkind.

I feel my face flush. I have to get out. I stand to hug her. "I love you but I have to go."

"Alright doll, I'll call you tomorrow. Drive safe," and she turns to pour the grey goose and soda in her now empty glass.

I leave the club quickly. Even with my head down, I notice if I'm noticed. I'm not. Not a smile, a stare, or even a passing glance.

I hand the valet my ticket stub and wait. I lean up against the building's exterior and pretend to text someone. I hear the snap of cameras—a lens pointed at someone else.

I Make Changes.

I grab a bit of belly fat and stretch my skin away from the muscles and bone. I turn my body to the right and look at the outline of my frame. I look closer and see dimples in skin on fleshy buttocks.

You don't love me. How could you—love this body?

I make changes.

Irony.

> One of the large California ironies is the way its very virtues seem fated to bring about the state's undoing. As the pressure on space and resources intensifies, one sees examples everywhere of how one cycle of nature is overlooked, or given low priority, in the rush to develop a parcel of real estate or maximize income or expand a city. Somewhere along the coast, a fragile slope, over-logged and over-built, is cut away by erosion, and six homes go sliding to the bottom.[124]

Somewhere within these hills, a bone is broken, shaved down, cartilage refigured. The natural body is over-stripped and always underappreciated.

Runyon Canyon.

You can reach the trails of Runyon Canyon from several different access points. The tourists usually start at the top entrance off of Mulholland Drive. The locals find space to park on the streets in Los Feliz and walk the steep hill to the entrance of the park. You pass celebrities. At least you think you do. Everyone here could be someone famous. Huge sunglasses hide faces and hats cover hair. They move quickly in plastique running pants or tight shorts and sneakers.

Run.

I'm up on the treadmill. I look at my reflection in the blank television screen. I am strong—ready to run. I just got off the phone with a man that does not love me. I don't think he finds me attractive. I'm too tall. I always have been too tall, big boned, a monster. My limbs, my bones are awkward. I can't shave down my bones, so now, I run. I box. I do yoga.

I turn the speed up to a 4 and begin to warm up. I turn up my music and take a deep breath. Run faster.

Up to a 6. I stretch my legs out. I begin long leaps, bounds. I'm not going anywhere.

Up to an 8. Sprinting now. I think about my weight hitting the belt. Too heavy. Don't pound down. Be graceful.

Flashes.

I move to open the front door, garbage bag in hand, I imagine John, the stalker, standing there. I walk past the green fence that separates my neighbor's yard from mine. I watch through the narrows slats, for any disruption in the spotty view like watching out a train window. My eyes move calmly with the blurry landscape. A building interrupts the flow, abruptly breaking the pattern of vision.

I look for his body, his eyes staring back at mine.

When I move into the bathroom to brush my teeth, I feel a presence behind me. I look into the mirror into the background. I see a figure— of her, of him, of them, shadowing me. Turn and they are gone.

Counting.

I go over what I ate today. I ate too much. I ran for forty minutes and took an hour and a half of yoga. I didn't do enough. I count calories.

two egg whites and cheese = 300 calories
two pieces of wheat toast = 150 calories

••• package of almonds = 100 calories
Oatmeal bar = 200 calories
1/3 vegetarian burrito = 400 calories
Kashi Cereal and fat free milk = 250 calories
Oats and Honey bar = 280 calories
Total calories = 1680 calories.

It's only 4pm and I have consumed far too many carbohydrates and not enough fruit and vegetables.

I hear him say, "I will only eat a salad tonight."

I hear her say, "I won't eat at all."

I see in both their eyes that they are hungry.

Surgeon.

She works for a prominent plastic surgeon in Hollywood. She files papers, makes sure people meet their appointments, moves fat from the fridge, and watches as people move in and out of their bodies; she sees the manipulation, the before and after. She knows when paparazzi will arrive and when they will leave. She knows that the ones that can't afford it are asked to pay full price, while the celebrities who bring business in get surgery for free.

I hear her say, "Do my hips look too fat in this?"

I hear him say, "I don't eat after 6pm."

Hair.

I go to the salon, to fill in the roots, trim the spilt ends. The woman talks about celebrity shoots, working with so and so and so and so. I listen. Flip through an *US Weekly*. Hours pass in a rotating chair. I thank her and move up to the front to pay.

I hear her say, "That will be three hundred dollars."

I leave and call Delila in tears. "Delila, I just spent three hundred dollars on my hair."

"Oh, I bet it looks fabulous," she says cheerfully.

"I think it looks ok. Do you normally spend this much? A haircut and dye job has broken my bank," I feel the sobs coming so I hold them back.

"I think it's a good price. I won't even tell you how much Sara spent. Ok, I will. She spent a grand. But it was this really famous hair stylist that everyone who is anyone goes to. So really, you got a good deal."

Being Seen.

I walk to the grocery store with my dog pulling me forward and past the light pink bursts of spring. I hear a honk. I see their eyes linger. I look to the ground.

I get on line. He starts to make conversation. "So, that's a nice bag. I like that it looks like it's been around a while."

I smile and look to the man who stands too close for comfort. "Thanks. It looks that way because it has been around a while."

I look to the attendant at the checkout. She looks at me, smiles knowingly. I turn my whole body around to block off future conversation.

I hear him ask, "Did you lose weight? I can tell. The bulge is gone."

I hear her say, "Doesn't she look amazing? I mean she has been working her ass off at the gym.

Date.

He waltzes into the bar, a spring in his step. He hands me a tiny flower he picked on the way in. His lyric voice lilts over the faded music. "Almost finished? Did you have a good day?"

I put the flower behind my ear and wipe the red counter with a dirty dishrag. "It wasn't too bad. Ethel just left. Oh, and Carl won 300 bucks in Keno."

"Well, that's pretty cool. Was Ethel smashed?"

"Do I need to answer that?" I grin and take a seat on my stool.

He laughs and leans into my ear. "I want to take you out. I brought my Maserati. Anywhere you want. Tonight. You pick. I want to take you out."

I pause and consider it.

An older man with money has just asked me out. I think of Delila, the fun she says she has, the presents, the dinners, the not having to pay for a thing. Her beauty offers the man a chance to be seen, but not for his ravishing good looks but because of his status, his wealth —his ability to make her feel beautiful through an exchange of commodity, a dinner, diamond earrings, a trip to Australia.

"Ok. But I look like shit. I don't have anything to change into."

"We can take care of that. I'll be back in an hour."

Replacement.

She had to have the silicone replaced. Like rotating tires or changing the air filter, replacing the light bulbs, tacking in the turf lawn.

Ritual.

Washing dishes in my kitchen sink is my nightly ritual. The sink has to be clean, scrubbed down, spotless, before I go to bed. I run the blue dish under the water. Miles growls at the front door. I peer past the dead rose stem in the yellow planter, out the kitchen window. Only darkness. He is out there. One foot from me. One layer of drywall and siding and my growling dog is my body's only protection.

I told myself I would not let this incident get to me so I kept my windows, my blinds, my locks open. To feel suffocated, in any scenario, is like a slow death for me.

But now, in this moment, I am vulnerable, exposed. I can't see him. His dark skin is camouflage in the night. I put the dish down slowly. In one quick gesture, I grab the rope of the blinds and tug it down fiercely. The slats fall with a snap. I turn the lock hard. I check the lock on the back door, and close all of the windows, all of the blinds. "It's ok Miles. I think he's gone now." It's pitch black in my house and I inhale stale air. Silence. Imprisoned. I hear someone whisper, "Jeanine."

Storm.

The storm is coming. The thunder grumbles. The rain chatters with the leaves and they fall in a swirling motion, flitter forcefully as the wind pushes them down to the ground and then back up again.

Maserati.

I get in his Maserati. "Hey Baby." He says joyfully. "So where are we headed? I'll take you anywhere you want to go darling."

"Well, I can't go anywhere fancy dressed like this."

"Alright, I'll buy you something then. We'll just stop off at the first store you see and pick you up whatever you'd like," he starts to drive up the winding hills into Topanga Canyon. "Now, this route would take us straight into Malibu. Would you like to eat on the beach?"

"I don't know. I don't feel comfortable doing that. Why don't we just go to the sushi place right here?"

"Because the way I see it, doll, is we only live once. Why not enjoy it? Money is meant to be spent, or it's no good to you, now is it? I dressed up, now let's go and dress you up."

I squirm in my seat in pretty woman hooker syndrome about to be cleaned up for the ball.

Caught Looking.

Walking down Sunset, his eyes meet mine. He smiles and ducks into a coffee shop. I pause on my walk. Without direction wandering the city streets, I figure, maybe the right direction to go is towards him. So I turn on my heels and enter.

This beautiful man tutors a woman in Italian. His dark beard runs along the edge of this sweet face, his smaller chiseled features, his lips. I feel a bit silly staring at this man. The woman he tutors keeps blushing. He's animated, unabashedly moving through the verb endings.

He looks directly at me. I turn my body away and bury my head in my book.

Capture.

Rap rap rap. My whole body tenses. It's him. I know it. I look at Miles and gauge his dog-like reflexes. He's up, barking, but not that concerned. Not like before. My neighbor rises slowly from the couch. "Oh, the police are here," she drones. I follow her slow footsteps to the door.

I've been spending more time at her house. Trying to feel safe in numbers. I fall asleep with my legs sprawled over the side of her armchair. I usually wake around 2am and stumble over to my house. Even in the midst of sleep, a groggy adrenaline pumps in my veins. I check each room of the house, closets, under the bed when I enter. I lock every open space. I hide, wound tightly under covers.

Police officer Sarkis stands on the tiny concrete stoop with his hand on his hips. "So we caught him. We found him over at 7–11. And good news for you, he resisted arrest. It was pretty brutal. He attacked an officer so that means he will be in for at least three days."

I can't help but feel sorry for the stalker John. I remember Orlando and the man who was swarmed by police officers. It felt like a coyote pack attacking the defenseless. He doesn't fight back. But the tazers, batons, and fists come out. I run over to yell at the officers to back off, and am held back by a stranger. "You don't want to get involved in that mess," he says holding my pulsing muscles with his fingertips. My flared nostrils shooting snot, snarling at the pack that is ripping at this man's flesh as he riles on the pavement.

I see John, flailing his arms defiantly, swarmed by angry officers of the law, then on his knees on concrete. I see his chin hit the ground. I see blood. I hear his mother scream. And in a moment of empathy, I say to officer Sarkis, "Maybe we shouldn't press charges."

"Ha. You better press charges. Actually, I recommend you get down to the courthouse first thing on Monday. We issued a temporary restraining order so if he comes within 100 yards of this house, this property, you call us right away," he shifts his weight from side to side.

"I have to tell you, and I don't want to frighten you, but he is a violent one. I don't want this to go under the radar. We will be here for you in no time," he grabs the buckle on his pants like a superhero.

I want to say, "Great. After the fact. After the fire, the intrusion. After he enters in this space and attacks me, you will be here."

All I say is, "Thank you."

"So hey, another question here, are you single?" Officer Sarkis asks with a glance to his walkie-talkie.

I ask myself, "Is this question relevant? Somehow he has phrased it so it seems important but not relevant at all. It seems more like a question asked at a bar after two rounds of drinks." I look at him sternly.

"The reason I am asking . . ."

And I think, "Yes, clarify, backtrack, do what you can to make this better."

He stumbles through the words, "Is that if you have a boyfriend . . ."

My anger rises in my inner monologue, "What if I have a girlfriend? Does that work for you, officer?"

". . . that you may want him to stay with you. His presence may deter him."

"We don't," My neighbor and I say in unison.

Owns.

Dee's boyfriend owns three houses in the hills.

One he rents to people for the weekend. His two sons and his ex-wife, whom he rarely sees, occupy the other mansion. He only stays in his four-story home in the hills for two weeks at a time and then he is gone again, to Paris, to Moscow, to New York. The only one who really knows him and his current habits is his housekeeper from Guadalajara.

I hear her ask, "So what if he uses me for my looks? Why would I give up all of this?"

I hear her ask, "Do you think he loves me or the idea of me?"

I hear him say, "I see her when I'm in town. It isn't that often."

For all of us, there is always another one.

Plastique: Between Attraction and Possession.

There is a line between attraction and possession in the plastique. The parallels between conquering nature and conquering women are still prevalent in these hills. A woman's body becomes the territory, the possession, the figure to be owned, framed, hung on an arm while mingling on a red carpet. A woman's desire to be beautiful to stand beside him, as his eye candy, is still very much a reality in this space. The cultural myth of man over nature, women as nature, is till very much alive and well. Think of Heidi Montag, the show, the Bachelor, the parading of female bodies on red carpets, men in dark suits. Since ecofeminists have been discussing the inequalities of biological determinism and woman's connection to nature, not much has changed.[125]

Dress-up.

"How about here?" He pulls the car into the lot of a boutique-clothing store.

"Are you sure?" I'm anxious. Nervous.

"Why of course darling. I mean you are so beautiful. You should feel beautiful. Can't have you going to eat at a five-star restaurant in camouflage pants and a tee shirt. You pick anything you want. Anything at all. I'm just glad we are here together."

We enter the store. The woman behind the counter smiles as we enter. She looks at him. Then me. I stand about a foot taller than his stocky build. My long blonde hair and long legs stunt him. She has seen this juxtaposition of bodies before. She has seen another woman like me before. Giggling in the dressing room. Thanking him for his generosity. She knows this pattern.

"How can I help you?"

Dress on, then off. Another piece of fabric drapes my body. I exit.

"What do you think?"

I liked the first one, the second one. Another piece of fabric. I turn and twirl and show off my new slimmed frame. Another twirl. I look at myself in the mirror. And again. A body that is not my body. An image I do not quite get.

California Dreaming.

Californians' versions of the American dream—celluloid images of prosperity, redemption and the human desire for reinvention—every day cross state, national and international boundaries. How accurately such images reflect California's reality remains debatable and opinions on this matter vary from Beverly Hills to Watts, from Barstow to Eureka, for amid the state's periods of growth and prosperity, Californians have found plenty of reasons for pessimism. In recent years natural disasters in the form of earthquakes, fires, and floods, episodes of major civil unrest, and economic and energy crises have repeatedly underscored the fragility of the Californian dream.[126]

I Know.

He doesn't actually have a lot of money. He just spends it like he does. He recently sold his Maserati to pay on his upside down mortgage.

Plastique: The Line between Over-objectification and Objectification.

We cut down shrubs to create the perfect view. We over-manicure the lawn by installing fake grass to reduce the amount of constant manicuring that needs to happen. We've created a monster in our visions of beauty, fantasy versions of ourselves. A fantasy, but not the reality. The Hollywood plastique is the perception of wealth. The perception of beauty. The trick on the eyes, the house in the hills, besides its location, is falling apart. It is not well maintained. The body within the hills in order to fit in is shaped and molded, manicured. To put on. To feel sexually desired.

After Dinner.

After wine and hundreds of dollars spent, on the drive home, he takes out his dick.

He pleads, "Suck me off while I am driving. Here, go ahead."

I turn to the window and scoff, "What? I mean, who do you think I am?"

Wax.

When the plastique becomes wasted, when you see her waste away, you just comment on her love handles, her wrinkles, the melting skin. When she really rots, she disappears from the public view but you still have her image—the image of her as she was. You can hold her there in your memory, or tacked to your refrigerator by a crayon magnet, hidden desire and nostalgia within the pages of photographs—your wax statue.

Plastique: Re-crafting.

I have been re-crafting, re-sensing, recreating how I feel beautiful in sexual relationships, how beauty, desire, pain, past and present fold into one another. The power of beauty creates attraction, but perhaps there is another layer here. A beauty that creates attraction also creates distraction from the other elements of physical and sexual connections. Sexual agency and image. I have a strong aesthetic for beauty. But there is the line of aesthetic for someone else's pleasure of consumption and a presence of confidence in beauty.

I made myself beautiful for someone else's pleasure.

But I don't know for whom.

Birthday Party.

We meet, the four of us for dinner at Katsuya, a popular sushi joint for the rich and famous. Paparazzi linger outside. I don't look around for the celebrity they are waiting for. I've gotten used to the idea that Jim, or Kate, or Nicole, may be sitting at the table beside us. I look at us, sitting around this tiny table. Each one of us is strikingly different from the other. We meet because Delila is our best friend.

Victoria, the hidden lust, the photographer, artist, we kiss in shadows.

Delila, the beauty, the rough princess, the soon to be millionaire's wife.

Sara, the snob with a romantic side.

Jeanine, the nerd, the teacher.

We are all 30. We are all turning 31. Successful, smart, educated, accomplished, and three out of four of us are broke. We are all still single and dating.

We are powerful women. They tell me not to get attached. It's ok to fuck. Live for now. The love, the right love just hasn't come along yet. I can hear the juxtaposition of power and worry. The myth that told us what we should be and shouldn't. In beautiful brilliant ways, each one of us is fulfilling these dreams. Just without solid, stable romantic relationships.

> I hear Victoria say, "In five years, we will settle down, the four of us and raise a baby."

> I hear myself say, "Yes, but not here. Please, not here."

Exposure.

The hills cover themselves. Winding up and through the Hollywood hills, the mountains provide both protection and then full exposure—once you hit the top.

green space, yellow, fence, fallen boulder, wall of clay. She can't see how beautiful she is. Tell her. And watch her cringe.

wind down.

green space, wall of concrete, yellow, fallen boulder, wall of clay. He can't see that he doesn't need that too. Ask him to share—if he actually has anything to give.

wind down.

green space, garage door, yellow, fallen boulder, wall of clay. They can't see how lucky they are. I do. But perhaps they aren't.

Look closer.

6

THE HOLLYWOOD HILLS, REVISITED

THE INSIDE AND OUTSIDE PERFORMANCE OF THE PLASTIQUE

In this chapter we move through the landscape of Hollywood Hills from the macro (the surface landscape) and the micro (the underbelly, the hidden view) in order to make sense of the perception of shifting and perceived forms of beauty. Beauty, and feeling beautiful, is intimately connected to feeling desire and being desired. It is connected to sexual agency. When we feel beautiful, we feel worthy of this desiring. Within the Hollywood Hills, in order to feel beautiful, I perform a kind of beautiful that can be understood as *plastique*.

We revisit the surface and the underbelly of four locations in this chapter: the house in the hills; my body; the club; and the streets of the hills. Each of these locations allows us to revisit the micro and macro politics of objectification and desire, the desire to be seen and not seen, yet also in the same moment, desired and desiring. It's a tricky line we walk between wanting to be desired and being objectified. It's an unfair balance, a trick on all of us. We are the brunt of some intense joke about beauty, wealth, and the elite. We are all working to be something other than we are and this struggle keeps us trapped in a cycle of attempting to obtain the unattainable. And perhaps, even if we do get there, we make it, we all still feel like we aren't enough. This is the performance of plastique. The underbelly of the plastique in the Hollywood Hills, once you get close enough to feel its rough skin, smells quite pungent.

In order to make sense of the landscape, we have to be able to look at the surface and its underbelly, be honest about the terrain, and its impacts on our consciousness and materialization of this consciousness in our everyday performances, our working knowledges. Although working knowledge can evolve into a mimetic performance of culture, which is the act of copying acts or performing representation without a clear connection to the original meaning.[127] It's like looking at a papier maché house (a representation of a solid wood house) and deciding to build your own house with paper maché, believing it will stand the test of time. Similarly, as we perform identities, we embody representations of territories, environments, cultural symbols, and aesthetic values.

The plastique is the mimetic process and performance of creating and maintaining the frame of your body, your house in order to fit and/or exceed social expectations of beauty, desire, and socio-economic status. The most important component to the plastique is the manipulation between what is real and what is projected as real to others.

I also felt the plastique growing up in one of the richest towns in New York. The struggle between the old and new money, the whispers of who really has and who really doesn't created stark class division between families and children. New money was considered more plastique because people who recently came into wealth didn't know how to properly use this money. They bought flashy cars, gaudy houses, and as those with old money said, they just used it wrong. In the hills of Hollywood, the plastique is also easy to identify. The elitism associated with the hills is quite clear as you navigate the micro politics of manicuring the body. The woman's body especially is a canvas for those with money. The woman's body must be maintained property, sculpted, crafted, arm candied and siliconed. But it has to be maintained just right, too much plastic surgery and you are new money, too plastique and grotesque.

Plastique is intimately connected to both the gaze and desire. Your body, your house, you, in Hollywood must be perfect just in case you are gazed upon. If your property might be seen as desirable you must maintain it, keep up with the Joneses. Even if, underneath the surface of the landscape, you do not have what you perform you have. My performance of identity, in order to maintain her plastique within the landscape of the Hollywood Hills, is one of a gardener, a manicurist, and a plastic surgeon. I navigate and manipulate the landscape of my body, and the actual landscape of the hills in order to understand beauty. In the story of these hills, my view is not as reflexive, but wrought with insecurity and fear. I both desire and loathe the plastique.

The Landscape of the House in the Hollywood Hills: Inside and Out.

The view from the hills of Hollywood allows the viewer to see the panoramic view. You see lights like fireflies. You may watch, like the rest of the elite, from above. Or perhaps you are at the bottom of the hill, looking up. The empty houses look like the shells of capitalist possibility. As you look up, do you imagine the landscape, do you feel the desire to be somebody, to have more, to participate in our capitalist society without struggle? As you move your eyes across the panorama of the city, the ocean, the mountains, do you see people there navigating the terrain? Do you feel special? Above ground? Do you feel like you are flying?

From the Surface: Landscape, Privilege and Lack

From the macro perspective, the surface, those of us that are allowed to see the landscape of Los Angeles sit high above the basin of the valleys. The landscape view is a privileged perspective. Those people who get to gaze upon the valley on a regular basis can afford to do so. They can purchase and rent the homes with the magnificent view. This creates a subjectivity that rests upon the insider–outsider relationship. The insider–outsider dichotomy creates a power struggle. Those on the inside know more than those on the outside. Those on the inside have, those on the outside have-not. This system of power is embedded within the local act of looking.

Mark Dorrian and Gillian Rose state that the eye of the viewer is the pivot point when assessing landscape:

And so we can continue: horizons move depending upon where the viewer looks, and frames demand a look as much as a look desires a landscape. Inside and outside then are held in tension together through a landscape, and the effects of a particular relation between them may also be called political. Who or what can see a landscape?[128]

There is something quite mystifying about the Hollywood elite. From the outsider perspective, we think we know the elite. We think we see them for who they are. They are the ones that have—everything. From an insider perspective, when you stand at the top of the Hollywood Hills you can see—everything. Well, from a distance that is. But the trick here is that we are all both insiders and outsiders performing an identity from and within a landscape that is constantly shifting.

Gillian Rose views "the material and symbolic dimensions of production and reproduction of society as inextricably intertwined."[129] For the most part, we make generalizations about each other from afar. These generalizations are part of the struggle for power. To look down upon the valley, see the lines of the horizon, imagine those other people navigating the terrain gives the viewer a perceived sense of power, of being above. To look up into the hills from the terrain of the valley offers this viewer a perceived sense of lack.

The distance between the person viewing the landscape and the person within the landscape creates a stark differential, a critical and poignant distinction between the haves and have-nots. The view from the hills represents the desired view and position of the upper class society, the hegemonic class culture, the view imposed upon us all. This view is sustained by the domination of the marketplace. "Free-market rules for corporate freedom are increasingly rules which exclude real people from the economic and political affairs of society and disenfranchise them from nature."[130] The market economy Shiva points to here is the market that is focused on capital, to the exclusion of how people perform to create the capital. She emphasizes that in this paradigm, relationship is substituted for profit and consumerism. Los Angeles is a glittering example of how profit and consumerism have come to mean cultural and personal worth.

From the Underbelly: Uncovering the Plastique

From the macro perspective we create a subjectivity and performance of identity that rests upon the generalization of privilege and lack. We compare ourselves to these perceptions. I was allowed to view the landscape of Hollywood from both an insider and an outsider perspective. On the cusp of the have and have-nots I discovered that at the micro-level the perception of wealth, elitism, is only plastique.

The plastique is the trick of the eye. This plastique exists only as a Cezanne painting. From far away you think you see the landscape. You know the view. It is familiar. But up close, it doesn't make any sense at all. We have a difficult time reading the painting. We may only see color, line, shade, dots of color and texture. Move one dab of paint and the whole landscape shifts. Move the silicone over too far and the breast is out of proportion. The landscape of the body shifts. Paint your house the wrong color, keep the broken down hot tub on the front lawn, and the perception of you and your wealth, shifts negatively.

At the micro-level, the underbelly of navigating the terrain of the house in the Hollywood Hills, I discovered the plastique is only a false sense of having. The house in the hills, while it has the view, is crumbling. It is rotting from the inside. The house is rented by five people and maintained minimally. The performance of identity within the hills is fueled by the desire to be seen as somebody who has, as if mimetically performing wealth will generate wealth. Yet, people in the hills may not have as much as we perceive they do. In terms of capital, and an ability to navigate and participate within the marketplace, there are people that live within these houses that still scrape by financially.

The struggle for power and the need to attain more, have more, the desire for more is fueled by our sense of lack.[131] But learning from the underbelly of the hills that people still struggle opens up the discussion and makes room for a renegotiation of power and privilege. The maintenance of the plastique is fueled by a false sense of having. How can the view from inside the truths of the hills offer all of us that feel disempowered financially, move into a different perspective? How can the truth about the plastique in the hills offer us all a newfound freedom? For me, learning the truth about the plastique allowed me a freedom from the desire to have the view of the landscape. The view is not privilege but the performance of having privilege. Within the micro-politics of this terrain, the insecurity and constant negotiation of lack and privilege is too much for me to bear. It perpetuates a never-ending mimetic cycle of false perception, and falsity of identity. To rest self-worth on perceived capital and privilege is a horrible, unfair cross to bear. The plastique is a lie.

Yet, most people that exist in the plastique do not know they do.

The Landscape of the Club: The Marketplace of Desires.

The booths are empty. The white linen shades draw away from the elite tables that normally close the view. The smell of after night party lingers in the satin ribbons. The coke and spilt vodka seeps into the chiseled concrete. The stairs now empty, the bar, the bathrooms, the space-vacant. In the daytime a club like this loses its mystery. It is the same as any other space. But can you imagine the woman at the front, not pretty enough to make it past the bouncers, calling on her cell phone to her girl friends dancing the dance floor. The rufie slip slides down the edge of the glass into her martini. A giggle, a wink, a pat on the ass. The woman with her exposed collar and pronounced cheekbones gets the number, her drinks for free. The man with the fat wallet, sweat faced and grinning feels her crotch on the dance floor. He tells her he is a producer. Can you feel the insecurity, the whisper of "You aren't good enough to make it past here." The glaring question, "Who are you with?" Can you see the money exchange sly, dry palms?

From the Surface: Outside the Velvet Ropes

From behind the ropes, those with the money to make it past the security, to ease by the lines of people and the bouncers, perform the plastique in the marketplace. The marketplace of desire is the exchange of commodity.

> For Marx, the *commodity* is the basic building block of capitalism. The commodity is not simply an economic fact or object; it is the manifestation of a social relationship in physical

form. The commodity hides this social relation as it appears as a reified object. The commodity, in Marx's terms, makes what are actually relations among people appear as relations among things. And vice versa—the commodity makes the relations among things the cornerstone of all social relations—what are actually relations among things, among quantities and objects, appear as relations among sentient beings. This is Marx's fundamental concept of *commodity fetishism.* When a commodity is fetishized, it undergoes a profound and spiritual transformation from a mere object (with a simple *use-value*) into a walking, talking, socializing creature (with an *exchange-value*).[132]

In the club, the commodity exchange is the dancing of bodies—thin, white, female bodes. The exchange of commodity at the door, buying the table, the bottle of alcohol for a thousand dollars, is not the actual purchase of the bottle, as bottles of alcohol sell for much less than that, but the purchase of status, the position behind the ropes, the ability to socialize as an elite figure in the club.

The commodity exchange is not a material good but an idea, an image, the ability to perform an identity on a certain privileged stage. The plastique offers most of us the perception of what it means to have wealth and access to the spaces behind the ropes. The ability to be on the stage increases desirability. On the stage, behind the ropes, you become the celebrity figure wealthy enough to have and exist on that stage for a few hours. Being on that stage makes people look up, literally and metaphorically, to you. They wonder, "Who are you? How did you get there?" Those on the outside of the ropes imagine themselves as the figure behind the ropes and, most definitely, in the spotlight.

From the Underbelly: To Market, to Market

From the underbelly of the marketplace of desire, the racism, heterosexism, capitalism, and body consciousness fuels the most intense cesspool of elitism. The commodity-exchange of image not only poisons our ability to feel good, but it intensifies the experience of lack in the world. The materiality of the ropes within an elite club in Hollywood is the actual manifestation of all of the images produced in magazines such as *Glamour*, *Elle*, *Vogue*, *OK*, *People*, etc., etc. The division is so obvious that it is hard to ignore the absolute absurdity in these created desires. We have fallen prey to an image we have and constantly self-create. In Hollywood, this desire and lack we feel becomes part of the performance of everyday life. We begin to perform an identity of having in order to have what has been dictated we should have—the six-pack, the ability to buy our way into and out of anything, the ability to make your way into and out of a body, any body.

The view behind the ropes is not satisfying. A person may buy an image but the image does not hold substance. The image only perpetuates the fear and anxiety associated with not having enough. The underbelly of the spaces behind the ropes is the honest recognition that the plastique offers the perception of depth but does not have depth. The fleeting and inconsistent connections that happen in the clubs are enough to make the vagina wet for a moment. But there isn't enough to make someone sustain an orgasm.

"To market, to market" people flock to perform an identity that they do not understand, but because of the constant barrage of images and societal expectations as marked by the ropes, the line at the front of the club door, the rented luxury cars and the thousand dollar tabs, people want to, and should, be aware. The club promoters have a quota they have to fill, certain people they need and are told to let in. These people fit, obnoxiously, the white, heteronormative framework of what we are told is desirable. Who is allowed to be behind the ropes? And why on earth would we want to be there?

As a commodity, we desire to become the image of wealth. My experience of wealth, of having, of aspiring to be the one that has, offers me nothing but insecurity, and this lack of self-assurance has mapped itself so much upon the body that my actual material body becomes the canvas in which to perform these desires. We map the terrain of my body in order to understand the value that could and would exist there.

The Landscape of Body: Plastique, Rot, and Manipulation.

If you look at my body as landscape you may see the hills of my stomach, the rolling skin pale between pieces of cloth. Like the landscape of the hills, my body becomes at once untouchable, a photograph, an image of, a distanced view. But the privilege of viewership allows you to know my vulnerable frame, the dips and peaks of bone, muscle, and skin. But you cannot feel me. You cannot smell me. Feel me shiver between your finger and thumb as you move your humming lips up to my cheek. You do not know me. But you can see me from this angle. And you can imagine me beside you. Look but don't touch.

———

From the Outside: Maintaining the Body

My body, once I navigated the terrain of the Hollywood Hills, became an undesirable landscape. From the outside perspective, my body was not the terrain that most would find desirable. The extra bulge around my thighs, the thickness of my stomach could not be revealed on the beach. The clothes I could afford to wear and the performance of beauty within the hills offered me a different expectation; culturally in the hills, the woman's body is perceived as desirable or not desirable by standards based upon thinness, lack of wrinkles, muscle definition, breast size, and hair maintenance. A woman's body in the hills is an important commodity, an object for the gaze. The body, like the houses, must be maintained. In this way the body is not seen as natural. Natural female bodies, in the hills, are few and far between. My body became a space to recreate, something disconnected, a terrain to manipulate in order to feel desirable. I perform the plastique.

The performance of the plastique is a myth, a false desire, a manifestation and materialization of insecurity drawn on years and years of being told a lie. But beauty, like our performance of gender, is not a fixed truth. Beauty is and has always shifted with time, cultural trends and societal pressures. Judith Butler states, "In this sense, gender is in no way a stable identity or locus of agency from which various acts process; rather, it is an identity tenuously constituted in time —an identity instituted through a stylized repetition of acts."[133]

The performative constitution of gender is similar to the repetition of actions within the Hollywood Hills. Each person repeats an action and learns with her or his body how to function within a capitalist, materialistic, fantasy-driven context. We perform an identity to fit a mold of beauty that has no origin or no endpoint.

The Body as Landscape, as Cyborg, as Plastique

Understanding my body as landscape reduces my body to the biological essentialism that women are more closely connected to nature than men. This connection to nature allows the woman's body to be colonized, used, and abused for her resources, seen as an object to be manipulated for another's personal gain and satisfaction. But Haraway notes, "There is nothing about being female that naturally binds women. There is not even such a state as 'being' female, itself a highly complex category constructed in contested sexual scientific discourses and other social practices."[134] Yet women in Hollywood Hills are bound by the social and cultural expectations that fuse the natural with the technological. Beauty is bound and created by scientific manipulation and natural bone structure. Women in Hollywood perform as what Haraway would call the cyborg. The actor as a cyborg opens up possibility because this definition of woman is not fixed. "Cyborgs are post-Second World War hybrid entities made of, first, ourselves and other organic creatures in our unchosen 'high-technological' guise as information systems, texts and ergonomically controlled laboring, desiring, and reproducing systems."[135] As cyborgs, we are also machines, "communications systems, texts, and self-acting, ergonomically designed apparatuses."[136] Arguing for ironic cyborg feminism, she states, "We are all chimeras, theorized and fabricated hybrids of machine and organism."[137]

Ingrid Bartsch, Carolyn DiPalma, and Laura Sells state, "The cyborg performs the function of radical nominalism; it names the condition of women's lives within the logic of late capitalism in which key boundaries between human and animal, human and machine, and physical and nonphysical have imploded."[138] These implosions set up an interesting dynamic between living and non-living things and rearticulate our dependence on identity politics. Our dependence upon the machine, the fusion of nature and culture has helped to perpetuate the plastique.

My experience within the terrain of the Hollywood Hills cultivated the desire to be outwardly beautiful, pumped full of collagen and silicone. It only fueled the performance of the plastique. Here, the actualization of the cyborg within my body problematizes Haraway's claim that this metaphor opens up subjectivities and identities. Our desire to be cyborg, to be the fusion of nature and culture limits our perceived freedom in possibility. Our dependence upon the machine to manipulate bodies to become beautiful narrows our definitions of beauty.

From the Inside: The Presence of the Plastique, The Absence of Presence

The presence of the plastique makes it almost impossible for the intimate to emerge.

The plastique is a performance of excess, whereby people embody the values of beauty and fame for the sole purpose of being seen as having more and being better. To maintain the plastique, one must engage with an overwhelming field of images and discern which beauty product, body enhancement, or fashion accessory will grant upward social mobility. Being in the presence of so much stimuli within the performance of plastique, one begins to wonder: When does the plastique become the real? And at what cost? To whose benefit?

Performing the plastique is a delicate balance between being seen and not seen, and the absence of being understood, listened to, and known while also recognizing each other as co-performers of the plastique. Derrida explains this relationship as *differance*: it is the condition for the opposition of presence and absence.[139] Differance is also the "hinge" between inner meaning and outer representation. In the Hollywood Hills, the differance is skewed towards outer representation, making the presence of inner meaning rather absent. Gumbrecht, in his work on the production of presences offers this: "I think that the aesthetic experience—at least in our culture [Western], will always confront us with the tension, or oscillation, between presence and meaning."[140] The tension emerges because in trying to capture presence through symbols, humans lose presence, making the quality of being an absence. A person performing presence instinctively does so, like a surfer that is one with a wave, she is simply being with the wave, not thinking about what it means to perform presence with the wave. If the surfer were to think about her presence, she would no longer be present with the wave. Thinking about Hollywood then, it is interesting to contemplate an industry—a place—that capitalizes on creating cultural meaning through the representation of presence on film; a place that is culturally identified by the image of meaning, not meaning itself. It's a place where the surfer is told to ride a manufactured wave as if it were real, and be one with it.

My body in the plastique became the desired image, a fusion of nature and culture, and the cyborg that performed beauty in order to be desired. But this performance of the plastique lacks intimacy and presence. As a cyborg in the plastique, I am not fulfilled. This desiring is inextricably linked to being seen and not seen in the hills of Hollywood.

The Street: Being Seen and Not Seen, Marked and Not Marked.

From the street, the viewer begins to peer into a life that is not theirs. Imagine standing outside of my window. You can see flashes of movement between the slats of the blinds. You can hear sounds, laughter, perhaps a moan or a sigh. You hear music. Smell banana bread baking in the oven. You see us playing a board game. You listen as I pour a glass of wine. Imagine the sip I take is your sip. You can feel the spice on your tongue. Imagine you can feel me next to you, my breath rising and falling in deep sleep. The blinds snap open. My eyes stare into yours. Caught looking, you flee. Caught being watched, I fall to the ground and sob.

———————

Passing Bodies: Being Seen and Not Seen in the Plastique

The performance of the plastique is also about looking, desiring looking, being looked at, and feeling objectified. As Peggy Phelan notes:

Since the given to be seen is always exclusionary, subject positions must attend to the affective consequences of the failure to be recognized. This failure implies that subject positions are always related to the negative, to that which cannot be or is not developed within the visual field. Therefore, subject positions are always partial.[141]

The gaze, the marked or not marked, in the Hollywood Hills seems to be a bit more complex, or perhaps thinly defined. Being marked in the hills always has an air of not being seen. You want to be marked as exclusionary, elusive, in the scene enough to be seen but not enough so you become the one who is around too much.

A good friend of the group in the hills wants to be seen. He works to always be at the right parties, to talk to the right people, to be present and known. His behavior becomes almost comic and for some, embarrassing. While he is an elite person in the hills, his desire to know everyone, to have them know him crosses the thin barrier between the seen and unseen. He doesn't stay in the liminal space, or on the tightrope of social expectation. And slowly but surely he is exposed. When he is exposed he moves on to the next group of elite figures in the hills. It takes them about six months to figure him out. He is a user, a snake in the grass. He is cunning. He embodies the plastique. He performs the plastique so much so that he crosses the line, becomes the image, the excess of the plastique. He is the danger that I am trying to avoid.

While Phelan argues that not being recognized is a negative state of subjectivity and identity, in Hollywood you want to walk in the liminal space. You want to be seen, recognized but not overly objectified, or overly zealous about the scene. You perform an identity that cannot be marked, you want to have the air of "don't look at me," but at the same time you want to be looked at. Foucault explains, "Hence the major effect of the Panopticon: to induce in the inmate a state of consciousness and permanent visibility that assures the automatic functioning of power."[142] By internalizing the gaze, one will constantly self-monitor and therefore follow certain societal rules. Hence, for Foucault and de Certeau, the gaze is omnipresent, but tacit and internalized.[143] This narrow path of performing in the plastique, fueled by the gaze, limits the way in which we perform desire within the space of the Hollywood Hills. There is a lack of intimate connection, a movement and fragile fluidity to relationships. Sexual agency, then, is lost in the performance of desire and being desired, seen and not seen.

Caught Looking: Hyper-Objectification and the Tourist Gaze

From the outside, viewing another person in the plastique is a difficult task. As you walk the streets, play in the Hollywood Hills, you watch others perform the plastique. You make sure your spectatorship is stealth-like. It is a careful observation of the other. The trick is to let them know you are looking, but not looking for too long. MacCannell claims that tourists are on a quest for authenticity, so much so that they accept a "staged authenticity," which hides the real backstage in favor of the fake front stage. In this transient space we are all tourists, watching, looking, wanting to feel authentic in the plastique.[144]

John, the stalker, became the manifestation of the tourist looking too long. He held his gaze upon me without my knowing. His gaze is the hyper-objectification of my body. The stalker behavior mimics the paparazzi in Hollywood, the celebrity sightings, the desire to know a stranger—intimately. The dialectic of Derrida's difference is clear in the moment of stalking: the cultural obsession with outer representation and the lack of presence of inner meaning leads people to seek meaning through excessive performances of outer representation.

Urry claims that tourists gaze in order to confirm their beliefs about a certain place. Most importantly, though, according to Urry, tourists look to find pleasure in looking at places, people, and things that are out of the ordinary.[145] Therefore, the tourist gaze constructs a very specific line of sight: the tourist gazing at the different Other. Yet in the plastique, we are all tourists, seeking out the other but also desiring to be looked at, seen as authentic, real in the space and terrain of Hollywood.

From the Inside: Hyper-Objectification Moving towards Active Subjectivity

I initially perform plastique to gain cultural acceptance and social mobility. Yet I realize that by performing a mimetic identity, I slowly lose my own subjectivity. If I repetitively perform the plastique, I can become a simulacrum of myself. Simulacrum is understood by Baudrillard as a process of simulation that occurs in four stages: the reflection of reality, a masking and denaturing of reality, masking the absence of reality, and finally, no relation to reality but pure simulacrum.[146] A simulacrum then is the object that emerges from the process of simulation. Baudrillard emphasizes that the simulacrum is held in place by the media and consumer society. Ironically, this concept was captured well in the 1999 Hollywood film *The Matrix,* where rebels try to reveal the simulacrum and those that construct it. The concern for me, then, in performing the plastique, is that I could replace my reality with the pure simulacrum of Hollywood.

The converse of losing subjectivity within a simulacrum is an active subjectivity. Lugones advocates an "active subjectivity"[147] that recognizes oppressed people as performers who "resist oppressive social worlds and who seek to develop and nurture counter-socialities in which their resistance can be recognized and supported by those who are able to interpret their actions outside the dominant words of sense."[148]

In the frame of the Hollywood Hills, a person performs an active subjectivity through critical awareness of the simulacrum and by providing spaces and places for inner meaning to emerge through conscious co-creation of reality. An active subjectivity in the plastique is navigating the awareness of the gaze and the creation of the simulacrum, the navigation of both your objectification and subjectivity. The danger of the plastique is losing your awareness of yourself in the image, in the desire to become something other than yourself.

My performance of an active subjectivity develops as I navigate the transient spaces of the Hollywood Hills. I reframe how I understand my body, my ability to desire and be desired. I begin to make eye contact, walk with my head held high, not because I became a part of and accepted within the simulacrum, but because I am aware of the presence of the plastique, its fragility and imbalance, and its falsity. I begin to see the underbelly and the surface of the hills, its slipping terrain, its rotting bodies, and the insecurity within the walls and veins of those participating in the plastique. The development of my active subjectivity allows me to see the landscape, *really* see the landscape and subsequently desire a different viewpoint.

Map 7.1 West Hollywood[149]

7

WEST HOLLYWOOD[150]

Image 7.1 Confetti

The Key with Three Teeth.

sunset strip.
Billboard. BIllboard. BILlboard. BILLboard. BILLBOard.
BILLBOArd. BILLBOARD. Hollywood hills backdrop.
Prada, Vitton, Gucci.
skinny jeans and crazy high heels.
yellow awning. people sit. fluff dog in an oversized purse.
Valet opens the door for a select few.

the avenues.
design studio. buffed glass. modern edges.
art studio. clean white walls. one piece hangs in the forefront.
Price tag. Price tag. Price tag. Is not visible.
you have to ask.

santa monica blvd.
rainbow flag. restaurant. concrete. awning.
she walks by. half mohawk. sagging pants. nose ring.
he walks by. muscles cut. chiseled tank top.

they do not look at me.

The Key.

West Hollywood is districted in the shape of a key. The city lines
create an almost haphazard configuration of streets and routes that
encompass the more upscale neighborhoods in Los Angeles County.
This is because activists and people with money were able to create
their own city within Los Angeles County.

The Drive.

To get to West Hollywood I drive from the beach, the PCH to the
10E to the 405N. I exit on Santa Monica Blvd and travel slowly. I
wait for the ten-minute traffic lights. The delay allows me to look
around, to really look at the manicured lawns, the gold of the Beverly
Hills sign. It is a fancy place. A slow travel through Beverly Hills permits
the soft gaze, the slow turn, stare and the shake of the head. The car
brands increase in value the further you move into the area. A BMW,

Land Rover, Range Rover, Mercedes, pass by, mostly all black and silver.

From Beverly Hills I turn a slight left, pass the Troubador, the famous music venue. I stood out there at 6am one morning. And took a picture of my friend's name in lights. I sent it to him from my phone. Smiling. So proud.

I look to my left. I know I'm in West Hollywood now. The Rainbow Flag hangs high on a flagpole right next to the American Flag.

Falling.

There is something magical about falling. Falling into your body, into the love, into a space where finally everything is clear, even in its chaos. The way two bodies meet, exchange energy, slide in and out of consciousness and desire. The difference for me, and for many others in the Los Angeles area, is that this meeting of bodies is not just physical. It is emotional, spiritual, contextual, full of pasts and secret caverns inside crevices of wholeness, two bodies, not of this earthly place, bodies that in the long run, mean nothing but the physical manifestation of our spiritual consciousness. For me, gender and sex do not matter when I fall in and out of love. The binary in between male and female does not suit me. Our bodies are our temples. And for sexual and loving communication between bodies, I can love any body.

But I have also learned this: the bodies that take shape in West Hollywood are as impacted by cultural and societal expectations as those in the Hollywood Hills or Chatsworth, or Burbank.[151] As open and brilliant as this space is for the queer community, it is just as unforgiving. Expectations set in the sidewalk, the pulse of the nightclubs, the expecting bodies that leave LA Fitness or 24 Hour Fitness with towels on their shoulders, muscles bulging, bodies sweating, and the look—over the shoulder, the sideways check-out. There are expectations here for gay males and lesbians in West Hollywood. And these expectations are seeping their way into our cultural consciousness through the manifestation of cultural myths. The expectations for transgendered and transsexual folk are different, still a different category within the rainbow. And even in these open spaces, where the 2.5 children and the white picket fence of the heterosexual kind are questioned, there are still people feeling lonely, wrong, or different. But there are even more people that feel like they have formed a tribe.

I would like to say this as a side note, I have learned more about humans forming tribes in the last few months than ever. Examples of people, no matter their sexual orientation or gender, that have come together to form communities, families, tribes of people that care for one another. And they take care of one another. I believe with all of me that if we put parameters on what a family should look like, we have missed the mark. In the cold concrete expanse of Los Angeles, lives colliding and supporting one another is certainly the greatest gift and grace we can offer one another.

I still have the potential to love any body, male, trans, female, and every form, without the binary. My spirit wants to connect to other spirit bodies, and their physicality becomes as generous and loving as their energy. Los Angeles is a materialistic place, the expectations for material bodies connect to the expectation of our landscapes. Like most places in Los Angeles, the walkable city, the creative city, the prideful city of West Hollywood, which includes two prominent neighborhoods: The Avenues and Boys Town, do not necessarily allow for this potentiality.

She

grabbed me in the bathroom years ago. Pushed me against the metal stall. Lips on mine. Her hands crawled up my body, under my shirt. Tongues entwined. Then parted. We separated then laughed. "No one can know," she said. "They wouldn't like it. It would get too messy." Then she slid out of the restroom before me so no one would suspect a thing.

The Pride Strip.

Pride, the iconic event of the LGBT community, happens once a year but is a framing performance. The pageantry, music, garish costumes, and floats, people connecting from new and far, all contribute feelings of acceptance and celebration. It is the time of year where whatever you desire or socially present yourself as, you fit in. But this performance of Pride only happens once a year. The performance of sexuality takes on many other forms throughout the everyday in West Hollywood.

The Walkable City (Santa Monica Boulevard).

I park my truck on San Vicente and Santa Monica. The crest of the Hollywood Hills covered by the mid-morning sun. This part of West Hollywood is the lower end of the key. Lavish houses, partially hidden by trees and shrubbery, back drop the clean suburban streets. I walk the length of Santa Monica Blvd from Robertson to La Cienaga. I follow the line of coffee houses, grocery stores, clothing stores, restaurants, and green spaces. I pass a packed Starbucks with people lounging outside, a lube store with sexy lingerie and neon lights, a bookstore, a bar, another club with overturned stools. It hasn't opened quite yet and the remnants of the night past waft onto the sidewalk. Another restaurant with white cloth that hangs on outside patio tables. People walk, jog, and move up and down this sidewalk. California cool.

I wander back to San Vicente into West Hollywood park. I stop at the edge and sit on a tree stump. A muscular man with perfect brown skin does back flips, ten in a row with an older man following him as he flips the length of the park. I watch his feet hit then spring up and curl inward then feet again, and again. He moves with grace. After ten rotations he plants his feet, claps his hands together and walks back to the coach. A young boy, his son (I assume), runs up to him and then begins to shake his hips from side to side in a funny dance, this three-year-old wants to entertain his father. The man takes him in his arms, spins him around then gently puts him down again. The boy with curly locks runs back to the mother, (I assume) and sits to watch his Dad go up again.

I take slow steps past the jungle gym and swing set where parents and caregivers watch their children move over the plastic and steel. I assume these are queer parents. I walk past the gate to the public pool, enter the tiny public library, huddled masses of books, a line for the four computers. It's cramped inside so I move towards the door and pick up brochures about the summer book fair, and whole living. I exit taking deep breaths in the summer air. A man in dirty clothes surrounded by two bags and a bicycle sleeps in the shade of an oak tree across the street from the Police Station.

West Hollywood is a perfectly compact city, one that has all of the necessary places for comfortable and functional living. You can walk from your apartment home or California bungalow with perfectly manicured fruit trees to the grocery, to the bar, to the gym and back. You can, that is, if you can afford it.

Spectacle.

A transgendered person walks by. Her red lips contrast against olive skin. She is pulling a suitcase. And stands ultra tall in high heels. She peeks in past the metal bars. Two women that look like visiting mothers from Nebraska in too tight white pants lean back in their chairs to follow her gait past them. They smile at each other and then turn back to their menus.

Surrounded City.

> Today West Hollywood is a completely developed, diversely populated area of 1.981 square miles, or 1273 acres, located approximately eight miles northwest of the Los Angeles Civic Center. It extends for a maximum east–west distance of about 2.9 miles and 1.25 miles from north to south. It is surrounded on three sides by the City of Los Angeles; on the north by the Hollywood Hills, on the east by the community of Hollywood, on the south by the Beverly–Wilshire district, and on the west by the City of Beverly Hills.[152]

Fresh.

I came to West Hollywood as a frightened, insecure being. It's taken me four years of true exploration and ratty experience to find stillness, a newness, and a freshness.

Our spaces and the places we cultivate impact our psyches. I know how much the burden of a drive through miles and miles of traffic can pound on our brains and the hunch of shoulders crunching into backs can weight our experience.

It's a new freshness, a consciousness that feels light. But when I walked into the past, the insecurity seeps in, fresh from the east coast, a body too big, an insecurity too large, a pain that seemed to hold itself in a body without any form of release. It's too big. All of this. The movement from past to present, into and out of feelings of true connection, a desire to feel as though I belong, somewhere. I started belonging to her, in a new space, trying to cultivate place together. And as we stood, freshly in the center of a space, we hauntingly floated in and out of possibility.

But we were defined distinctly by our queerness, two women in one house, in one bed.

We fell into a new fresh crop of people, possibility, women, and men to connect to. We wandered into West Hollywood and I felt a different heaviness of insecurity. Ani, my ex, performs and looks queer, I do not. She gets hit on. I do not.

Ani would survive here without me. Find a community, another wife, be desired. I don't know if I could. A fresh wave of discontent washes over my body.

Phobias.

> I hear him ask, "How can you like both men and women? What if one day you decide you want to be with the other sex?"

> I hear her ask, "Are you going to want threesomes, cause I'm not into that."

> I hear him say, "Your sexual decisions do not fit with your politics."

> I hear her say, "A heterosexual relationship is so much more fruitful."

> I hear her ask, "So, do you miss the vagina?"

I hear this barrage of homo/hetero/bi phobia phrases on a weekly basis. But I only hear it from people who know me well. They have to know me well enough to know about my sexual practices. They know I have had sexual relationships with men, women and trans folk. These words come from people that are closest to me. That's the worst part.

The Abbey (Morning).

I enter into the Abbey at 11am. It's a beautiful sunny morning in southern California. Ornate decorations, slab metal, rusted statues, slate floor, elaborate red chandeliers, wooden beams, and terracotta walls make this fit for a queen. A Virgin Mary statue with arms outstretched looks down upon us alongside the Gargoyles facing the street protecting us. There are large rooms upon rooms with four full bars. The remnants of a night, last night, the stench of party in the bathroom masked by cleaning spray and wiping down tables, mopping floors with beer drenched mops. A night washed almost clean for the breakfast shift. The music still thumping, music that is not, in my mind, daytime music but pop, dance music.

The waitress introduces herself to me. I order a Bloody Mary and she IDs me.

I show her my California license and she says, "Wow. Really?"

"Yep, I'm 32," I say with a smile. She puts up her hand in a high five and says, "You go Girl."

Since I've moved to Los Angeles, I've worked hard to stay in shape. Today I am in my workout gear, still sweaty from my morning boxing class. I intend to stay in shape for the rest of my life. I watch my food intake. I have the privilege of buying wheat-free, gluten free, organic foods. I have the income to self-support a healthy lifestyle. I know this is privilege. I know my skin color, my gender, my body, and my outward appearance allows me several privileges. I am not naïve.

And yet still, sometimes I feel so negative about myself. It's scary.

She brings my plate of food, egg whites with cheddar cheese, wheat toast and avocado.

The lesbian couple to my left drink coffee and talk about their friends that work at Crate and Barrel. Their short hair, styled spiky and tight, gives them away. Other markers stand out, such as the striped masculine shirt or the way they lean in to each other when they talk. I look over. One catches me and smiles a sweet smile. I turn back to this Macbook computer.

Kiki, the waitress comes back, notices that I haven't touched my plate and says, "Babe, your food is going to get cold." She is a sweetheart.

The framed poster of Elizabeth Taylor catches my eye and makes me laugh. Her arms are outstretched like the Virgin Mary statue but she, Liz, is covered in gold. Short hair, fluffed like my mother used to do. I can't help but think, "What a cliché."

I think back to my student coming out to me a year or so ago. I think of him now because his boyfriend works here, or used to. He asked me for advice on how to come out to his parents, introduce them to the man he loves. I remember telling him my story.

***

My mother washes dishes over the sink. I know I need to tell her. I love my girlfriend. I want them to know about her, to take her in, to really understand and appreciate my love, our love. I say, "Mom, I need to tell you something."

"Yes?"

"I am in love with a woman. And I want you to know and meet her." She laughs her sweet laugh and says, "You're kidding right?"

I storm out of the kitchen and say, "No I'm not. You are so awful." I throw myself on the bed in a dramatic heap. She follows me in. My sighs and sobs are heavy. My head pushed into the pillow. I turn away from her when she sits on the edge of the bed.

She puts her hand on my back and says softly, "Honey, we are going to love whomever you love no matter if they are a man or a woman. I just want you to know that. Ok?" I open my wet eyes and smile.

"Thank you."

West Hollywood Neighborhood.

Behind the main strip of Santa Monica Boulevard are rows of houses, part of the West Hollywood West division. While closely packed, the exterior and interior design of the houses expands the city's property values, each one a bit better than the next. These houses are manicured with an artistic flair.

This has been said about the gentrification process: first the artists move in, choosing cheap living over safety. Then, the homosexual men come in and clean the neighborhood up, designing and crafting the space with perfect precision, then come the corporations, then the upper-middle class straight white families that are attracted to the artistic. They ruin the area by allowing for Panera Bread to take out the neighborhood bakery and the Starbucks to capitalize on the local caffeine addicts.

The artists, and the lower income population that once thrived in this area can't afford the raised rents so they move to where they can survive. And it happens all over again somewhere else.

Here in West Hollywood, it is different. The homosexual population moved in and never moved out. The history of West Hollywood is based on a political and activist desire to carve a space in Los Angeles that is home to a population of people who are proud of and are marked by their sexual orientation and the performance of this identity. And, here, we can be open about it. And yet, my being open is marked as straight. As a bisexual woman who loves people, the wholeness of people, over their bodies, it can be quite difficult to meet other women.

She

pushes me up against the kitchen counter. Our tension pulsing, present, clear to us, only us as we make fajitas for the gathering downstairs, outside on the lavish deck, they wait for their vegetables and tortillas. We push against each other's bodies, digging deeply into the possibility. "We would be the perfect couple. A power lesbian couple," she whispers as her hand moves underneath my dress. "Can't you just see it?"

Footsteps up the winding staircase. We push back and away. She grabs the spatula and stirs as I wipe the saliva from my chin.

Homebody.

The bartender talks to the red-faced man at the bar. His pickled skin signals to me that he is an alcoholic. I am sure he is here every day when they open. He reminds me of my patrons at my bar.

I over hear the bartender say, "I love my place now. I mean I am close enough that I can walk to work but I am far enough away that I don't feel like I am right here."

The man says, "I know. Can you imagine living right here on San Vicente?"

"OH No!" The bartender waves emphatically. "Never. I mean, my last place and my place now were perfect."

A truck backs up with the warning sounds, "Beep Beep Beep" then releases the brake with a huff of air, a sizzle. The bartender breaks in and says to the older man with a giggle, a shake of his head, and a soft taunt, "You are so cute. On the rocks." Then he says, "Your partner is working, isn't he?"

"No, not yet. He is at home."

"How come he doesn't come here with you?" The Asian bartender with tattoos on his upper left arm, Chinese symbols in an armband pattern, leans in.

"He is such a home body that he likes to stay in."

"Perfect Friday or Saturday night for me is staying home, making dinner then having friends come over for dessert. I don't like going out to bars."

The hostess enters and says hello to the family at a table caddy corner to me. She is dressed in tight black skinny jeans, a thin black top. Her long and skinny body is given height by her tight black boots. Her long black hair frames her beautiful face. She leans back against a chair and her tiny belly inches forward. She is beautiful. One of the men gets up and carries his small pincher dog to the bathroom with him. His casual slip-on shoes and light blue preppy shirt remind me of my hometown in the northeast. The bus boy, an older Mexican man stares at the young hostess. He looks at her ass and then sees me catch him. He turns back to the plates in his hand.

Two men walk in. Kiki walks up to them and says, "Hello. How are you?"

The man in his late thirties with a black tank top and Ray Ban sunglasses says, "Gooood. How are you Darlin?" The lilt in his voice marks him as gay. It's an upswing in tenor, a lengthening of vowels, almost like a slow drawl. They sit behind a wall. I can't see them anymore.

An Abbey bartender walks in. His tight red tank top accents his perfect arm muscles. His black spiky hair, chiseled cheek bones, Ray Ban sunglasses, and his strut in black cargo pants makes him the envy of the room. People turn to watch him. I'm sure he gets picked up on by everyone. He disappears behind the bar.

I ask for my check. The sun is starting to heat the back of my arms. I'm going to wander the streets, drive through the neighborhoods. Encounter and listen.

The check arrives and I realize just how expensive this place is: $10 drinks, $15 breakfast. Not many people can afford to eat here. Most people eating are white, middle to upper class, framed contextually in the Abbey, marked as queer. But perhaps they aren't. I may be making grand generalizations, leaning on the fact that this space is marked as queer, which may mean that people in this space are themselves queer. I should never lean on these assumptions.

As I type these words, a man and a woman get up from the table behind me. They slowly saunter out the restaurant and he lovingly puts his hand on her lower back.

Cop Cars.

In West Hollywood the police cars have the graphic of the rainbow flag plastered on the side of their doors. Even the police cars are proud. Or at least they want the people in this area to feel comfortable, to forget the past when the police would arrest you or beat you for being queer.

> I hear her say, "Queerness is celebrated while hetero folk are almost looked down upon."

I wonder if that is the generalized truth.

Her Body (a Dream).

With sweaty palms we pass the bouncer at the front door. she hangs her body over the rail and twirls. "hey baby," she calls to me. "ah. come here." she begins to twirl again. her tank top cut so close to her nipples. the edge of her breasts exposed. the bouncer smiles as I pass through. im wearing my flowing attire. always flowing clothes. I look out of place. I feel out of place. naked breasts. but pasties. The bartender leans in and asks if I want a drink. "Vodka soda please."

a woman, it her, a version of Jill, striking brunette with a thin yet curvy body. legs crossed at the bar. sips a martini, three olives swim in her glass. she stares at the clock. grabs a toothpick from the plastic caddy on the bar. and glides the point over the edge of her teeth.

the announcer.

the brunette stands. She pulls at her fishnets, adjusts her corset. to the stage. up the three steps. she's on.

song: *American Woman*

man: with tweed jacket and large rim glasses. throws her a dollar. she dances for him. turns her back and bends from the waist. holds her ass in the air.

he imagines he has her by the waist, the hips. thrusting.

she shakes, thrusts. her skin moves, jiggles.

she grabs the pole. and gracefully flies around it. her leg parallel to the floor. an acrobat. a gymnast. a dancer. a sex kitten. she lands on one foot. and slaps her ass.

she looks over at me.

he throws another dollar. she crawls the floor to him. his glasses fog. he leans in.

her breasts. his face. he inhales.

she exhales. shakes a bit.

another dollar.

another spin. tight abs and muscles ache as she climbs the pole. flips over and slides back down. juices and sweat. in her pores. his juice and sweat on sheets that night. alone.

song ends. she collects the crumpled bills from the floor. he adjusts his glasses. announcer on. Red is next. tip them well. they make what you give them. another girl shifts from the seat, from the bathroom, from the lap of that man, to the stage.

"you wanna another drink honey?" the bartender with a voice like liquid candy asks.

"yes please," I murmur but can't take my eyes off her.

she moves back to her drink. pounds it. the bartender pours another.

"wow. that's impressive," I say as she chugs the next glass. and another.

she dryly says, "it's water in a martini glass. the olives for effect. we can't drink on the job."

she seems bored with me. she glances up and down my white linen pants and soft cotton shirt that do nothing for my figure, my frame. I feel boxy, bland next to her. she twirls the olives in the glass.

"that was a great dance." I say shyly.

"what do you want?" she barks.

pause. Silence.

I look up.

"to know you," I whisper.

"why?" the olives twirl in clear liquid.

"I want to *know* you."

Red Tour Bus.

In the distance a double decker tour bus packed with tourists passes by. Binoculars, floppy white cloth hats, sunglasses, and arms stick out the side point towards this or that building, this or that history, this or that celebrity sighting.

Rooftop.

Sam looks at me with pain in his eyes. A larger man, with a robust belly, and a really handsome face, "I don't get looked at by other men. I'm too fat." He looks around the open patio. "Oh. That one is sexy. You think I could get him?"

"You should come running with me? I would love that."

Susanne looks at me and laughs out, "Yea right." She looks at Sam and says, "He is not going to run. Walk, maybe."

She has always been far too honest.

"God, could you be ever more cruel? You are such a bitch," Sam says with a sense of real hurt in his voice.

I ignore the comment and say, "Well, we have to start somewhere. A walk is just as good as a run. We will have you running in no time," I say with a full sense of empathy. I know what it feels like to not feel good enough, to feel too big to be loved. I know that once I discovered that to be loveable has nothing to do with the body, I felt freer, ever more loveable. I look at Sam and say, "Sam, you *are* loved."

"See Susanne? That is how you speak to a friend. Jeanine is my wife. I love her. Not you." I can tell he doesn't mean that. He is just trying to get a rise out of her. I can see how much he loves her and wants her to respect him.

Jake, a small picture of a man, with dark brown eyes deep set in his skull, greasy black hair styled in a waved coif, looks at me with disgust, grabs Sam and says, "Come on. Shots."

Jake, Sam, Susanne and Michael line up against the bar. When I approach, Jake doesn't move over, or look at me. He stares at Susanne, with this strange lust, or control, or desire.

"Susanne you bitch, come take this shot with me," he says with a layer of disdain, or pointed hatred at my exclusion.

I look at Susanne, with that "I told you so" shake of the head.

She takes the glass filled with green liquor, "Jake, where is her shot?"

"SCOOBY SNACK!" he screams with a snort. She stops him from downing the drink mid-air. "What about Jeanine's shot?"

His lips purse. "Oh, I'm sorry. I'll get one more." He turns back to the bar.

Sam comes over to me and says, "Don't worry about him. He's a little testy."

"Whatever. I think he is gross." I dismissively wave my hand. I wonder what really bugs me about him.

"Scooby Snack," Jake says as he hands me my own shot. We hold up the glasses, clink and down another one.

The Gay Wife.

Whenever I enter West Hollywood, I am marked as heterosexual. I am not hit on, nor watched. Women may glance up, but then mark me as straight, not worth their time. If I am with a gay man, I am considered the gay man's wife, or the fag hag. When I am with more masculine women, they may mark me as the lipstick lesbian. They assume she is more dominant than I am.

This is not a new story.

Performativity of Limited Survivability: A Queer Identity.

West Hollywood, the west side, is a created place for the performance of queer sexuality. The businesses thrive off of consumers that relate to the rainbow flag. WeHo is a perceived place of pride and safety. But it is limited in this freedom. Folks are marked by a perceived performance of queer. These expectations of the performance of queer are versions of queer identity that is framed by heteronormative expectations of queer. The heteronormative expectation of queer is based on the binary of queer and not queer, the categories of gay male and lesbian woman on one end of the spectrum and heterosexual males and females on the other. While there has been movement in queer communities to accept and understand versions of sexuality that are neatly packaged in this binary, we have not envisioned or enacted these multiplicities in our daily practices or performances of queer so that our spaces and places shift.

Art/Design/Fashion.

The front of the Chanel store is one large screen.

   Film footage of models walking the runway.

   This movement is very posh.

   No one walks on the sidewalk.

The Falcon.

L-word screening night. At the Falcon, women and men that watch the L-word for critique and pleasure gather at the Falcon. The four of us are late. Most people are seated in the levels and floors of tables. The buzz is like a sexualized hum, word, and laughter. Fedora hats and fingerless gloves. The perfectly tailored blazer over engineered ripped jeans. A flash of a smile and eye contact.

   Jill and I wander through the space, up and down stairs looking for a free table, any table. "We just passed the creator of the L Word. And some of the cast." Her hand grabs mine and she squeezes it. I think it's too obvious that we know these celebrities are right behind us. I do not turn around. At least not right then. Jill giggles nervously. And we keep walking. Down to the first floor. We find a table too close to the screen. I feel like people can see us. So I pull my scarf closer to my neck and take a breath. The white candles on the table in glass bowls cast a dim glow on the white tablecloths. I pick up the small menu and peruse for a light snack. Don't want to eat too much. The lights do dim and there is a collective 'hush,' then one woman laughs almost too loudly and her friends giggle. I am sure she appreciates the attention.

A red-haired mousy girl comes up to our table and awkwardly says hello to Jill. She extends her hand to me and asks to sit down beside me. I let her and position my body to engage in conversation. I always try to be polite but I don't feel attracted to her. I can tell she wants to talk with me, for more than just polite conversation.

She stammers, "I, uh, I work security." I look at her tiny frame and wonder how on earth she is security. I imagine her swimming in her security guard uniform. I imagine the fabric drags on the ground as she yells, "Stop! Thief!"

"Wow, that must be an interesting job." I whisper and turn back to the big screen. She continues to chatter as the television show's opening credits start. I now think she is a little rude. I position my body away from her and towards the screen. People begin to clap and hoot and holler.

They lounge, the group of them in their VIP seats, soak up the glances and praise. I don't see my favorite character there. Maybe she doesn't like these events. Women in twos, hold hands, defy gender expectations. First couple sits two tables away. Their gendered performance—feminine and feminine, white silk shirts, make-up and high heels, paired with long dress with skin exposed, a slit up the fabric so the leg is exposed. Or another couple, short-cropped hair, with gel and spikes, a tie, holds hands with tight purple pants punk rocker, with ripped t-shirt and a nose ring.

Back to the screen and I order a vodka martini. After the end credits of the television show that is supposed to represent lesbians in Los Angeles, I feel slighted, disappointed. That is not my life. Or maybe it was at some point. Certainly not here. I felt part of the queer community in Florida when Ani and I loved each other, when we had circles of lesbian, bi and trans friends. Here in LA it was just the two of us trying to get acquainted, trying to make it. And that fell apart.

A Latina woman comes over and speaks with Jill, her back-less t-shirt exposes beautiful skin. She doesn't look my way except to say hello when introduced. Jill laughs at her joke and then stands up to say hello to other people she knows.

I feel exposed, unattractive, and stuck talking when I don't want to. I gulp the vodka down and order another.

The Creative City.

West Hollywood, also known as WeHo, or Boys Town, is also known as the creative city. Over 40 percent of the population in WeHo is comprised of gay males. West Hollywood is a model of androcentric privilege that becomes the image of and product of design–interior and exterior, fashion, and high end art. Most think this section of town is Beverly Hills. The Avenues, an elite part of West Hollywood, with its line of the most expensive of shops thrives off of lack, desire, consumer profit, and image. In WeHo, they acknowledge that those that create and wear and furnish with our designed desires, or objects of aesthetic envy, are mostly gay males.

Chanel Heteronormativity.

Is there a gay male aesthetic? Is there a gay male affinity for fashion, design, and art? Is this affinity or expectation of fashion sense and aesthetic in the gay male community reinscribing the consumerism of heteronormativity? As gay males corner the market on fashion design do they push forward a queer agenda or a reinstatement of the hetero world? Are these worlds actually that distinct?

The gay male figure in fashion loves the skinny girl aesthetic. The model body is the pinnacle of bodies. And the model body that can wear art is the pinnacle for fashionable bodies.

I instantly think of Andy Warhol.

The Avenues.

The Avenues—Art, Fashion & Design District, located in West Hollywood, California has been the West Coast's premier shopping destination since the golden days of historic Hollywood, filled with boutiques and ateliers that catered to movie stars and the elite of the new metropolis. Officially organized in 1996, the Avenues seek to protect this legacy of quality, style and experience. Respected brands, outstanding service, impeccable workmanship, and cutting edge design give visitors outstanding value in fashion, interior design, furniture, the decorative arts, food and spirits.[153]

Jaguar is its official sponsor.

The Gay Male Body.

I hear her say, "Being chubby in the gay male community, unless you are a Bear, is like a cardinal sin. My friend Trevor spends every waking moment in the gym."

I hear him say, "Ugh. I was so worried he was going to think I was too big."

I hear her say, "You are so sexy and handsome. No matter what size you are."

I see him scoff.

Urth Café.

In the Urth café, an obvious haven for celebrity culture, rich and not so famous, a man holds the hand of a teenage-looking Russian woman. She is thin, the ideal looker. The age difference is obvious.

I take a steep inhale. My favorite sitcom actor just walked in. He is handsome. Looks kind, with a book in his hand, my favorite type of man. The intellect. He went to Harvard. And is now working in television. I wonder if I will see my dear friend Scott here. I also wonder if I should sit outside. I'm inside waiting for my green tea, a white middle to upper class drink. He is writing in a journal that I have. I used it when I traveled to San Francisco. I wonder if we are connected. This is the third time I have seen him out and about. Places like an art show, across the room, he saw me looking. I am pretty sure he is in a relationship with a beautiful Hollywood actress.

In West Hollywood, the Avenues are an elite place to thrive. On the corner of Westmount and Melrose people sit with sunglasses on. They look bored, despondent, and rich. Perhaps these judgments are based on nothing but the few markers I see and make sense of—the gladiator sandals, the high heels, the bling of diamonds on the Russian girl's finger. The actor leans against the metal post in his too California cool casual button-up shirt and tied leather bracelets. The iPhone, the large gold watch, the plastic surgery face that seems a bit too shiny, the conversation that has turned quite loudly on to the Hollywood topic, the creation of movement, of television, of a sitcom, a heart that feels closed, the Ray Ban sunglasses and unfinished plate of food that was not boxed up to go. There are far too many markers of elitism here.

The greatest marker is the ivy on the buildings, ivy that clings to the concrete, a faux head nod to nature, the natural can exist here, in this line of buildings, boxes with large windows for peering through, the ivy hides the grey, corners of fences covered, rounded by the green.

They speak about the value of the house, the silver house that is valued at a "not too expensive price of four million." The price, for me, is impossible. The price, for them, is easy. This is the difference. The largest expectation of West Hollywood is to be able to afford the posh lifestyle, or at least act like you do. I flash back to my parents' house, the elitist behaviors of those that lived around me, the egos that fed into an entire class of people that thought about whose house was biggest, whose car was the nicest, whose body was the fittest, which inheritance was oldest.

But underneath the façade, there wasn't the substantive desire to care for each other. The ego became so big, so important. Soccer games were about parental flaunting of new cars or fancy digs. My friends and I talked about trust funds. I whined to my father that I didn't have one.

I like what my favorite actor just said. His new book is about the ability to spot ego, the blindness that comes from that. He also said, "It's hard to write about my personal experience because it always feels like a time capsule." Maybe we are more connected than I originally thought.

Coffee House Connection.

I hear him say, "I am juicing my dinner. I had a late lunch."

I watch her eyes light up as he says, "Well, I want to sit down with the both of you."

I can hear the sound of money dropping in her proverbial bucket.

Celebrity.

When I first met her I was nervous. Really nervous. The celebrity of the interaction overshadowing the reality that she is a real person. In the coffee house with low bucket seats, French bread, and white linen tablecloths, I wait for her to arrive. My laptop open on the table signifies to her that I am ready to work for her charity, not ogle at her, or use this opportunity to say, "I know so and so . . . ."

She is a lesbian icon. A heroine to some, a crazy character to others, but one thing is for sure, if you mention her name in the queer community, most people know it.

I shuffle my papers around. And there she is, a miniature person, short, really short and stunning. Her black hair and deep blue eyes sparkle as she says "Hello" in this soft syrupy voice. She extends her pale hand and I shake it as I offer her a kind smile.

She sits. "Nice to meet you. Jill tells me a lot about you. So how did you hear about the charity?"

"Well, Jill first introduced me but then I did a lot of research about it and I just have to tell you that I think what you do is just fantastic. You are saving lives, telling their stories, giving back to the underserved. We need more people like you in the world." I mean these words but worry I sound like a kiss ass. She smiles and says, "Oh well, I'm not the only one. There are so many people that make this organization work." Her blue eyes strike me. I pull open my laptop and ask, "Well, how can I help? What do you all need?"

When I tell people later that I work for her charity organization the response is varied. She is, after all, a lesbian icon, the character on a lesbian show that discovered late in her life that she was in fact a lesbian. Her struggle was fodder for debate for most fans of the show. People either loved her character or hated her. She was for some, "not enough of a lesbian." She was "the crazy one that couldn't make up her mind." Her character's chaos and journey was uncomfortable in its truth.

Her character was someone I identified with and sitting across from her soft skin and full lips, I find myself attracted to her, thrilled by her activist sensibility and turned on by her low rustle of a voice.

I discover that she does not like to go out in public.

She

asks, "Can we do back rubs?" I run through the many scenarios. With Jill, it is, perhaps, frightening, exhilarating, that we could at any moment be thrown against a piece of furniture, tongues moving over tongues, hands on breasts and skin. I flash back to her dinner party, Carter, my new date downstairs, the other guest mingling. We said we would get the dessert. My back against the wall, her fingers underneath my skirt. Lips and skin and passion and cum, then kiwi and sorbet.

"Yes," she says, "We can do back rubs." I sit on her butt and move underneath her thin red shirt. She has the softest skin, delicate and pale like origami paper. I'm careful with her skin. I'm careful with my heart and her skin. She could break me and I know that. She doesn't self define as lesbian or bisexual. She hasn't been with women for more than a night. She certainly hasn't dated a woman. She can tame any vagina, any penis, grab people by their crotches and drag them towards her heart. She's a stunner, in more ways than one. So I'm cautious.

I wonder if she feels the hesitance in my touch. My hands, usually strong hands, but what I give in massages is my energy, the heat from me. But with Jill, I purposely hold it back. I wonder what my touch feels like when I'm holding back. I should ask my exes. What does my touch feel like when I am holding back?

My fingers move, but stay focused on the knots, the one on the right side of her spine. If I tickle, I may arouse her, wake the sexual energy inside me. I could flip her over, kiss her. But I stay focused on the knot. I don't move a muscle except to loosen hers.

Pride Parade.

Colors. Everywhere there are colors. Bright colors adorning almost naked skin. A feathered peacock, a man, several men with 8-pack abs and a black jock strap thrust atop the float, black leather, headdresses, signs that read, "Out, Loud, Proud." And "My Mother Loves Me and my Husband." "Here, Queer, Get Used to It." Cheers from the lines of people, laughter and public displays of affection.

A line of police officers surrounds the church-going protestors, with signs that read, "You will burn in Hell," "And God said . . . ."

I begin to snap photographs of this juxtaposition. A lesbian couple walks in front of them and I yell out, "Hey. Stop right there. I think you should kiss. I'll take a picture." I smile and they wave and turn to one another. The religious leaders begin to point and scoff. I take a photo.

The layered imbalance, the showing of anger and disgust frames the women's love, their passion. They stop and turn to say something to the men watching, jeering. I don't know what they said, but I do know the men laugh. At them.

Then, a police officer walks by them, a female police officer. She dismisses their call to get the lesbians away from them. "Well, you shouldn't have shown up to a gay parade then." I laugh and give her a grand smile.

In Los Angeles, the LAPD can ask to be on this assignment. I assume that most officers that arrive to work the pride parade are allies, gay-friendly. I assume that in this neighborhood, most are queer or at the very least allies.

It's been ages since Ani and I have spoken but in a moment of nostalgia and desire, I text her. "I'm at Pride. You coming?"

She meets us at the corner bar on La Cienaga. We order champagne and pour it in plastic cups with the rainbow flag. Swarms of people move in and out of the bar, swarms more line the sidewalk. I can see Ani look at Elle, a beautiful redhead, a folk singer. She is just Ani's type. They begin to make small talk and I turn to Ani and kiss her. Out of jealousy, nostalgia, claiming my territory.

She pulls me outside. "Why would you do that? That isn't fair."

"Well, I still miss you," I say as I let my fingers grace her skin. I know deep down that this isn't fair, to her, to us, maybe even to Elle.

"Let's go. Sam wants to meet up with his wife." She smiles sweetly.

We find Sam on the sidewalk. "Oh my God. Good thing I found you all. Hi love." He pulls me in for a big bear hug. "See, she is just so nice to me, unlike you." He takes a jab at Ani. She smirks. "Of course you would think that. Jesus."

She puts her arm around my shoulder and we make our way through the crowds of people, to get a better look, to begin to separate from the rest of the group. Ani and I always found a way to make it just about the two of us.

PRIDE for Sale.

We wander away from the parade and pay $20 a piece to enter the festival. The festival center holds beer tents, vendors selling artwork, clothing, buttons, and hats. There are organizations offering services, promoting the AIDS clinic, the health care services, lawyers, queer allied businesses. The list goes on and on. What most business owners, corporations, town and city managers, have figured out is that the Queer community is a profitable consumer. And that money is more important than social politics. West Hollywood is an upper to middle class city.

Performativity of Survivability: The Act of Consumption and the Creation of Queer.

While there is something extremely valuable about a gay man and a lesbian feeling safe, allowed to express their queerness out and proud, there is something lacking in the West Hollywood creation of queer. The place of queer is not so. It is a shaped landscape that rests on the consumption of heteronormative objects and things. People thrive in West Hollywood if they have money. You can meet people in the bars, if you can afford to enter in. You can live in the perfect houses designed by queer folk if you can pay the rent. You can purchase the performance of queer.

The Abbey (Evening).

The Abbey is infamous in the queer community. It is always busy, day or night, filled with tourists and locals alike. People come for the drinks, the company, for the eye candy and flirtation, the possibility of meeting. They come for the dancing, and the laughter. They come to the Abbey for the high ceilings and grand dance floor. They come for the bathroom kisses, the hand down the pants, for the energy of the evening. And the swing of the daytime.

We push past the gates, past the tables filled with laughing people, covered by sunglasses and fedoras flooded by California sunlight.

I turn to Amber and say, "I wonder if Tolstoy is here. God, he is such a dick."

"Who is that?" She asks with her compassionate eyes.

"Ani's friend. He has such a crush on her."

"I thought he was gay?"

"He is."

We glide past tables. A handsome server stops me. "Hi. How are you? Aren't you Simon's professor?"

I look at his tousled hair, his dark brown eyes, and olive skin. His muscles exposed through the work-ordained tank top. "Yea, I am. Jeanine."

"Nice to meet you again. Simon speaks really highly of you." He leans in and says, "Thanks for the advice you gave him about coming out. I am sure he will tell you but it went pretty well."

"Anytime. He is a doll. I am happy to help," I say as he gathers his cocktails from the service bar.

"Well, I hope to see you soon."

I smile and say, "Yes, thank you. Tell Simon I say hello." It feels nice to be recognized here. I put my arm around Amber's shoulder. I can see people looking at her. She is attractive, an energy that everyone wants to grab on to. We move to the back room and make our way to the bar. Amber leans her back on the rail, watching as I lean forward to grab the bartender's attention. She nudges me to turn around. I look and there is a woman almost swallowed by another tall, full woman with short blonde hair and baggy pants. Her white tank top hugs her breasts that she smushes against the woman with brown spiky hair's smaller, slender frame.

I see Tolstoy there, in the circle, laughing. He looks my way furtively and then says, "Oh hi" with a sneer. He is enjoying this exchange, watching the drama unfold.

I get a vodka soda. Amber and I slide into a booth behind this group of drunken buffoons. The woman with brown spiky hair slides into the booth next to us. She moves closer to another woman. She saddles up close, way too close. It's a fuck fest. The blonde woman watches. Then, another woman, younger, long brown hair walks up to the blonde and kisses her in front of the first woman. The crowd seems to be moving in circles, moving between women. I ask Amber, "How can they all act like this?"

The brown-haired woman in the booth leans over and kisses another woman. I slither out the words, "I can't believe they would act like this." I know they are wasted. The brown-haired woman stands up and the blonde woman is on her, she kisses her and they fold over onto our table, inches from my drink. I look at Amber and say, "We gotta go." We stand to leave.

I glance back at the woman on top of the blonde woman. Her hands are down her pants. On the table, in the Abbey, in public—fucking.

Perception.

I hear her say, "You just don't look gay."

I hear him say, "I don't have the abs. But fuck, he looks good."

I hear her say, "They are a fabulous couple. An architect. A designer. They have just such big hearts. You would love them."

Love.

In the middle of a city's travesty, there is so much love here. I need to say that once in a while. There are people that thrive, relationships that thrive, and circumstances that do and can provide for us. In the middle of a nation's tragedy that still needs to recognize and appreciate various forms of love.

In the middle of a city's travesty, I am searching for real love.

A Queer Body.

She asks me, "So, which guy are you dating now?" She always assumes I am dating men. As if she never believed I was queer at all. I've dated four different women in my life. I've flirted with far more. For me, love isn't about the body. It is about the person, the energy between souls, the desire to talk, to hold, to feel, to listen, and to honor their life's path and process. It is about loving all of them, penis or vagina, transgendered or not.

But she pulls at me to answer. "I'm not," I say softly. "And why do you always assume that? I don't think you are being fair." My words move into memory. Our memories. The way we left each other. The many more ways we leave each other now. And we come back, once in a while. I think to try and see, what if?

She is also the closest person to me out here. She knows me inside and out. And there are times I almost feel the love again and other times when I feel the disgust.

"Come on, are you sure you are really queer? I don't really see you as a lesbo." She picks up the guitar and looks out over the mountain.

"What about that guy at the Bistro?" She asks with almost sincerity. "You deserve someone like him, someone who will be kind to you rather than use you. Come on, you know that most guys just want to stick it in you. They are all pigs. Find one that actually respects you." She flicks her cigarette over the railing.

In some ways she is right. I need to respect myself enough to find someone who will respect me. But my body, this queer body doesn't exactly look the part of a queer-identified woman. I don't know how to meet women romantically anymore. And so far I haven't met anyone that interests me physically, emotionally, personally.

"I don't find him attractive. He's too small."

"You like women when they are small. Why not small men?"

I think about this for a while. I don't want to admit that men that are smaller than me make me feel big, whereas female bodies aren't given this parameter. I don't mind small female bodies, big female bodies, or bodies in between.

"I don't know. They make me feel big," I respond sheepishly.

"You are so weird."

The Performance of Sexual Survivability.

Sexual identity is created through the act of doing. Not of categorization. Agency is local action, the acts of sexual connection within the day to day. Choices we make constitute our identity. It is these choices that are shaped within and with the space. Identity is not being but doing. Sexual identity is created within the act of physical connection and intimacy. It is also made up of the choices we make after the physical connection has left us. What do we choose to do with our bodies within space.

Sexual identity is connected to the carnal, nature, the human as nature, as natural beings, naked, thrusting. Bodies upon and within bodies. For me, this sexual connection occurs without attachment to gender. Rape, the act of domination and pillage was that man's choice. His choice. He did not and will not take my agency from me. I will not exist as a victim anymore. My choice, to be with bodies, not sexual categorization, is also an action. And a desire to be without category. Once that recognition is fully realized, fully embodied sexual choices and sexual agency can shift. Our sexual choices can be made into the performance of clarity and wisdom. This is what I understand to be sexual survivability.

The non-reaction.

I tell my brother. "I'm dating a woman."

"Cool."

"What? You don't have anything to say?"

"No. Isn't that what you are all fighting for? A non-reaction? A normalization?"

Stunned, I nod. My brother is so smart.

But perhaps it isn't the normalization that falls in line with heterotopia but a normalization that allows people to expand possibility, widen and lessen expectation.

Santa Monica Boulevard.

To the ocean and back, Route 2, is both a tourist route and, just east of La Brea, one of the most infamous sidewalk stretches for prostitution—male, female, and transgender.

She

tells me we could have been perfect, in another lifetime. If we got together, friendships could be ruined. People just wouldn't understand.

We let the fantasy, the possibility, the sexual bond, die.

The Key.

the avenues.

design studio. buffed glass. modern edges.

art studio. clean white walls. one piece hangs in the
forefront.
Price tag. Price tag. Price tag. Is not visible.
you have to ask.

I do not ask.

santa monica blvd.
rainbow flag. restaurant. concrete. awning.
she walks by. half mohawk. sagging pants. nose ring.
he walks by. muscles cut. chiseled tank top.

they do not look at me.
I want them to.

8

WEST HOLLYWOOD, REVISITED

THE QUEER PERFORMANCE OF
LIMITED SURVIVABILITY

Throughout my experience of West Hollywood, I struggle with the notions of community as I confront the invisibility of my queerness. At the same time, I champion this community as the place in Los Angeles that explicitly invites queer people to express ourselves safely. Like much of Los Angeles, there is a slippage between the dream of inclusion and access. While West Hollywood is a safe space for some, it is not a space for all that may consider ourselves queer.

We revisit WeHo through a critical parade route of Santa Monica Boulevard. We revisit four locations in West Hollywood. Although there are several other locations, such as the Russian community that immigrated to West Hollywood and still thrives there, we focus primarily on Santa Monica Blvd, aptly named Boys Town or WeHo that sets up an expectation of queer norms and values, and yet even as it protects and defines queer *community*, it shrouds other queer possibility and futurity. Second, we move into the design and fashion district. A *terrain* named The Avenues, which capitalizes on the commoditization of the queer aesthetic. Third, we revisit the Falcon, a nightclub that only on certain nights is designated a lesbian bar, which creates a limited survivability of a *home* for female identified queer folk, because of the lack of queer female defined or identified places. Finally, we move into the non-place, invisibility of my queer *body*, as it moves

against hers in hidden places. In this parade, we examine the relationship between the queer community and heteronormative logics, in
particular, we address the performance of limited survivability in the
queer community of Los Angeles, noting that for a queer community
to thrive, members need to resist commodification and normalization.
In addition, we examine the demand of aesthetic accuracy of identity.

Santa Monica Boulevard: Queer Logics.

Imagine you are right there, next to the man in the tighty-whitey shorts
that cling to his perfect muscles. The backdrop, the American Apparel
store situated between a Starbucks, a restaurant, another bar, across
the street from the lube shop. It's just another day as the twink with
thin limbs and a pierced lip strolls past a drag performer with his
clothes packed in suitcases, wheeling to prepare for his show tonight
at Hamburger Marys. WeHo, framed by shops that line Santa Monica
Boulevard, and made energetic and vibrant by the people that reside
there, is not unusual. It is a queer community. Imagine you listen to
the cars pass, honk at the man with no shirt on, and turn right down
Roberston Ave.

––––––––

Pride sets an expectation for the queer community; whatever your
inclination, there is a place for you. However, this expectation falls
short outside of Pride. The epic nature of Pride places it as a special
performance, a window in time where queer reigns and all things
heteronormative are diminished. But throughout the rest of the
year in most US locations, all things queer still take a back seat to
heteronormative privilege. In West Hollywood, this push and pull is
a bit more blurry. The area itself is a proclaimed bastion for those that
are queer to feel safe in performing their identities. Although for this
to happen, the queer community itself must be supportive of varying
performances of identity, to operate out of a queer logic.

What exactly are queer logics?[154] Both queer theory and gay and
lesbian studies "seek to link research with politics and liberate sexual
and gender 'minorities' from oppressive forms of heteronormativity and
sexual and gender prejudice that have been, and continue to be, harmful

to those that do not fit gender and sexual norms."[155] In other words, LBGT studies emphasize the stability of sexual and gendered identities and queer theory aims to dislocate and critique the performance of fixed sexual and gender identities. Queer theory emerged as a result of the AIDS crisis and surrounding activism (Queer Nation and ACT UP),[156] postmodern and poststructural theories, feminism, and the homophile movement.[157] In short, queer theory emerged to encompass the multitude of ways one may express (through time) the self through sex, sexuality, and gender while also trying to remain connected to the political realities of homophobia, transphobia, and the privileging of reproductive systems.[158]

Consider also that a queer experience is completely rooted in place. In the text, *Love, West Hollywood*, a trove of writers comment on the ways in which West Hollywood shaped their queer identities. Greta Gaard frames her identity in the following way: "As an adult I've given a lot of thought to place and identity, yet it's surprising that my view of my coming out years is so entangled with the built environment."[159] Queer identity is discovered, played out, and realized in and through queer spaces and the surrounding landscape.

Halberstam offers us a vision of queer community that goes beyond queer as simply sexual or gender orientations. Being queer is inherently about existing outside of linear, heteronormative timelines and about inhabiting space in ways that transgress the capitalist, heteronormative frame. So that, "futures can be imagined according to logics that lie outside of those paradigmatic markers of life experience—namely, birth, marriage, reproduction, and death."[160] Munoz builds on Halberstam's notion of queerness and calls for a utopian, queer futurity, an economy about "desire and desiring" and opening the self to embody a hopeful, ecstatic future beyond heteronormative limitations. And to lean into the future of this possibility is where queerness begins. "Doing, performing, engaging the performative as force of and for futurity is queerness's bent and ideally the way to queerness."[161]

The Abbey: Heteronormative Logics.

My experience at the Abbey highlights the struggle of crafting and understanding one's queer identity. Heteronormative logics render queer identity as errant and therefore, devalued in society. For many queer people, the key to being in queer community is to feel accepted and valued. To overcome the social stigma by a heteronormative society, many queer people strive to find acceptance in the queer community through idealizing certain body aesthetics. The quest to achieve an ideal queer body and subsequent sexual–social performance creates a web of aesthetic demand, whereby one must meet a certain level of aesthetic accuracy to find acceptance. I recognize this pressure and feelings of my body being too big and looking too straight. Because of my perceived performance of a straight identity, I feel unseen, hidden, unattractive, and perhaps not queer enough. While certainly, to perform a socially understood queer identity enables people to identify others like them in a safe way, it is also a limiting logic as performing queer is more than looking a certain way.

The performance of queer identity within the Abbey, especially at night, is to be explicit with sexual desires. Some even act out these desires on tables, in the bathrooms. Other folks within the queer community are not as openly explicit about their sexual acts but are part of the terrain, watching, commenting. Critiquing. The performance of queerness in these explicitly sexual moments marks the sexual act as the doing of queerness. And yet, this is also a limiting logic as performing queer is more than the doing of sexual acts in a certain way.

I experience WeHo as a place that marks me as invisible because my identity performance transgresses the community demand for aesthetic accuracy of identity. In the gay and lesbian community, certain aesthetic markers exist to indicate identity as gay or lesbian. Certain styles of clothing communicate group affinity or sexual preference. For example, tight t-shirts that accentuate upper body muscles or leather vests. Certain styles of hair can also communicate this affinity such as a short haircut that is styled to shape the face in a feminine but rough way or jewelry that is simple and strong. While there are many ways to perform gay or lesbian, there are aesthetic choices that are more normative within these communities. Importantly, these kinds of very public aesthetics are rooted in political purpose. Representational visibility is about creating social awareness, acceptance, and ultimately safety for those that exist under a queer umbrella. Still, as Galewski points out, the iconic markers of lesbian or gay identity are often viewed as the only legitimate identity performances at the exclusion and invalidation of other identity performances that are not as visible.[162]

I do not aesthetically perform my queer identity in a normative or visible way. Yet my identity is queer in that I am open to all kinds of people as potential sexual and/or relational partners. Questions around visibility and invisibility are important ones because they call attention to issues of political possibility and interpersonal acceptance. While I may be overlooked within gay or lesbian contexts, I do have passing privilege within straight contexts, which is a kind of political power. My bisexual, high femme identity is a queer performance in that I elude others' attempts to concretize me. Like all identities, there is a historical arc and constitutive fiction surrounding bisexuality. The identity paradigm—a homo, hetero opposition—is reproduced under discussions of bisexuality. There is a failure of both LGBT and queer theories to account for the relation dimension of bisexuality as marked identity.[163]

The Avenues: Commodification of the Queer Aesthetic.

Walk down the avenues. You pass an empty building, a "for lease" sign. Then empty walls with one sparkling chandelier. She walks by with Chanel sunglasses on. You stop and stare at a video screen with models strutting down catwalks in Milan. You can feel the immense pressure to be something else. Ivy hangs on concrete buildings, a bit of nature in this row of strip malls. The ivy heightens the aesthetic and hides the fact that these are just buildings with fabric, wood, and people inside.

I do not wear clothes that mark me as having money. I do not wear designer sunglasses or shoes. I do not carry a fancy handbag with designer initials printed on the side, or carved in fine metals. As I walk the street of the Avenues I am prompted to feel as if I do not have enough. As I walk by the designer furniture stores I think of the furniture in my house, never designer, always thrift store bought. I look into the store. I like the eclectic funky vibe but cannot afford what is behind the glass.

Alexander writes of how capitalism and heteronormativity function together to frame the queer community as white and male.

> Heterosexual capital makes it appear that the only gay people are consuming people, and that the only gay consuming people are white and male. In this universe, whiteness and masculinity operate together through a process of normalization that simultaneously overshadows lesbians, working-class gay men, and lesbians and gay men of any color of any class.[164]

In the fullness of being queer, there are certainly others that fall outside the parameter of white, gay, and economically privileged.

From Connolly's perspective, the world within capitalism is held together through webs of minorities, to include: illegal immigrants working for unfair wages, women working in underpaid, socially necessary positions, child slaves, underground economic networks, and gay communities working to establish credibility. "The capitalist nation-state, organized around a putative linguistic, religious, ethnic, and gendered center, has devolved into a world of interdependent minorities."[165] While such communities of people keep capitalism afloat, the center of this system, which is mostly white, male, and Christian, continues to exclude and punish such groups.

A huge issue across queer communities is the level of corporate interest in promoting Pride. At the Pride Parade, everywhere you look you see a corporate logo, reminding you that this bank or that bank, this insurance company or that insurance company, has an economic interest in the "gay" community. The involvement is similar to the logic that some Americans use to advocate the acceptance of queer marriage: gay people spend money, and they will spend more of it if we offer them mainstream access. Of course, many questions emerge out of identity as commodity. First and foremost, the question becomes: If a queer identity can be manufactured as a commodity tool, then what is the sustainability of this identity? And from Althusser's perspective: If the market is interpolating the appropriate queer identity, what does it mean to perform queerness as an individual?[166] The marketplace is a toxic player to queer identity even as it promotes it.

The Falcon: Fleeting Home.

The white walls and wooden tables, benches, and lounge chairs. The VIP section of this lounge offers tables like cubbies with high walls to create invisibility. You peek inside one of the areas and see them, their bodies close. You ask, are they just friends? Lovers? Is that a man or a woman? You watch as she slides her hand over her leg. It's confirmed. Lovers. With the sweet smile and the knowing giggle, they show affection towards one another. They look up and catch you looking.

As a queer identified woman in Los Angeles, I find that looking for spaces that are designated as female-identified is quite difficult. In Burbank I knew of one female-identified bar and most of the patrons were men. In West Hollywood there are three female-identified bars, Here, East/West and The Palms. Each of these places has their own expectations. I remember entering Here bar and feeling as if I stepped into an LWord club scene with women dancing on the bar. After waiting on the line that wrapped around the building and watching as my ex Ani was checked out by most of the people in the place I wanted to leave. I entered into East/West a more lounge bar; I felt more at ease, with 25–40 year old women mingling in dark clothes, sipping martinis. I have never entered the Palms but after 40 years it is a West Hollywood staple. While these three places thrive each in their own ways, it feels as if this isn't enough.

WeHo is an androcentric space like many queer places. There are many more places for gay men to congregate and express themselves. But this should not be a shock. For those that identify as women or trans, there is a general lack of access, respect, and economic stability compared to cismen. The Falcon is not normally a queer space. On select nights during the month, this bar hosts lesbian events. While some places exist that are primarily marketed to women, there is still a lack of public space for them to congregate. Part of this reality is the arc of history; gay men, or men who enjoy having sex with other men, have had public places of connection since the eighteenth century in the form of men's clubs.[167] Women on the other hand, do not hold such a history. Of course, the main factor in this arc is social privilege and disposable economy.

Yet, The Falcon, like other bars that are inclusive once or twice a week, are engaging in a kind of queer practice. Queer geographers are increasingly interested in and championing "more fluid, ambiguous, and contingently sexualized spatialities such as circuits and fields."[168] In other words, movement through WeHo from bar to bar or place to place in and through shifting identities is a layered queer performance. If WeHo were to become more queer, we would see places that are not fixed as "the gay bar" or "the lesbian bar," but rather places that host events across identity fields. Most certainly, the way WeHo is spatially represented now lacks the possibility for this kind of queer movement. The individually fixed bars limit a full embrace of fluid identity performances.

The Body: Non-Place, a Transition, a Hiding.

Imagine yourself in the space of a neighborhood park. The green space etched by others fits snugly between buildings and parking lots, stores and restaurants. People walk by holding hands. You hear a child laugh. Smell the familiar smell of grilled cheese from the restaurant next door. Perhaps you are hungry. Lay in the grass. Look up at the sky. Breathe in. Exhale. Pay attention to this body, your body as part of it all. Now imagine your body, your sexual body was invisible, unseen as a potential romantic or sexual partner. Feel the grass against your back. Move your finger against the blade. Focus in.

Who lies beside you?

––––––––––

As we end in the quiet space of a WeHo neighborhood park, I make sense of my own identity within queer identity. As I watch parents and a child play, I catch myself making assumptions of identity and relationship. In one glance, I capture the three as a family: father, mother, and child. Contextually I expect them to be so. As if West Hollywood is the designated place to be queer and elsewhere is not. But this assumption is not always true. Queer folks live and thrive throughout Los Angeles. And heterosexual folks live in West Hollywood. I chastise myself for making this assumption. Yet, I can, can't I? West Hollywood prides itself on crafting a city inside Los

Angeles County that is designated as queer. And perhaps when I walk these streets, sit in this park, smile at strangers, I too, am marked as queer.

Yet I struggle with my own characterizations because I know my story can be anything. The body that lies in the grass beside me or holds my hand on the street as you walk by marks my queerness. It is difficult to know by looking at another the gender, sex, or sexual preference one may prefer. Perhaps this couple is only connected over raising the child. Perhaps they all live together but the parents are polyamorous. Perhaps one of the parents identify as intersex or trans-gender. At the same time, maybe this triad is a cisgendered father and mother in a monogamous relationship with their biological child. It is clear that the only way I can know the story of this family is to ask. Because the fact this family group is in WeHo suggests they may be queer in some way. At the very least, queer friendly. Yet, no assumption can be made despite the identity expectation of the place.

I think back to my brother and his non-reaction to my announce-ment of dating a woman. I think for him that queer, while different than the heteronormative expectation, is not so different. When we differentiate ourselves as queer, mark out separate spaces, we are both creating safe spaces and separating ourselves. My brother's non-reaction means queerness is accepted and I do not anticipate from him expec-tations and snap judgments. I want a world where generalizations for others to be "this way," "that way," easy to read, and placed in our mental maps is no longer a part of our consciousness. I think back to my brother and I want to re-imagine queer space as all spaces, all families as family. I want to not react.

West Hollywood: A Call for Queer Possibility and Futurity.

It is from these questions that we posit the queer performance of limited survivability in Los Angeles. This performance is one borne from oppression of the past and present, a performance to carve out safe space for queer people in a context that can be quite homophobic. It is necessary in a hostile environment to create spaces of safety, and part of creating and maintaining safe queer space in a country that does not federally recognize queer partnership and marriage, is to align community performances with heteronormative values. For example, two gay men getting married and committing to a monogamous relationship, holding corporate jobs, buying a house, and having two children. Two men following a heteronormative script is far less threatening than two men in a partnership that is polyamorous with work outside traditional occupations, no house, no kids, and with no plans to contribute to a 401k.

If, as Munoz advocates, queerness is a performance of embodied futurity that seeks to create inclusion, then it is also a disavowal of capitalist webs that entrench minorities into working to support those that continue to oppress them.[169] Is it a full and utter disengagement from heteronormative space and time logics, whereby one shrugs off the pressure of reproduction, marriage, and even the process of how to die? And from this vantage, how are we to understand the queer community of West Hollywood? While certainly it is a community that has created safe spaces for people to create family in a myriad of ways and to establish queer space as normative space, do these efforts simply reinforce the oppression of free "desire and desiring" and performances of futurity that seek to acknowledge intersectional politics through normative consumption? This space seems to privilege whiteness, binary gay and lesbian identities, and cisgendered perform-ances. With so many possibilities being left out, West Hollywood is not a place that is unequivocally queer. It is a place that exists within Los Angeles, which is a place of plastique, consumption, and exploita-tion. West Hollywood has moments of fissure whereby it shrugs into and out of the capitalist framework, moments that are marked by inclusive community and desire that exceeds heteronormative boun-daries. It is in these moments that queer performance emerges most strongly.

I think of her, the one I wrote about, her body against mine. I think of our possibility and the desire we held and still hold for one another. I feel her soft skin and lips and miss her, our desire and desiring. I think of the "what if?" What if we held on to each other and didn't let expectations seep in? What if we decided to be a couple and not let the expectations of others or the possibility of torn friendships owing to our heteronormative social circle influence us? I wonder how everything would have changed. The reality is that everything would have changed, marked as queer, and then made into another expectation.

It feels as if there is the dual binary that bears on my sexual body, my desiring body. My queer body is not visible in the place of Los Angeles and more specifically in West Hollywood. It feels as though I only have two options, to be marked as lesbian or heterosexual. What about the fluidity of desire, the movement of bodies, and the desire to be seen as queer without meeting a particular aesthetic?

Our queer lenses and frames need to keep expanding and moving queerly forward. My queer body, the one that desires, loves bodies, the multiplicity of identities and the beauty that resides not just in the body but beyond the body, feels eclipsed by the community that seems to not have room for a spectrum of possibility. My desires feel silenced, muted by demands of identity, accuracy, and authenticity. It seems that in order for me to exist on the Avenues, The Abbey, or The Falcon, I need to be seen with another queer body. Then, I can be marked as queer.

But for my own futurity, my ideal queer place is one that does not expect, but allows. I have a longing for both inclusion and non-reaction. Inclusion is to be seen and accepted. And I want inclusion in a place that does not expect. I think of her, our possibility. It feels lovely, the possibility to be seen next to her body. But here is the catch: there would have been a reaction and a shifting of relational commitments and acceptance.

I think back to my brother and his non-reaction to my coming out. His non-reaction creates a space of openness, a space of normativity. The real promise of queerness is the space to be open and to feel as if queerness, in all its fluid categories through time and space, is normative. At the moment, most queer people do not hold enough rights to feel safe or to survive which necessitates a separation. This separation is what is needed right now. Yet the future begs us to imagine more. I know how I want to exist in my queer performances in the future and how I want spaces to hold this existence—allowing and embracing a kaleidoscope of desire. I'm just still not sure how we are going to get there from here.

Map 9.1 Topanga Canyon[170]

9
TOPANGA CANYON[171]

Image 9.1 Morning fog and sun

Green space.

A lull. a bird chirps. a dog barks. wind. a car whizzes past.

guitar strum.

A lull. a spider moves up its web. a dog barks. wind. a car stutters.

she sings.

A lull. a hum. a crow caws. a neighbor sighs. wind.

high hat.

Sentience.

In the mountains of Topanga the rumors of spirits past, people past, a dream of peace in Los Angeles is embedded in its rock and soil. The canyon is a thick space of green and hearty yellow. Where roots find nutrition in the memory of music, of escape, of a sentient nature. People come to transcend the nastiness of the city. The soot and grime of city smog folds away in chunks, carried by the ocean mist that covers the mountain range at dusk and again at dawn. As if nature were hauling the muck on its back, cleansing the lungs, the skin, the bones.

Home.

I've scoured the streets of Venice, CA for a place to live. I can't live in Burbank anymore. Too many memories rest and wake there. My hesitation in moving to this artistic beach community is spurred by the looming 405-freeway traffic, the necessity of driving to work in hours and hours of bumper-to-bumper exhaustion.

> Alone in his Civic, I hear him scream, "Where are you all going?" The solo commuters inch up the freeway. Brake lights and horns. Brake lights and horns.

I am desperately clear. No, not Venice. I wind north up the Pacific Coast Highway. My eyes move from the winding road to the immense cliff face only feet away from the crashing ocean. Cars move slowly, to allow the gaze. I gaze and inhale and exhale a relief. I can't believe I haven't lived here, right here, all along. Close to the ocean, against a mountain. The California dream—to be one on the sand, in the water, staring at mountains.

I turn right up Topanga Canyon Blvd, Route 27, to the northeast and wind in and out of the narrow roads. The steep S curves demand a slow and cautious drive. My nerves tighten, if I make a sudden move, I could careen off the side of this cliff, into the creek hundreds/ thousands of feet below. I follow the guardrail and yellow lines. Stay on track.

The S curves straighten. A yellow sign, painted with full letters, reads, "Slow Down Through Town." Another demands, "Slow Down: Kids and Dogs Here." Fences, crooked fences, line the creek and hide the sunken houses on the right. Trucks and cars are parked on the side of the road. I go over one short bridge and I spot a blue angel statue in the bushes, then a wooden sign that says, "Pine Tree Circle."

The signage in this space reminds me of New Paltz, NY, where my parents live now. I feel most at home (in my psyche, my body and my identities in New Paltz). Here, in Topanga, I feel the familiar bohemian pulse of freedom and artistry. I see women in flowing dresses, thin tops, relaxed hair that falls long. I see flowers and green. A barn and feed store. A psychic reader, a hum of bees. A yoga studio and the Waterlily Café.

I sigh. I'm home.

A Place Above.

The Native American indigenous Tongva tribe gave this area its name. Tongva means people of the earth. It is said that Topanga may mean "a place above heaven."

Universe.

I stand in front of the hand-written advertisements for places to lease posted on the Real Estate office door. Leasers in Topanga don't use Craigslist. It is a test, or a way to keep non-locals out. If they are worthy, they will know the space already. They will know to look on the door. They will know. And if they don't, they don't want them. I scan the prices, the locations, and look for a posting that says Dogs OK. Nothing.

A woman climbing into her Prius looks at me and stops her descent into the seat. She asks, "Are you looking for a place to rent?"

"Yes. I am. Hi. I'm Jeanine." I extend my hand, thrilled by the possibility.

"Well, I just love how the universe works. My friend Joan was just telling me on the phone this morning that she is looking for a new renter. And you look just perfect. Young, thin, beautiful. Good energy. I think she would love you."

I blush a bit. And wonder why my hair or body would mean anything to this Joan or this stranger in front of me.

She grabs her black notebook and rips a piece of paper out. She scrolls through her cell phone address book and copies the number in scrappy handwriting, blue ink. "She's a great lady. Here is her number. Call her and let her know I met you in front of the office."

"Thank you so much. I really appreciate it."

"Appreciate the universe. Things always seem to work the way they should," she climbs into her car and leaves me there, smiling.

Packs.

They form packs and small tribes.

Coyote.

My mother holds the door handle of my truck and I wind up and through the mountains of Malibu. We reach the top. And I slam on the breaks. A coyote, the size of a wolf, blocks our path. I stare deep in its glowing eyes. For a minute it stares back then lazily turns and trots to the side of the road.

The Path.

I climb up the long and steep path from the gravel parking lot and enter Froggy's, one of the five restaurants in Topanga, with my book in hand. At the top, my lungs feel a bit heavy. I open the swinging door and assess how this place works. It has a cabin-like feel, with rooms upon rooms, a huge deck that leans over the gravel parking lot below. People form a line at the counter. I get in line and listen for how to order. The man in front of me with long hair pulled tight into a ponytail, a tee shirt, and cargo shorts greets the woman with red hair behind the counter. "Hey Stew. Long time no see."

"Yea, I've been traveling a bit. Following the path, ya know?"

"How's your girlfriend?"

"She's good. Thanks. Can I get the taco plate? And a Bud Light."
She hands him a white number on a metal stand. I follow his
movements. Next to the bar, he picks up his beer and greets the tall
bartender with large fleeting eyes.

My turn. I order one veggie taco and a glass of red wine. She looks
me up and down. She says without prompt, "I didn't used to look like
this. I was a model you know. I was in a car accident. They didn't
think I would walk again. But here I am. Still standing. But with a
body I don't really love anymore." Her eyes look stained.

"You look beautiful. Absolutely. I'm Jeanine."

"Miranda. Nice to meet you."

I move from the counter to the bar and pick up my glass. I'm
beginning to recognize faces, the man in front of me at the counter
works at the local coffee shop. He talks a lot about surfing. The
bartender just proposed to his girlfriend on stage at Topanga Days, a
music festival in the canyon. I open the door to the deck and find a
seat on a stool facing a windowpane. Grab an ashtray. And open my
book.

A Local.

In the mountains of Topanga, there is a hierarchy of living. Locals
versus newcomers. There is a certain pattern to the canyon life that
newcomers have to respect in order to get by, to make new friends and
connections, to feel at home. But the newcomers are always known as
such. Locals, the ones that were born here, grew up here, or came to
this space in the sixties and know the rich history, move through the
canyon with a heightened pack mentality. This is their territory. Don't
fuck with it.

Spirit.

In the creek bed, his spirit moves up and over rock. He was found
with his head cracked open. There are whispers of suicide, or a drunken
fall. When his name is mentioned the Wiccans chant and ask for his
spiritual release.

Belonging.

A sense of acceptance and love. A belonging to others, to our surroundings.

A belonging is shelter with others, a part of our hierarchy of needs,
yet not high enough on that list. I believe we strive, day in and day
out, to find that sense of belonging, to feel love, to feel a part of something other than our own thoughts and processes. To belong is to know
the movements of a space, to listen and feel at one with a community.
Steps taken as a pilgrimage, with slow breaths and presence.

I am still waiting to find and know the community here, to root
myself in the soil. To allow my being to thrive in a space that feels so
much like homes I have known, filled with nostalgia and desire. I've
been told it takes time and openness.

House Hunting.

Sue's house. Up Old Topanga Canyon Blvd, where cell service is
obsolete and you have a house phone. I imagine a rotary phone with
a long winding cord that weaves in through crooked banisters. I imagine
I will let it ring. Here, I can hide.

Her ski lodge-type house is a wooden A frame with three floors.
She sees me coming up the steep driveway and moves from her rocking
chair to the patio gate. She invites me in up narrow stairs. She directs
me how to open the gate, "No, not that way," she says with a con-
descending tone. "This way." Her wrinkled hands click open the gate
and she waves me through. Her paintings stand upright on the ground.
One big blue flower with a pink backdrop.

"That's lovely." I say and point at the canvas.

She waves me off, "No. Just a test run. Let me show you the place."
I follow her up through her backyard, with a narrow path through her
garden. She stops and waves me forward. "I used to be a bit more
nimble. I can't make it as far as you can but you should really take a
look at the planters."

"Planters?" I think to myself and wobble on a path that cuts down
a steep hill. I wave at her from a far and lie loudly, "Yep. They are
really pretty." The crumbling planters don't have much to show for
themselves. She definitely hasn't been back here in a while. I wander

back, and she leads me to the apartment underneath her house. Her dogs aggressively follow my heels.

The converted apartment is a long and narrow space with one front room and a living room. The small kitchen without a stove ends the room. It is a nice size. But there is no privacy. Sue says, "Louisa, nice girl. She is from Germany. But she, like the rest of the single women in Topanga, met an older man and is now moving up to his house. I can tell she really doesn't want to but I think she made some sort of contract. She can't seem to get out of it now, I hear her cry about it." Sue's admission of hearing her cry makes me cringe. No privacy.

I look over the wooden balcony at the side of the mountain with huge slanted rock framed by green shrubbery. Here, I would be watched. I thank Sue and leave, telling her I will be back tomorrow so Miles can meet her dogs. I have a feeling they won't get along.

Town Mayor.

The tall barstool digs into my ass as I flip the page of a new read. I'm bored by it and to pass the time I watch and listen to everyone around me. I'm still learning this place, this space, these people. I do not know a soul.

I overhear a pack of men talking. There are two younger guys and one older man. Age doesn't seem to define groups of people here. But rather, age is the one thing that seems to be defied. Young girls in conversation with ancient men and women, young guys talking to the neighbor's mother. People connecting with people, connected by the space.

This pack of men discusses radiators and wood being stripped down. I think about the desk I need to protect from the rain, the light green desk I positioned to face the mountain while I write. So I boldly ask the boisterous one with a confident stance, "Hey, do you know how to protect a wooden desk from the rain?"

"Keep it inside?" One of the others, with a half grown black mullet jests.

They all start to laugh and I smile and say, "Funny. No, I'm serious." The leader of the pack nods at me and begins to explain. I listen and check off the supplies I bought yesterday to complete the task. I'm already ahead of him. "I can come show you sometime." He hands me a piece of paper with his name on it.

His friend laughs, "What are you like the town mayor? The welcoming party?"

He grins, "Something like that." Then he looks at me again. "Call me."

Neighborhood.

I hear him ask, "Oh you live in Topanga?"

I hear her say, "Only in Topanga would you tell a complete stranger the street you live on. And then talk about how nice the neighborhood is there."

I hear them say, "Welcome to the neighborhood. We get the best weather in this part of the canyon."

In the Minutia.

I've moved to the mountains to reconnect to nature. To feel the physical embodiment, the need to reconnect to the sounds of birds, sunshine covered by trees, frogs when it turns to dusk, and the fear that comes when I hear a coyote howl into the night.

Sparrows and woodpeckers. A yellow monarch butterfly. A hummingbird. A deep breath. And a new start. I've moved from Burbank and a house that held years of both joy and pain, stalker and neighbor, Ani and anger, into a space I can make my own . . . into the image of who I believe I am. Who I have always been. I can reconnect to nature in ways I haven't in the four years of living in Los Angeles.

Territory.

The town mayor wanted to take me under his wing and show me around, introduce me to all the locals. What I didn't realize was that on the tours through town with me, he was also trying to mark me as his territory.

Indoor/Outdoor Space.

I call Zack, the owner of the house on Topanga Canyon Blvd. I navigate the huge stone steps up to the white house converted into a two-story duplex. I listen to the cars rumble below. The house is right on the Blvd. I reach the top of the stairs and Zack greets me with a big smile. His chunky black glasses sit atop his long nose that matches his thin frame. "This is the garden terrace with two small decks on the first level. It would be a great place to entertain people." A white fence cuts the yard up and separates the deck from the roof of the garage that sits on street level. It's a small yard but right above the white fence is an expanse of mountain. The creek across the street is home to frogs that rumble out a patterned ribitt. "Check out the rest of the property." I thank him and wander into the 570 sq feet of inside space. A hobbit house. I have no time left. I take it. I tell my friends that my house is an indoor/outdoor space.

Predator.

"The female mountain lion," he says with a surfer-like tone, "cries in the canyon. You'll hear her and she sounds just like a woman screaming for help. It's a high pitch and then a moan. Listen for her. She cries right up there." He points to the mountain across the street from my house. He points to the green and smirks.

I should have known then that he knows the sound of a woman screaming, a woman crying for help. He knows that sound intimately. They are screaming because of him. Women are his prey. He just doesn't recognize that he is the predator.

Black Flies.

After a family reunion in Seattle, WA, I return home. I pull my suitcase out of my truck with a thud. Miles jumps the four feet down to the pavement. I tell him to wait as I grab the handles of the paisley bag. We climb, slowly, the two flights of hand-placed stone steps. Miles' hind leg is wobbly, fragile. He is getting older and these gigantic steps, while beautiful, are only aging him faster. I know I need to move. The colored fabric draped in the trees moves softly with the wind.

Then I hear, thud, thud, thud. Tiny thuds, not loud thuds, but a repetition of thud, thud, thud, thud, thud, thud. Then, I see them colliding with the front window. A pattern of flies, thud, thud, thud, trying to escape. My heart starts to pound heavily in my chest. I can't breathe. I start to sweat.

Miles is just happy to be home. His tail wags frantically. I open the door. Miles begins to run in and stops. He pulls his head down low. And begins to shrink in size. He backs out of the room slowly.

Black flies, the size of quarters, buzz low and slowly, weaving in the air. Black flies, some dead, lay in patterns on the ground, on the windowsill, on the coffee table. Everywhere. Black flies. At least 20 flies per square foot.

I want to throw up and cry at the exact same time.

"Miles, Let's go." I move him out the front door. My panic rises. I run to the refrigerator and grab two beers and slam the front door shut. I go to the bottom deck, sit, and begin to sob.

Whenever Miles hears a fly now, he comes over to me and puts his head on my lap. He knows they don't agree with me.

Mountaintop.

He lives atop the mountain, up a dirt road that falls into cliff on either side. It winds the length of the peak, the ridge, and reaches the last piece of mountaintop before it meets the ocean. He walks slowly, deliberately, with a walking stick and straw hat, the acres of property. He can see, everything. But the years of mushroom tea and acid, have blinded other sensibilities. He can't see, anything.

Compromise.

I climb back up the steps to Froggy's. I know the pace now, the way I should navigate the concrete steps, the use of breath, the stillness in movement.

I rest my laptop on the painted wooden table faded by weather and time, a pulse and scent of memory. A feeling of wholeness in the nostalgia. And I sip my Bud Light. I listen to the little girls around the corner asserting their subjectivity, their feeling of agency. I hear the whisper of my sister Marisa and I competing for the best imaginary character to be in our seven and six-year old brains. These little girls embody the struggle of all of us people, to become who and what we imagine ourselves to be.

She says, "I'm Bella."

She says, "No, I'm Bella," the sweet voice creaks and whines in the background.

Then, the moment of compromise.

"We can both be Bella."

Then a second pause of silence. And the cycle begins again.

"I wanna be Bella."

"No. I'm going to be Bella."

The voice of childlike authority, "No, I will be Bella."

And it rests for a moment.

Then another creak of a voice rises up.

"Can I be *Isa*bella?

Yes, Isabella. Versions of themselves navigated and compromised, balanced and negotiated within context.

The voice of adult authority chimes in, "Leo. That's your name. I remember. You're Leo." The mother speaks calmly to one of the little girls that I cannot see because they are hidden by a green fabric that corners off my private section of the patio.

I want to be Bella. Isabella. And Leo. Combined.

I want to be the landscape, the rock, the machine, the bird and the preying mantis. I want to feel freedom in all of these decisions, in all of these identities. The consequence rests in the ticking pulse of judgment and expectation, the materialization of myths and experiences, the sounding fury of lost dreams, and fantasy.

Traffic.

Traffic moves past the window at 8am in a long pulse of engine and horns.

Something about this house doesn't feel right. In the mountains but so close to Los Angeles, the traffic, the commuters that move from the San Fernando Valley into Santa Monica take this mountainous road; most people try to avoid the 405. So I listen to the scraps of metal break the silence of this space.

Motorcycle.

Mimosa Café. With papers in hand, we park my truck and he enters in front of me. Seth, the Town Mayor, always walks ahead of me, a strong walk, large steps, chest puffed out. "What the fuck. Why would he park his bike like this? This is fucking ridiculous. Now no one else can park their cars." I feel the weight of his steps get heavier, fuller, with purpose.

"Can you please just calm down, Seth? I told you I don't like anger." I feel the aggression seep from his skin to mine. I feel it cover my body. I hang my head low, avert the eyes of three men sitting on the front porch. They watch him with pacing eyes. They hear his anger and shake their heads. I put my computer down on a metal table. And listen. The wooden screen door opens and closes with a snap.

"Craig. Move your bike man. If you don't park it the right way then I am going to move it for you." Seth ignores the comments, the sighs of exhaustion from the now stilled café. They saw him like this before. He is from these mountains. A mountain lion, growling.

"Calm down Seth. It isn't your place," Craig says but there is no sound of movement. I hear their voices rise. "Fucking move your bike, man."

The man with long grey hair, John Lennon glasses, and a beaded necklace looks at me. Then looks at the rounded man with thinning hair and a ponytail. The rounded man stands as Seth swings the door open furiously and stomps to the bike. He tries to roll it off of the kickstand. "Move your bike. Last warning. Or I'm going to drop it on its side."

I can't watch. I enter the café, move past Craig, and order a coffee at the front counter. I don't want to turn around. Silence. I walk back to the front patio. Seth comes to sit near me. I tell him, "I came here, to the canyon, for peace and quiet. To get away from anger and violence. I can't be near you."

I get in my truck and drive the mile home.

I do not speak to Seth, the Town Mayor, for months.

In this small town you speak to everyone again.

There is no hiding.

Animal.

A single female that is new to this canyon is prey. Jesus. Going to the local restaurant, is like getting fed to the wolves. Each masculine character in the canyon that is not already in a relationship is there, watching, talking, listening, wanting whomever shows up.

Demons.

I hear him say, "You confront your demons there. You confront them and then you have to let them go."

I hear her say, "I found peace here."

I hear her say, "They found them atop the mountain practicing witchcraft."

I hear him say, "He found a memory about his childhood. He said he saw them sacrifice a human. He hasn't come back."

Reminder.

I turn on the faucet and walk down the redwood stained steps to my garden terrace deck. I grab the black garden hose. I direct water over the dry dark earth, over agave plants with think sturdy arms, green vines that climb up the rock wall, bright pink flowers with reaching stamen. A lizard moves from the earth up the tree and bobs its head at me, a nod, a warning. A few grasses, green weeds peak up through the cracks in the stone path. Ants crawl up the oak tree that dumps its browned leaves in piles. There's a hum of crickets. The fabrics, bright pink and reds and orange, hung from the trees, a Moroccan flair swims in the air. A peace in the stillness.

Then, I see it. A plastic bottle filled with soft soil. I didn't leave it here. He left it. And on top of the green cap the misspelled words, "Diametorus earth."

He was here. Without my permission. And I feel the remnants of fear left in my body from the stalker John, who now lives in a mental hospital. I know *he* can't hurt me. But this reminder of people coming too close, without permission, feels intrusive, uncomfortable.

And I will not let it happen again. This is my space, my home. I leave the bottle on the bench. A reminder now. A warning—to not let the gaze encapsulate me, to not become the object of their desire. I need to claim my territory, my body, my space, my identities.

Earthquake Dream.

I had two of them. In one night. The first—I am on campus. People are all around, milling about, in a condensed version of the campus quad. Then, the earthquake hits. We are running, people are screaming, the earth is being torn apart from underneath us, the sky begins to split. I look for anyone, someone I may know to comfort, to run to. No one. Then, a big palm tree falls on top of four people. I watch as their bodies bounce to the ground. Others run to help them. They pull their bodies from under the tree but the force of their yanking them sends their bodies flying across the grass. They land again in a horrific thud. I know they are dead. I do not go help. I find my truck and get in the front seat. I then feel so much fear, I turn around slowly. There are two men in the back seat. I look one of them dead in the eyes. I ask, "What are you going to do now?"

He seethes out the words from behind slanted brown eyes, "We are going to rape you."

I turn slowly, open the truck door and say forcefully, "No. No, you are not."

I get out of the car and close the door.

I wake myself up.

The second—back on campus. The aftermath of the earthquake. People are searching, looking, for each other. I find one colleague. She hugs me as she always does. They are beginning to show a movie. We watch. The screen rips as the earth begins to move again.

I wake myself up.

I am in transition.

Cultural Myths Materialized.

They sit across from me on the hard wooden benches of Froggy's. A poster signed about Goodfellas. I think he is the director. They talk in a patterned rhythm. No, he is the writer or a character in the film.

He is the one that moved the film through. Henry is the one on the phone with the director. The man signing the poster is the one that leaked the story. He's an old man now, talking about his experiences back in the day. About Jimmy and Tommy. About street smarts and card games, drug deals, and connections. Calculations and smooth talking. The way of the old New York. Something bigger than everything I've ever experienced.

> I hear him say, "I used to look over my shoulder. But that was a long time ago."

> I hear him say, "I'm struggling now but I don't regret it. I should have done a few things differently. But hey, those other guys have life without parole."

> I hear him say, "I know I saved a lot of lives, put a lot of horrible people away, deserve to be in prison, that was the way, ya know that's the way you answer to that lifestyle."

> I hear remorse. Not regret.

> I hear the reality that these mobsters are, the mafia is still alive and well, running the unions in New York. I hear, I hear, I hear.

And I watch the interviewer lean in intensely and listen with wide blue eyes to this man's story in an attempt to capture the story. I watch and I feel dishonorable, not for me for eavesdropping, yes, but for the idea that we can understand, can feel the embodied moment through the words of another. Only this man knows his glimpses into his own past. The movie Goodfellas, as much as it captured, was not the *real* story. Is it ever the *real* story, and whose story do we feel compelled to tell?

This is the way of Topanga, the memory, the history, the stories that layer and pulsate throughout the space. The stories are as old and faded as this table, but these cultural myths, made by people such as the man telling his stories across the table, have defined our reality, shaped and shaved the rock of our embedded desire, like the creek bed, that now sits dry, scraped, and chiseled by the intensity of the water.

The cultural myth of Goodfellas resides in the pulsing veins of young men searching for masculinity, camaraderie and connection, dues to be paid, and risk in moving ahead in a culture defined by gangs and drugs. The water, these cultural myths, metaphorically names the rush of experience, the movement of power in the moment. The power, in being in the here and now, is still as pungent and powerful, even if it sits in stagnant pools festering with mosquitoes and soaking lizards. The water will always come back. It's actually never left.

The cultural myth, the story of this man that leaked the truth of the scenario has ruptured and sustained the overall myth of masculinity in the United States.

And here he sits in the shade and hollow of Topanga, hiding.

But still speaking loudly.

Change.

I ask my friend Amanda to come to Los Angeles, to work with me at the University. She does. Arrives with suitcases in hand, stacks them into my tiny apartment. Her colorful suitcases add a spice to the crammed house. And we begin to house hunt. For her, and subconsciously for me. I have to leave this house. Restless energy, claustrophobia, black flies, and intrusive behavior. It's time to create real change.

Belonging: Cultivating Physical Change.

Real visceral change only happens when we make a move, when we create a new embodied experience. We can talk a big game, but every life experience, every actual change happens because we make it, we do it, feel it and create a new memory, a new embodied experience. That way, we can look back and say, "Yes, I did that and it changed me." And then, after some time, we say, "And this is how that experience changed me." To say we are just rationalizing feels too practical. We are creating and recreating lives we want to lead. The agency in the decision is the important part. Choice. And when we don't have a choice, how we make sense of the lack of choice is ever important. The past and present are entwined. And because of both the actual moment and the ones we carry with us, we can look into the future.

My father is a psychologist. He speaks to his children and patients about action therapy, that in order to feel changed, you have to create change, take action. And with talk and action we can make sense of our lives. Create and lead the life we wish to have. I know, wholeheartedly, that he is right and has always been right.

I reread pages of this book and I weep. For the choices I have made and the ones I didn't. And yet, here we are, in this moment of your reading and my writing, together. A past, a present, and a future that has not been realized. I made choices to make sense of some really serious trauma. I made choices to reconnect to a body that did not feel like mine in a place that, for me, felt alienating and superficial. I made choices to find a version of myself that felt like home, and is, now, a home. It takes some time. And I always know and am prepared for the possibility of another earthquake, another shattering. Wiser now, I know I will survive.

We, Amanda and I, begin the search for a house together.

Music.

Topanga is filled with music.

When Pigs Fly.

Atop a tall pole, right off of the main boulevard sits a replica of a flying pink pig. The pig's snout is raised upwards. Attached to its robust body are two white wings. I do not think there is a story behind it. I think the artist that lives in the house next to the pig, made it and stuck it high in the air. Now, the flying pink pig hangs in wind chime form at Froggy's. Most people ask about it, for its story. For me, there isn't one. It is just a reminder that there will be a time, a possibility that pigs may fly, that things and perceptions, and identities can shift so dramatically. We can change our consciousness, our desire. We can. I will. I am.

It is time that pigs fly.

Blue House.

The bottom half of a house, atop the mountain. The bathroom is hand tiled with bits and pieces of scrap tile, bright colors that don't mix line and frame the mirror, the claw foot tub. A kitchen with a wood-burning stove, two wood-burning stoves, a room for painting, and a small bedroom with a perfect view of the mountain. But it's dirty. The cracks of the floor show the years and years of dirt and grime.

But I give the older woman with thick grey hair a deposit, anxious to leave my current house, anxious for more space, a view, a full kitchen, and anonymity. I call her back an hour later with a changed mind. She scolds me. And rips up the check.

Run.

I turn my truck up the winding entrance to the Topanga State park. The wheels grip pavement as I glide past a house hidden within trees, behind crooked fences and painted mailboxes. The eclectic tick of artistry and a carpenter's hand slows my gaze, rumbles a rhythm that soothes me.

On the trail, I open my legs, stretch out and begin to trot up the hill, past a woman on a tall brown horse, past a lizard, and a team of young children guided by the park ranger. He points out the snake track wiggled into dust. I smile and feel a wave of nostalgia.

And at the top of the dusty trail, the peak of eagle rock, a jagged outcropping of yellow sediment, I wander up the slanted slope. At the edge of this cliff, with hundreds of feet of possible air to fall through, I open my mouth, inhale deeply and begin to sing the melody of a song that has been carrying me these past few months.

Belonging.

I hear her sing a Beatles song over an acoustic guitar. He stops her too often. I want to hear more of her voice as it sweetly runs parallel with the birds above me and the circular saw screeching and sanding wood in the distance.

In Topanga, I feel a sense of belonging to my intimate surroundings. It reminds me of my childhood, suits my desire for a peaceful disposition. I do not wish to feel and know violence anymore. I've been there. I do not wish to know and feel fear so intimately, fear of intimacy, fear of openness, fear of love. I feel at peace listening to them strum a new love on the balcony below. I listen and close my eyes and dream of the moments in my life when I knew and felt love. A black fly tries to disturb this peace and I whisper, "go." It moves as the wind does.

Town Center.

Amanda and I sit outside of Waterlily; people pulse in and through this small town center. Hellos and how are you, and how is she. The farmer's market is in full swing. It is a smaller market here in Topanga. The market is made up of six tents with limited choices. But everyone stops. And here in front of the café, people move in and out of the glass door surrounded by rustic wood. In the forefront of the greatest green mountains, the Town Center is full. The café is enriched with an eclectic group, a mix of homeless hippies with purple beanies and rich middle-aged women with plastic surgery but in jeans and flip-flops. Teenagers in almost fitting t-shirts and white sneakers talk to each other outside surrounding the small round tables. Topanga is about hippie chic and the very real sense that all are welcome here.

The town plumber, Scott, talks to Amanda. She asks him about surfing, and his eyes light up. He talks about the way a long board moves versus a short board. The time he went out in tsunami waters and lost his board, almost his life.

A woman with a beautiful dog, a bulldog of some sort with the long snout, walks up and says, "Hello." To him.

"Hey, that's a good lookin' dog." He says with this glowing smile, and calm presence.

"Thank you. He is a rescue so I can feel a sense of pride with that. How is Ali?" I inhale and exhale.

"She's doing good. Thanks," he smiles then lovingly pets the dog once more.

"Well, tell her I said hello."

"Will do," he nods, smiles, then she is gone.

The homeless woman comes up to me. "Did you know that they stole my jewelry and all of my tools? I mean I don't know why they would do that. But it's that guy who is always messed up on meth and the other guy who has spent four days drunk. I don't know how they can then all blame me. I mean I didn't do anything wrong. I think its elder abuse." I nod and look up at her sun-baked face, a face now etched with wrinkles and years of street living. The narrow cheekbones and thin frame browned into a long frown. She keeps talking. Scott listens and watches. "I'm just gonna make wind chimes. I still have the wire and wire cutters. I mean they can take the material goods away but they can't take your creativity or art." She wanders back to her own chair surrounded by bags of cloth.

Peter, the local musician that lives in an RV, walks up, says hello. He pulls out a necklace from under his ripped brown t-shirt. His painted fedora cap matches his bearded face. The necklace is heavy, almost too heavy, two large stones weighted with all of his worries and fears and consequences. "Yea, do you know what? These have been keeping me really balanced."

I hear him say, "I just kinda want to say fuck it and throw my hands up in the air and go up North and get blazed and play music for a little while. You know, center."

Jimmy with his cowboy/sun hat covering his scalp, arm muscles strong, his body thin and toned, his long brown hair pulled back in a ponytail jests, "I don't think that's big enough." Peter makes a gesture as if stone weighed him down. Jimmy talks to Amanda, a conversation clouded by ear length. Jimmy turns to me, "How do we know one another?"

"We met in front of the natural food store," I say remembering that day vividly.

A teenage boy and his girlfriend look flustered. They surround the red hatchback. Scott notices and gets up to help them. I watch Scott, also a well-known surfer in the area, as he holds open the window, pulls and pries it back so the teenager can get the wire hanger down between the crack to open the latch. He is patient. He doesn't tell him how to fix it unless the boy asks. Then he shows him gently and slowly. They work and he looks up at me, only feet away and smiles.

"Hey, are you Scott?" A woman with red hair pulled into a short ponytail asks.

"Yep," his kind voice seems to smile as he moves his head to look at her.

"I was told that you are the mechanical genius. Can you help Rita?" I smile.

He walks away from the still locked car.

Then he is back again. When they finally open the car he turns and addresses me directly, "Jeanine—look." Like a proud Dad he grins.

"You got it open? Great work," I say beaming. Then he is gone.

Over the course of the day, just one day, I see everyone, the staple figureheads of canyon living—the man with the white parrot, the girl that fell into the meth world, the ancient woman who is a spit fire. The child named Luna who can't sit still. The children of the canyon reflect the care free spirit of this place, the adults fall prey to the lightness or the darkness. For me, I feel somewhere in between. Stuck loving so much, knowing that it isn't the right time to love him. Sometimes, you can't help it.

But I also know that somewhere in the near future, it will be the right time. Sometimes, you just know.

Trailer House.

Up Fernwood Pacific Drive, a windy road that weaves up the mountain stands house alongside house that each holds a certain mystery, a possibility, a treasure behind slanted fences and Buddha statues.

I make my way to the trailer house. It is a half converted trailer, with a front room built on. The deck is gigantic with the perfect view, a view to entertain guests. I imagine dinner party after dinner party with twinkling lights and so much laughter. So much laughter. I can imagine my life here, staring at the expanse of deep green, the peak of mountain that carves edges into the sky. I can see Miles curled at my feet as I type pages of this book and sip a glass of red wine. Outside, this house is perfect. Inside, well, is another story.

The kitchen is a kitchenette, with molded cabinets and a tiny refrigerator. The bathroom, a foot away, separated by a sheet of vinyl. The toilet almost inside the shower. I can't imagine space here, feeling good cooking a meal with the ceiling so close to my head. But then, I walk back out to the converted living room with a window for a wall that faces this mountain. And I see a life here.

I realize, my desire to stay in the space is connected to the landscape, the view of the mountain, as if I were part of it, one with the tall trees, the dust, the soil and green.

Yoga.

In the middle of Pine Tree Circle, nestled between an art gallery, near a bistro, is a yoga studio. One small room, with wood floors, clean walls, the Om symbol crafted out of twisted oak wood hangs in the center wall. Unrolled mats, the space fills softly. Shoes at the front door, bags hung on the line of hooks. Soft hellos and neighborhood chatter. This is a place of opening. I sink into breath, into the present, deep inhales and strong exhales through a wide-open mouth. Like a lion sighing, I dig into my body, begin to know the lines and stretches of muscles, the way our shoulders learn to curl into themselves, I correct my posture, with an open heart I sink my shoulder blades down my back. I breathe into my center. A core that glows. Opening. Opening.

Lucid Dream.

Surrounded by men in an apartment that looks a lot like Hunter's Ridge, a college complex in Harrisonburg, VA. They talk over and around me. Then I'm pulled down on a bed. Hands and arms pulled tight. Poked and prodded, laughter. I recognize one of them. He is a Topanga local that I despise. I think he (in real life) is a creep. I scream and cry for help. I look to the other men in the room and they turn their heads, think it's normal. No one helps.

I get out of their grip and run out of the house. I see in the corner of the parking lot a small hatchback car. My old friend Brooke is there. I tell her what happened. I need to get out of here. I say. We get in the car. Amber is there. Her dog. My dog. Several dogs and women begin to pile into the car. We can't leave unless all women and dogs are in the car. They hop and move. I bring them in. I look at Miles, my dog calmly laying on another dog. The most calming dog I have ever met. His calm presence calms me. And we are off.

To somewhere.

Labyrinth.

Hike early morning with a new friend, the town coffee shop queen. She is friendly, a chatterbox, with a voice so full of life and honesty. She and I travel the dust path, wet with morning mist and rain.

Our shoes crust with the brown earth. As we walk, my feet become weighted. And her laugh keeps me guided.

I am in it now, the town. An almost local, I know names of people now, stories, and community. The longer you stay here, the more everyone knows about you, your choices. I don't say much about me to anyone but I laugh and listen, to it all.

We come to a labyrinth at the end of the dirt road. Maintained by someone, we do not know whom, but it is cared for, loved. In the center, a crow flies low, circles.

breathing. listening. laughing.

My House.

Amanda and I find one more listing. We call Stella. She directs us up Fernwood, but higher up the mountain than the trailer house. My truck hits a ditch, then moves past the 'End County Maintained Road' sign and a row of garbage cans. Up a steep incline then a sharp descent down the driveway. Stella, a tiny woman with a Latin American accent, greets us with shining eyes. She brings us up a stone walkway to a two-story green house. Up short wooden steps to the first deck, a thin deck with an extraordinary view. Then we weave around the house to another stone patio, step up to a top deck. Inside, it feels like home with a wood-burning stove, two bathrooms, two bedrooms, tile floor, and large windows. We gasp. Yes, this is it. This is home. And this is the view.

Topanga Days.

I look for him in the crowd. A glimpse. I know he is here. I can feel him.

The heads bob to Zoot Suit Riot as the man on stage twirls his upright bass between his swinging hands. My friend Frank talks in his southern drawl about the two young girls holding coconuts. In between songs the group of teenagers, boys with mullets freshly cut in a rock-a-billy style call out "Coconuts, get your coconuts here." Most people ignore them, or stare at the young teenage girls' stomachs exposed between a pair of short shorts and a halter-top. They know they produce envy.

Then I feel it, a body brushes into mine, an accident. I turn to say, "It's ok" to a stammering stranger but I see him. He smiles his knowing smile. As if to say, "I'm here, beside you." He apologizes then turns to his friend, pretending we don't know one another. My heart moves into my stomach and I breathe in that full breath of anticipation and giddy, a feeling I have not felt in years, a fresh journey, a love, a compassion, a need and desire so strong my stomach aches. I turn to where I imagine him standing. He is gone and my heart sinks. I furtively turn a bit around and I see him with his twenty-year old son. He looks up. Grins. He is watching me. Aware. I watch him move up towards the stage, his salt and pepper hair, his lean arms and muscular frame, he turns back to me again, a quick glance, a smile. A nod. A glow. He takes money out of his wallet and gives it to his son. Then he is gone again.

I look for him, all the while not letting Frank in on the game of cat and mouse. No, not so much a chase but a looking for, a wanting to hold him, his hand. A real couple, allowing others to see and feel the absolute love we have for each other. I hear a good rhythm and move my body to the music. I take a sip of the cold beer and laugh at another one of Frank's infamous jokes. And in the laughter I move my head to the left. There he is again, leaning on the back of a pick up truck, he looks and smiles. He is ten feet away from me. There, guarding me, watching me. I smile interiorly. I feel safe. Knowing he is there. I watch as he moves to leave.

He stands at the stage and turns to me. From 50 yards away I can feel him say I love you. He climbs up past the stage. From 70 yards away he turns back to face me. He puts his hands on his lips and throws me a goodbye kiss. I nod, savoring his look, his love. He sees me receive his gesture and nods as he turns away. His head down as he climbs the dusty trail. On his journey.

Wash Away.

I know my demons now, intimately.

> The body.
> The rapes.
> Trust.

Being the object.

Not being heard.

The expectations crafted by different terrains, of nature, of culture, of place and pain.

I've seen them unpack themselves in each process, each moment, each area, each location, town, and terrain, each broken promise, each destructive choice. A punishment for an experience I did not self-create. And yet, I respond viscerally to the places in which I exist. I move from place to place learning, intimately, the terrain of my identities, the terrain of my body, the terrain created for and by us, the places in which we thrive and survive. The places we cultivate and the places we choose to turn away from. We are the terrain, we are bodies, we are the community.

I will never let my demons swallow me whole. They exist as a part of my past, my present, and future, fading as love overwhelms me and I choose to love.

And I know I am blessed.

Belonging: To the Terrain.

Geographically, Topanga Canyon is nestled between the San Fernando Valley and Malibu. It is an exquisite landscape, with high peaks, and jagged rocks. A creek runs through it. After years of living in Burbank, exploring the previous locations in Los Angeles, I moved to the canyon for respite, retreat, and reflection. Topanga welcomes scavengers, squatters, and people searching through demons. Famous musicians and artists such as Woodie Guthrie and Neil Young found and find respite in the canyon.

There is much to say about the choice I made to become part of this terrain, where houses are smaller on more space of land, with wood-burning stoves instead of the ceiling to floor window plan or the infinity pool. People in this space honor and privilege the natural beauty and much is done to stop new building construction. I rarely see plastically enhanced bodies in this space. It's a small town nestled away from Hollywood. And for now, it feels like home.

He feels like home.

Under Our Tree.

He pulls his truck into the furniture store at the bottom of the mountain, next to the crashing waves of the Pacific, the Pacific Coast Highway lined with cars on this Memorial Day. His two surfboards tied into the bed. He smiles. I nod. He points towards the south. I turn my truck and follow him down the highway then up winding roads then into a suburb with perfect houses, each a little fancier than the next. Picture-perfect houses that I scan, imagining our life there, in that house, or the next. We come to the end of the road and there is a stretch of green space right before the cliff that descends into the ocean. He parks his truck and I come to a stop a little further away.

I walk towards him. And gaze out to the ocean a mile beneath us. We kiss, softly. And he hums in my ear as his arms wrap around mine. He smells delicious, like healing. We walk towards the edge and sit on a stone bench. "It's beautiful here." I say as I feel his hand take mine. "My son and I used to come here. I lived just a block over with my first wife. We would climb down this trail. You want to go?"

"Yes" and we weave down the dusty trail and find a spot underneath a twisted tree. "I have a blanket in my car." "I'll go get it." He kisses me on the forehead and moves towards the truck. I sit in a squat not ready to let my white lace flowing dress get dirty. He's back in a flash and we curl up on the purple and white Aztec blanket. He pulls me in close and we kiss, and kiss, we move lips and limbs, hum into each other.

And this is where time stops. Everything else around us stops, the click of the everyday drone. Everything is about us, here in this moment, fingers delicately moving over skin. He is love, kindness, presence. We ask each other about our first times. And I giggle out the story of my first long-term boyfriend at his parent's house. The pain and dissatisfaction. "It wasn't like this," I say and smile into his tie-dye shirt. I inhale his scent then exhale.

He pulls back to look at me, into me. "Your eyes are the color of the ocean, no, all of the oceans in one."

A plane overhead begins to draw circles in the sky. "A hug." I smile. Then an x is drawn in the middle of it. "A kiss."

"I wonder if they are writing that for us."

He shakes his head from side to side then says, "I haven't felt like this in a very long time. Not since High School."

"I don't think I've ever felt like this before."

"Yep, me neither." Our admissions of pleasure and presence seem to overwhelm us both. We hum into one another. This is right.

"If this doesn't work, then I don't think I will ever believe in love again," I say with my entire being invested in him.

"Me neither. It will work," he says as he nods his slow nod, that knowing nod. And I believe him.

"I was scared that you would turn on me, end up crazy and then that would be it. But you are not, you are exactly who I want in the world." We kiss and fall, our bodies shifting slowly down the slope.

"Do you see that house over there? The one with the ivy growing on the roof?"

"Yes, it's perfect. I would live there."

"Now scan your eyes across all of the houses. Which one would you pick to live in?"

I scan my eyes and the only one that stands out is the ivy house.

"The ivy house."

He grabs me in his arms and pulls me back down to the blanket, he wraps his legs between mine and we curl into one another.

"I like smaller spaces."

"Me too. I built a miniature house out of cob. Sand Clay and Straw. You mix it with your feet."

"Yea, like Adobe." I love that he knows, works with his hands, can fix anything.

"Where?"

"In Tampa. I worked with a youth organization and we built it from the ground up.

I would love to build my own cob house. With wood."

"Yea, we could do that. I would love to do that." And for a proud moment I can see us, outside, hands and feet dirty creating our house, a labor of love.

Suddenly a man runs up from behind us. He throws white powder on the ground near us.

"Hey, what is that?" He asks. I can feel him get protective but not aggressive, never aggressive.

"Flour." The man shows us the plastic bag in his hand. He stammers a bit then says, "There will be a race down here. I'm marking the trail." He starts to awkwardly descend the steep slope.

"Alright, when?"

"In ah, one to two hours." And then he is gone.

I pull my head away from his shoulder and ask, "What? How is anyone gonna run down that hill? There isn't a trail." We laugh and he pulls me in closer. My hands trace his face, memorizing the lines, the corners of his eyes. We stare into each other, really stare into, looking, holding, embracing. I memorize the layers of color in each eye, a golden hue, a deep brown towards the center, a faint swirl of maroon. His hands trace my shoulders, my neck and he buries his mouth in my skin. After hours of this, of us, we stand to leave.

He gets in his truck, I in mine, and I follow him out the neighborhood roads. He puts his arm out the window and points. There is the man, with his plastic bag of flour jogging down the street. He throws one puff of white in the air and is gone again.

The Fog.

Watching the fog roll in from the Pacific. The Topanga Mountains cradle the plumes of fog, hold it, allow it to slowly crawl from crest to valley. A slow drift. That cleanses the air. Angel clouds slowly descending. Cleansing. Cleansing.

Green Space.

A lull. a bird chirps. a dog barks. wind. a car whizzes past.

                                             guitar strum.

A lull. a spider moves up its web. a dog barks. wind. a car stutters.

                                             He says, "I love you."

A lull. a hum. a crow caws. a neighbor sighs. wind.

                                             I sing.
                                             high hat.

10

TOPANGA CANYON, REVISITED

A SENSUOUS CONSCIOUSNESS

Geography is concerned with both a physical and human world. Literally, geographic is earth (geo) drawing (graph). It is a representation of an experienced world, both perceived directly through the senses and mediated by the mind. Perception as a process by which data is collected and ordered is therefore fundamental to geographic inquiry. Geographical perception is identification of distinctive places—to recognize our situation in a world and to have a sense of a world.

—*Paul Rodaway*[172]

It wasn't until I moved to Topanga Canyon that I really began to dig into the terrain of my body, my memory, tilling the soil of the sensuous terrain of a place that, for the first time in a long time, feels like home.[173]

I wouldn't say that it has been an easy process to cultivate home here. I have confronted many demons in this canyon, the mirroring reflection of memories past, patterns I have recreated by allowing people in my life that were not positive or beneficial for personal and collective growth. I have confronted the basic need embedded in my bones to live in a place that reminds me of my childhood homes, and the geographic complexity that now soothes me. I have felt the incessant shake of fear and finally, the calm inhale and exhale of a knowing, a kindness, and a desire to feel at peace.

I recognize, as Rodaway suggests, the different geographic locations in Los Angeles that impact perceptions of each recreated sense of a world. It was my move through Topanga Canyon and the people that have welcomed me here that opened me to a different possibility, the possibility of belonging. Human beings need to connect, to belong to their bodies, terrains, and locality, to survive. In order to create these connections we have to cultivate what I call a *Sensuous Consciousness*.

We move in this final chapter through the different elements of belonging. And to do this we re-enter my new *home* in the mountains of Topanga. We look closely at the turns of wood, the balcony, the wood-burning stove. I bring you into the intimate cracks of the wooden floors, the wind chimes that tangle in the wind, so you may feel at home. Next, I invite you into a healing, loving sexual experience with my *body* and new love that created space, intimate space, and belonging in my body. Next, we explore the *terrain* of the canyon, my embodied experience of connecting with the elements of the land that houses all of us here. Finally, we walk into the Café where the local folks meet and connect, reconnect again and again. The centrality of this place cultivates a sense of *locality* and *community*.

Pollini, a sociologist, suggests that belonging involves social, cultural, mental, and ecological dimensions.[174] Psychology also theorizes belonging, most prominently in terms of place identity,[175] place attachment,[176] and sense of place.[177] Across disciplines, place and one's relation to it, significantly impacts identity formation and maintenance. Critical to connecting to a place is the feeling of belonging, or the sense that one feels home with the land or the people inhabiting the place. Place is the container, catalyst, and catapult for the performance of personal and collective identity. This sense of belonging is integral to our perceived sense of survival. I also argue that we need to develop sensuous consciousness in order to develop this sense of belonging. We need to be conscious and aware of the ways in which our senses develop understanding and identity in order to survive.

Survival: The Roots of Sensuous Consciousness.

Survival is a local practice. The roots of sensuous consciousness start with our desire to make sense of and survive this life. And survival exists, not only in our discourse, but also in our everyday action. Physically and ideologically, creating home in a place is about cultivating movements and moments of survival. As a form of survival, creating home is a creative action as well as a discursive and ideological practice of survival. Homemaking is artistic, ecologically aware, communal, and a consciousness-raising practice.

Learning to survive is to envision, articulate, and to materialize proposals for new consciousness and ways of living in terms of environmental, social, relational, and political change. Strategies for material change and a consciousness of our terrains exist within a reciprocal relationship. Understanding our terrains is an integral part of our survival. Moreover, the smallest change can shift a terrain. We need to be aware that these shifts happen as we shift or others shift. We can enact strategies that spur personal and social change through the rooting of *sensuous consciousness*. And part of this survival is connecting to the sensuous geographies of the *home*, the *body*, the *terrain* and the *community*.

And yet, the idea of survival sounds so basic, of course we want to survive. Perhaps then, what I am searching for, perhaps what we are all searching for is to belong. This belonging is motivated out of sharing love, connection, intimate conversations; an acceptance that is unbiased. Belonging is wholeness within us as well as with others. Belonging is created through a development of *sensuous consciousness*.

Sensuous consciousness is comprised of memory; complexity of story; sensory knowledge of place; process. Our perception and colliding senses create a relationship to the world that is not simple or direct but complex in its negotiation. Consciousness is the heightened awareness of these complexities and the ability to understand how in each moment these complexities impact your shifting and ever-changing identities. The delicate balance is the ability to be aware of these complexities but also present, cultivating a sense of belonging within your own home, your body, your terrain, and your community.

Belonging Home: A Sensuous Place

Imagine you make your way up the winding canyon road, just narrow enough for one car. It's a steep road that winds by houses tucked into the hill, tucked into the mountainside, nestled by trees. You climb up and up, further almost to the tip of the mountain. You reach the driveway that dips in broken concrete down onto a pocket of land. A house in the shape of a treehouse reminds you of the Smith Family Robinson. You climb the shifting stairs, made of old railroad planks and railroad ties. You find the top deck, a crafted sanctuary, made of bamboo poles and a sheet of dried heather. You sit and feel the softest warm breeze through—yellows and browns. As you gaze out into the canyon, you see houses, trees, deep green. You inhale. There is a stillness, a calm in knowing. and breathing—deeply. softest warm breeze through—yellows and browns. There is a stillness, a calm in knowing. and breathing—deeply.

Talking about place, where we belong, is a constant subject for many of us. We want to know if it is possible to live on the earth peacefully. Is it possible to sustain life? Can we embrace an ethos of sustainability that is not solely about the appropriate care of the world's resources, but is also about the creation of meaning—the making of lives that we feel are worth living.

—*bell hooks*[178]

The sensuous place of home is connected to memory of our own childhood homes. These memories can be delightful, aching, full of pain and passion, a place we wish to return to or one we never wish to embrace or know again. I watched my family maneuver through the bureaucratic and capitalist structures of land ownership. Home, in these times, was scattered between the moving vans, the rhythms of packing and unpacking our things, showing the house to potential buyers and waiting for the sale to go through.

My father and my uncle were involved in the construction business together. They built homes together. On a plot of connected land, our two families built a small community. We were close in proximity and in familial love. It was the only type of house I knew. So I keep searching for such a loving household, with several people that make up the terrain and the family. I search for houses in terrains that are green, lush, open. I find myself at ease in Topanga, navigating the lush landscape, away from concrete and strip malls, closer to the open sky, listening to coyotes howl.

Awareness of the sensuous terrains of memory, or our past experiences within the crafting of home, allows for us to make sense of our blockages, our choices and our connections to the intimate spaces of home. These memories may not be as picturesque as we might desire. But our intimate memories of home are tied to the way in which we make sense of home space now, in the present moment. I wonder which terrain, which would I connect to if I grew up in New York City rather than the wooded expanse of land on Long Island. What if I never knew snow, or cultivated a desire to hike or connect with the land? What would my home look like? Where and how would I feel safe?

The sensuous place of home is also fueled by the ways in which we connect to and process our immediate surroundings. As we make sense of home, we take part in the sensuous engagement of all of our senses, letting them breathe in and through our bodies, connect to our consciousness, our sense making, and our re-experiences. Rodaway states:

> When the information of the senses seems to agree with the expectations of a given culture, that is, compatible, it reinforces them. When the information of the senses conflicts with expectations, that is, incompatible, the information is either not comprehended, or is ignored or dismissed as an anomaly or illusion—or contributes to a doubt which fuels new ideas and practices.[179]

The sensuous place of home is also engaging within the incompatible experiences, negotiating the pain and pleasure of establishing home space. To claim that our experiences of home will always be compatible with our utopian vision of home seems to be, well, utopian. Rather, we argue that creating home is allowing us to move through the survival practice of negotiating memory and the present state of home cultivation.

Belonging in Body: Sensually Conscious of Place, Body, and Safety.

Imagine you feel safe. Imagine you feel safe in the place of a bed within the space of a bedroom, next to a body that you are sexually attracted to, connected to. Imagine you feel completely safe. You touch skin, fingers light on their back. Mouths connect. Lips linger on lips. You inhale each others' breath. Imagine again, you feel safe. Inhale, exhale, touch lips, and organs, and skin. Within each other, you climax. Imagine, once more, that you feel safe.

––––––––––

The body is an essential part of sensuous experience: a sense organ in itself (including the skin), as the site of all the other sense organs and the brain, and our primary tool for movement and exploration of the environment. Geographical experience is fundamentally mediated by the human body, it begins and ends with the body. This is the basic corporeality underlying all sensuous geography.

—*Paul Rodaway*[180]

I watched a television show on BBC about how the brain functions. The brain responds to embodied action. For example, when you learn to ride a bike your brain begins to create new synapse pathways for this new body movement. When you learn to pick up a spoon, you learn about the spoon as a tool. You learn about the weight of each material that fills the spoon. Is it heavy or light? How do you hold the spoon to get the food into your mouth? The spoon creates learning beyond the spoon. Once the food gets to your mouth, you learn about texture and taste. As you move through these motions, you are creating new synapse pathways in your brain. The mind and body work together to create mindful action. Sinking into the performance of my sexual identity in the place of Los Angeles, I took the embodied risk to try new things and to renegotiate my body as part of these various terrains. And in the place of Topanga, I found another body in place within which to feel safe, whole, at place, and in love.

And as I process place, memory, and consciousness in the place of Topanga, where I reside and thrive now, I take part in the doubling of consciousness; remembering and reminding myself of a past that is part of the process. My relationship with my body changes in Topanga as I allow myself the space to change through a sensuous consciousness with my body, the embodied memory of past actions, and the presence of mind to cultivate change.

Part of these changes and deeper understandings developed because the action was striking, abrupt, painful, and perhaps grotesque. Other actions were softer, kinder differential movements. Through the process of these differential body movements, and the process of writing and processing, reflection and consideration I come to know myself anew. There were times that I did not want to move through a terrain, or face my choices and actions in certain terrains.

There are times now that I reread the text and re-experience the place so much so that I find my body responding viscerally, emotionally, fraught with the pain of this exploration. Sometimes I find myself sobbing.

And from all of my experiences in Los Angeles, I have processed the ideological and discursive truths of manipulated beauty, manu-factured plastique, grotesque sexual acts, and honest and open connections that resonate love and respect. It wasn't until I reached Topanga Canyon that I felt as if I belonged in my body; found a place in my body.

Belonging in the Body

As a woman with a past experience of rape, it isn't possible for me to have a healthy sexual relationship, a sexual conversation, or a bringing together of bodies if there is no safety or comfort. This comfort is also what allows me the space to explore the terrains of my body, without feeling anxious. Or when the anxiety creeps in, to breathe through, to look into eyes, and know that this movement, this gesture, this sexual act is for one another, for pleasure, for joy, bodies in dialogue.

Safety, honor, love, an openness, and a listening. To come to the body, honor your own body. I have learned to honor my own bones, skin, blood vessels, and pulse of breath. I have found place in the body.

And this place in the body begets a conscious presence with the past that is written on this skin. A past that, while it may define parts of my being, can be rewritten, crafted into a narrative that allows for a loving of my own body and the loving of another's body. I will also allow myself to feel agency in sexual choices. I have made the choice now to only connect sexually with someone I love. I will allow my body to feel love. And I will only connect sexually with someone when I feel safe, honored, listened to, respected.

A sensuous consciousness allows for the complexity of the world around us without blocking the pain, the truth, the history, and the weight of history that scars our bodies. We can't deny that we have a past. We can't deny that this past, all of our experiences, past and created now, have twisted and will twist our skin; like the Indian burn from aggressive classmates or the soft caress of a lover, our skin knows the sensation, remembers the sensations. I won't do arm balances in yoga because I connect it to my top heavy balance as an infant, leaning over too far and I bruised my skin far too often. Photographs mark the scar, and my memory tells the story but I feel it viscerally in my hesitation to lean forward. I have to tell myself to trust my body. And trust my body alongside other bodies.

Belonging in the body is also consciously reflecting upon the body as situated within a specific context, terrain, and historicity. I argue that we must consider the terrain as part of place. The terrain is also the institutional, social, and cultural contexts that frame these elements. If we can reconfigure one of these positions, the reconfiguration impacts the other definitions.

Geography: Sensuous Consciousness of our Terrain.

Imagine you hike through yellow dust trail, weave through the chaparral and oak trees, you weave thinly, softly. You can hear the coyotes break the morning silence as the sun lifts over the tall trees. You inhale the mist that floats in from the ocean. You wonder how far this trail winds over and through the mountains. How far until you reach the ocean's edge. You keep walking. Hear the twitter of the Topanga birds, the tiny ones that hide. It isn't until you stop, and really look between the green that you find them there jumping from branch to branch, leaf to leaf. You find stillness. And all around you there is movement, diversity of energy, intersecting beings colliding. You are in the middle of a symphony of sound, scent, image, touch, taste. Here in the chaos, within your stillness, you are aware of your part in it all.

———

In the Topanga terrain, I feel at one with the sky, the stars, the moon, and sun. I give myself the space and time to connect to the terrain, to develop sensuous consciousness with stimuli that I identify with. "Therefore, perception involves the sense organs (including the body) and the minds, but it is also situated in and mediated by a geographical and cultural environment."[181] The experience of finding place within this terrain, while a process, was much more pleasing to my senses. I felt to be a part of this larger system, interconnected.

In Topanga, unlike Chatsworth, I am reminded of my deep ecological approach to environmentalism, as developed by Aldo Leopold. The deep ecological approach portrays the land as an intricate system, an "intricately interwoven and interdependent intersection of elements that functions as a whole organism."[182] This branch of environmentalism looks for interconnections, diversity, and richness, and sees human beings as a part of a whole system. This approach rests on the holistic assumption that everything is linked and that all actions have an impact on all parts of the system. I feel part of the terrain, not separated from it.

According to Sandoval, one creates social change by living in it and learning to navigate that terrain effectively.[183] Within that terrain, we are but one part of a larger whole. The locality of terrain also includes the complexity of beings that exist in that space. In a call for social and political change, Chela Sandoval asks us to work within local sites of political oppression. Sandoval proposes that the site of political struggle, in what she calls the "neo-colonizing postmodern world," should be the eminently unstable, constantly changing, and adaptable immanent territory.[184] These territories while unstable are also connected to community. The sensuous consciousness of place is also very much connected to those we allow into it.

Locality: Communing Sensuously and Consciously

You enter the coffee shop. The door swings close to the brown table and blue chair. A little girl with brown bobbed hair just misses getting hit by your bag as she weaves towards her mother. You say "oops." And you watch her fall into her mother's lap. The mother smiles at you and you set your bag down at the back table. The man behind the counter smiles and says hello. He knows you now. He asks, "How are you?" And he really wants to know the answer. The girl tugs on your shirt and pulls you down to her. She says, "I'm Callie. What is your name?" You giggle and extend your hand to meet her tiny palm. The mother smiles again. The door opens and you walk to greet her. You ask about her father. "How is he feeling?" Her face turns into a frown, a bottom lip quiver. You extend your arms and pull her into a hug. You connect.

————

In this small town I have begun to develop many friendships. Others begin to know my name, what I do, who I love. The trick is I have also begun to know their lives, their histories, and their stories. I am one body situated with other bodies in this small town.

> Corporeality subsists both in the structure of the body, as a physical object situated with other "bodies" in a wider environment and with basic physical properties and needs, and the subjective experience of being a personal body, owned by an individual with a particular biography and situated in (and conditioned by) a given culture.[185]

I have begun to be a part of this community, through local action and connection. We have begun to co-create community.

John Dewey believed that the Great Community is not solely about association. While people may be physically connected or proximate, there may still be a lack of community.[186] Those in the West are constantly being hailed as performing subjects "through countless articulations of 'Individuality.'" Yet we need to incline towards one another to create community. "There is no subject prior to infinitely shifting and contingent relations of belonging."[187] An individual, no matter how pushed and inspired to be an individual is at once a member of a community. In the smaller space of Topanga, it is easier to find and cultivate a sense of community.

Materially and geographically, a community is based in a local space. Rather than defining community based on social or political boundaries or similarities in identity, I argue a place of community is based on creating, the act of working together. It is a form of community in the *doing*. Commune works through the current definitions of community and argues that geographic locality and community action can cultivate movements of contextual, relational belonging. Iris Marion Young argues that the ideal of community is a dream that "expresses a desire for selves that are transparent to one another, relationships of mutual identification, social closeness and comfort." This ideal "privileges unity over difference, immediacy over mediation, sympathy over recognition of the limits of one's understanding of others from their point of view."[188] But the building of community is based on a bundle of complex relationships, disagreements and agreements, complex discussions, and interrelated subjectivities. In order to build a community that might thrive and survive, people must first commune.

As a verb, to commune is the act of coming together. To commune is to create through mindful action and sensuous consciousness a state of intimate and heightened receptivity. To commune is to collaborate, to work together, in a joint intellectual effort. As a noun, community is a material place, defined through and by spatial and geographical relations. The space of community offers a heightened awareness of the features of each potential definitional space. Antonio Gramsci calls for engaged knowledge: "The intellectual's error consists in believing that one can know without understanding and even more without feeling and being empassioned [. . .] that is without feeling the elementary passions of the people."[189] Community is based on the intersection of subject positions and the cultivation of relationships through engaged knowledge. A community is the bundle of relationships that create these spaces of negotiation.

Within these spaces of negotiation, a sensuous consciousness allows for the complexity of another person's story, another's experience of the world. If everything in nature is part of a cycle, then there is no end-point. There is decay that feeds other life. This too connects to how we relate to others. Examine local action and interaction between people and positionalities. Local actions and interactions cultivate change. Our embodied experiences connected with the way in which we make sense of these experiences shifts our life path and plan. Our sense-making of our sensory experiences fuels our next action, our next narrative, the next story we tell about that past, and the stories we tell ourselves and others about our lives. As part of the larger interconnected whole, our local actions impact place, each other, memory, and the body; they impact the narratives we tell of place, of space, and of larger meta-narratives and ideologies.

Sensuous consciousness is the study of relationships between living things and their environments through a re-engagement of our senses to uncover a system of relationships within a particular environment. Sensuous consciousness is made aware of living and non-living beings, not only in terms of our natural environment, but the people and organisms that live and exist within it.

Belonging: Sensuous Consciousness and Mindful Action.

Sensuous consciousness is based on balance, compromise, relational negotiations, and an intimate understanding of the land. Survival strategies are contextual. Working on the local level frames the discursive elements that map each person's specific mode of survival within a specific terrain, each person's ability to use their multidimensional senses to explore their locations, processes, histories, and presence. However painful this consciousness and action, within certain places within Los Angeles, I argue that social, interpersonal, and personal change is cultivated through mindful action.

Cultivating mindful action happens in three cyclical steps. First, I act. Next, I reconsider. And finally, I act again. I have reconsidered how to move in the world through each personal conflict, through anxiety, fear, and each push to keep trying. I have reconsidered and acted in the world motivated by the desire to cultivate loving relationships with the terrain, with others, with my body. Finally, these reconsiderings fuse together in a process to create mindful action.

Following Augusto Boal's belief in the human capability to reflect on emotions, intentions, and themselves in action, with a moment or moments of witnessing,[190] I have reconsidered each developing relationship and how my actions have an effect on the rest of the process. While some scholars argue this momentary or brief interaction with a place or with people is not as consequential or as important as other more depth-full periods of time with a culture, the body in juxtaposition with a situation, context, experience, people, and a sense of identity that has not been previously understood or acknowledged will feel an immense jarring, a cacophony of senses, perhaps overrun by fear, which turns into a desire to make sense of a place, or can turn into a desire to turn from this place. This sensory engagement is a survival instinct that if developed turns into a doubling of consciousness. This jarring moment is a collision that provides us the liminal space in which to make sense of our values, beliefs and allow for these systems of belief to be suspended, perhaps even ripped to pieces.

Augusto Boal states, "Humans are capable of seeing themselves in the act of seeing, of thinking their emotions, of being moved by their thoughts. They can see themselves here and imagine themselves there. They can see themselves today and imagine themselves tomorrow."[191] In this way, we are able to image ourselves on new planes; we can then imagine new ways of interacting. From a Boalian perspective, one can enter a place, imagine what it is to really be there in all its socio-cultural complexity, and then process how this knowledge will aid in further experiences.

That written, I am quite sure that in a few days, I will have a different vantage point, a new learning, and new insights, and different questions, all of which will shift the writing I have done in these pages. I will navigate the terrain again, doing, reading, writing, and recreating. This is the beauty of processual work. This is how I understand my work as human being, creator, and scholar. These actual, tactile, and habitual actions are what create change, first on the local level and then in the reconsiderations of discursive and ideological negotiations. Sensuous consciousness is moving with the process and letting the process shape you as much as you shape it. And each day, I will look for another terrain for exposure, connection, and creation.

CONCLUSION

HERE

Never.

I never wanted to move to LA.

But here I am.

Connected to the Terrain.

In all of these other places in Los Angeles, I see potential insights, discoveries.

I could come to know them as intimately as the others if and when I find myself there, really there.

Within these pages we encountered several places in Los Angeles, locations and terrains that I came to know intimately. These places— Burbank, Chatsworth, Hollywood Hills, West Hollywood, and Topanga have become terrains that are familiar to me. When I move in and through these places, I find memories tucked in the architecture, in the people past seeped into the cracks in the concrete. I have embodied reactions to the stories that live there in the branches of an old oak, or the reflection of the local general store window.

As I was in those places, I will not be again.

Within the terrain of my body, I have uncovered through the process of culling painful memories and how they have impacted my material decisions in sexual relationships. I have connected with presence, a newfound safety and pleasure, desire without pain, a *place* with my own embodied empowerment. I have felt and come to *know* the terrain of my body.

I know now the terrain of home, the ways in which I need to and can feel safe, comfort in a home. I know the terrain of this comfort is a privilege and I cherish it. My actions will continue to cultivate safety for those that enter this place of home.

I know the terrain of community, creating community through localized action. I know how to cultivate a mindful relationship, one that is open and honest, kind and generous. We can cultivate community, all the while knowing that without each other, we wouldn't survive. I will approach people without fear, with love.

I have come to know the terrains of many locations in Los Angeles, engaging my senses consciously. And know we are connected to the terrain. It is a part of us as we are a part of it. The terrain shapes us as we shape it.

Move Along.

> Grey space. Concrete. Flash of red.
> Grey Space. Concrete. Plastic Bag.
> Human body.
> Extend your hand.

> Roar of truck. Exhaust puff. Silence.
> Listen.
> Grey Space. Plastic Bag. Blue tent.
> Look.
> Human body.
> Extend your hand.

> Lost sky.
> Breathe.
> Extend your hand.

NOTES

Introduction: Los Angeles River

1 Visit www.concreteanddust.com/#!la_river|c1enr.

2 Philip L. Fradkin. *The Seven States of California: A Natural and Human History* (Berkeley, CA: University of California Press, 1997) 33.

3 Mark Kingwell. *Consciousness and the City* (Toronto, ON: Viking Canada, 2008) 146.

4 Jane Jacobs. *The Death and Life of Great American Cities* (New York: Vintage, 1961).

5 Kingwell 150.

6 Michael Keith. *After the Cosmopolitan? Multicultural Cities and the Future of Racism* (London: Routledge, 2005) 181.

7 Jan Cohen-Cruz, Ed. *Radical Street Performance: An International Anthology* (London and New York: Routledge, 1998).

8 Fradkin 33.

Introduction: Los Angeles River, Revisited

9 Fradkin 326.

10 Steven Solomon. *Water: The Epic Struggle for Wealth, Power, and Civilization* (New York: Harper, 2010).

11 Gary Bridge and Sophie Watson, Eds. *A Companion to the City* (Oxford: Blackwell, 2000).

12 Yi-Fu Tuan. *Topophilia: A Study of Environment, Perceptions, Attitudes, and Values* (New York: Columbia University Press, 1974).

13 Tim Cresswell. *On the Move: Mobility in the Modern Western World* (London: Routledge, 2006).

14 Cresswell; Yi-Fu Tuan; de Certeau, Michel. *The Practice of Everyday Life*, trans. Steven Rendell (Berkeley, CA: University of California Press, 1984).

15 Elliot Eisner. *The Arts and the Creation of Mind* (New Haven, CT: Yale University Press, 2002); Elliot Eisner and Thomas Barone, "Arts-Based Educational Research," *Complementary Methods for Research in Education*, Ed. Richard M. Jaeger, 2nd ed. (Washington, DC: American Educational Research Association 1997) 73–94; Susan Finley, "Painting Life Histories," *Journal of Curriculum Theorizing* 17(2), 2001: 13–26; Susan Finley and J. Gary Knowles, "Researcher as Artist/Artist as Researcher," *Qualitative Inquiry* 1, 1995: 110–142; Carol A. Mullen, "A Self-Fashioned Gallery of Aesthetic Practice," *Qualitative Inquiry* 9, 2003: 165–181; Rita L. Irwin and Alex de Cosson, Eds. *A/r/tography: Rendering Self through Arts-Based Living Inquiry* (Vancouver, BC: Pacific Educational Press, 2004); Maria Piantanida, Patricia L. McMahon, and Noreen B. Garman, "Sculpting the Contours of Arts-Based Educational Research within a Discourse Community," *Qualitative Inquiry* 9, 2003: 182–191; Rhonda Watrin, "Art as Research," *Canadian Review of Art Education* 26, 1999: 92–100.

16 Patricia Leavy. *Method Meets Art: Arts-Based Research Practice* (New York: The Guilford Press, 2009).

17 Karen Scott-Hoy. "Form Carries Experience: A Story of the Art and Form of Knowledge," *Qualitative Inquiry* 9, 2003: 268–280.

18 Mullen 2003.

19 Mullen 178.

20 Stephanie Springgay, Rita L. Irwin, and Sylvia Kind. "A/r/tography as Living Inquiry through Art and Text," *Qualitative Inquiry* 11, 2005: 897–912.

21 Irwin and de Cosson.

22 Harry Wolcott. "The Ethnographic Autobiography," *Auto/Biography* 12, 2004: 93–106.

23 Lyall Crawford. "Personal Ethnography," *Communication Monographs* 63, 1996: 158–170.

24 Carolyn Ellis and Art Bochner. "Telling and Performing Personal Stories: The Constraints of Choice in Abortion," *Investigating Subjectivity: Research on Lived Experience*, Eds. Carolyn Ellis and Michael Flaherty (Newbury Park, CA: Sage, 1992) 79–101.

25 Carolyn Ellis. "The Other Side of the Fence: Seeing Black and White in a Small Southern Town," *Qualitative Inquiry* 1, 1995: 147–167.

26 Wolcott.

27 Carol Rambo Ronai. "Multiple Reflections of Child Sex Abuse: An Argument for a Layered Account," *Journal of Contemporary Ethnography* 23(4), 1995: 395–436.

28 Norman K. Denzin. "Aesthetics and the Practices of Qualitative Inquiry," *Qualitative Inquiry* 6, 2000: 256–265.

29 Deborah Reed-Danahay, Ed. *Auto/Ethnography: Rewriting the Self and the Social* (Oxford: Berg Publishers, 1997).

30 Tami Spry. "A 'Performative-I' Copresence: Embodying the Ethnographic Turn in Performance and the Performative Turn in Ethnography," *Text and Performance Quarterly* 26, 2006: 711.

31 Norman K. Denzin. *Interpretive Ethnography: Interpretive Practices for the 21st Century* (New York: Sage, 1997) 217.

32   Carolyn Ellis. *The Ethnographic I: A Methodological Novel about Autoethnography* (Thousand Oaks, CA: AltaMira, 2004) 30.

33   Ellis, 2004, 30.

34   Ronald Pelias. *Writing Performance: Poeticizing the Researchers Body* (Carbondale, IL: SIUC Press, 1999).

35   Julia Kristeva. *Desire in Language: A Semiotic Approach to Literature and Art*, trans. Thomas Gora, Alice Jardine, and Leon S. Roudiez (Oxford: Basil Blackwell, 1982).

36   Craig Gingrich-Philbrook. "Autoethnography's Family Values: Easy Access to Compulsory Experiences." *Text and Performance Quarterly* 25, 2005: 297–314.

37   Patricia Geist Martin, Lisa Gates, Liesbeth Wiering, Erika Kirby, Renee Houston, Anne Lilly, and Juan Moreno, "Exemplifying Collaborative Autoethnographic Practice via Shared Stories of Mothering," *Journal of Research Practice* 6(1), 2012: Article M8. Retrieved March 1, 2010, from http://jrp.icaap.org/index.php/jrp/article/view/209/187.

38   John Agnew and James S. Duncan, Eds. *The Power of Place: Bringing Together Geographical and Sociological Imaginations* (Boston, MA: Unwin Hyman, 1989); James Duncan and David Ley, Eds. *Place/Culture/Representation* (London: Routledge, 1993); Dolores Hayden, *The Power of Place: Urban Landscapes as Public History* (Cambridge, MA: MIT Press, 1997); David Harvey, *The Limits to Capital* (London: Verso, 1999) and "Cosmopolitanism and the Banality of Geographical Evils," *Popular Culture* 12(2), 2000: 529–564; Doreen Massey, *Space, Place and Gender* (Minneapolis, MN: University of Minnesota Press, 1994); Gillian Rose. *Feminism and Geography: The Limits of Geographical Knowledge* (Minneapolis, MN: University of Minnesota Press, 1993); Mark Dorrian and Gillian Rose, *Deterritorialisations . . . Revisioning Landscapes and Politics* (New York: Black Dog Publishing, 2003); Yi-Fu Tuan. *Space and Place: The Perspective of Experience* (Minneapolis, MN: University of Minnesota Press, 1977).

39   Cresswell 2006.

40   Yi-Fu Tuan 1977.

41   Yi-Fu Tuan 1977.

42   Hayden 16.

43   Massey.

1 Burbank

44   Visit www.concreteanddust.com/#!maps_mobility|c24pc.

45   Visit www.concreteanddust.com/#!burbank|cihc.

46   www.burbank.com/channel/History/1593.

47   www.ci.burbank.ca.us/index.aspx?page=43.

2 Burbank, Revisited

48   Anne Lamott. *Bird by Bird: Some Instructions on Writing and Life* (New York: Anchor Books, 1994) 266.

49   Yi-Fu Tuan 1974.

50   Natalie Goldberg. *Writing Down the Bones* (Boston, MA: Shambhala, 1986).

51   Lynda Schneekloth. "The Frontier is Our Home," *Journal of Architectural Education* 49, 1984: 210–225.

52 Schneekloth 222.

53 Schneekloth 214.

54 Wendell Berry. *The Unsettling of America* (Berkeley, CA: University of California Press, 1996).

55 Victor Turner. *From Ritual to Theater: The Human Seriousness of Play* (New York: Performing Arts Journal Publications, 1982).

56 Michael Dear and Steven Flusty. "Postmodern Urbanism," *Annals of the Association of American Geographers* 88, 1998: 50–72.

57 Susan J. Brison. *Aftermath: Violence and the Remaking of a Self* (Princeton, NJ: University Press, 2003) Xx.

58 Brison 46.

59 Ken Gale and Jonathon Wyatt. "Inquiring into Writing: An Interactive Interview," *Qualitative Inquiry* 12, 2006: 1117–1134.

60 Laurel Richardson. "Getting Personal: Writing-Stories," *International Journal of Qualitative Studies in Education* 14(1), 2001: 35, 33–38.

61 Laurel Richardson. "Writing: A Method of Inquiry," *Handbook of Qualitative Research*, 2nd ed., Eds. Norman K. Denzin and Yvonna S. Lincoln (Thousand Oaks, CA: Sage, 2000) 923–948; Ellis, 1995.

62 Roland Barthes. *The Pleasure of the Text* (New York: Wand Hill, 1973) 39.

63 James Agee and Ealker Evans, *Let Us Now Praise Famous Men* (Boston, MA: Houghton Mifflin, 1941) 232.

64 Denzin 1997, 217.

65 James H. Olthuis. "Otherwise than Violence: Toward a Hermeneutics of Connection," *The Arts, Community and Cultural Democracy*, Eds. Lambert Zuidervaart and Henry Luttikhuizen (New York: St. Martins Press, 2000) 140.

66 Sarah Pink. *Doing Visual Ethnography* (London: Sage, 2001) 18.

67 Mary Beth Cancienne and Celeste N. Snowber. "Writing Rhythm: Movement as Method," *Qualitative Inquiry* 9, 2003: 237.

68 Chandra Talpade Mohanty. *Feminism without Borders: Decolonizing Theory, Practicing Solidarity* (Durham, NC: Duke University Press, 2003) 126.

69 Biddy Martin and Chandra Talpade Mohanty. "Feminist Politics: What's Home Got to Do with It?" *Feminist Studies/Critical Studies*, Ed. Teresa de Lauretis (Bloomington, IN: Indiana University Press, 1986) 209.

70 Susie Harrington. "Responsive Design: Integrating the Spirit of Place with the Vision of Home," *The Art of Natural Building: Design, Construction, Resources*, Eds. Joseph F. Kennedy, Michael G. Smith, and Catherine Wanek (Canada: New Society Press, 2002) 52.

3 Chatsworth

71 Visit www.concreteanddust.com/#!maps_mobility|c24pc.

72 Visit www.concreteanddust.com/#!chatsworth|ctzx.

73 Women in the adult entertainment industry are not just porn actresses. They are also the directors, producers, camera people. Several of the big name porn actresses such as Chloe and Stephanie Swift have become prominent directors and producers.

74 To enter into first person experiences of being a porn star and direct involvement in the adult entertainment, Legs McNeil and Jennifer Osborne, *The Other*

Hollywood: The Uncensored Oral History of the Porn Film Industry (New York: It Books, 2005); Jenna Jameson, *How to Make Love Like a Porn Star: A Cautionary Tale* (New York: It Books, 2004); David Jennings, *Skin Flick* (Fairfield, CA: 1st Books, 2000); Tera Patrick, *Sinner Takes All: A Memoir of Love and Porn* (New York: Gotham, 2009).

75 San Fernando Valley Economic Research Center, *Report of Findings on the San Fernando Valley Economy* (California State University Northridge, 2007–2008).

76 US Department of Housing and Urban Development, *City of Los Angeles Five-Year Consolidated Plan (Program Years 2008–2013).*

77 Gillian Rose. *Feminism and Geography: The Limits of Geographical Knowledge* (Minneapolis, MN: University of Minnesota Press, 1993).

78 US Census Bureau. *Population Estimates*, July 2008, www.census.gov/popest/counties/CO-EST2009–01.html.

79 Rosemarie Putnam Tong. *Feminist Thought: A More Comprehensive Introduction* (Boulder, CO: Westview Press, 1998) 247.

4 Chatsworth, Revisited

80 Bronislaw Szerszynski, Wallance Heim, and Claire Waterton, Eds. *Nature Performed: Environment, Culture and Performance* (Oxford: Blackwell, 2003) 11.

81 Henri Lefebvre. *The Production of Space*, trans. Donald Nicholson-Smith, (Oxford: Blackwell, 1974/1991).

82 Bryant Keith Alexander. "Telling Twisted Tales: Owning Place, Owning Culture in Ethnographic Research," *Opening Acts: Performance in/as Communication and Cultural Studies*, Ed. Judith Hamera (Thousand Oaks, CA: Sage, 2006) 49–74.

83 Gilles Deleuze and Felix Guattari. *A Thousand Plateaus: Capitalism and Schizophrenia*, trans. Brian Massumi (Minneapolis, MN: University of Minnesota Press, 1987).

84 Frederick Corey. "Performing Sexualities in an Irish Pub," *Text and Performance Quarterly* 16, 1996: 150.

85 de Certeau 117.

86 Tim Cresswell. *In Place/Out of Place: Geography, Ideology and Transgression* (Minneapolis, MN: University of Minnesota Press, 1996).

87 Deleuze and Guattari.

88 Cresswell 1996.

89 Lefebvre 86–87.

90 Lefebvre 86–87.

91 Duncan and Ley.

92 Dwight Conquergood. "Performance Studies: Interventions and Radical Research," *The Drama Review* 46, 2002: 145–156.

93 Clifford Geertz. *The Interpretation of Cultures* (New York: Basic Books, 1973); Victor Turner, 1982.

94 Italic in original. David B. Ingram and John Protevi, "Political Philosophy," *Columbian Companion to Twentieth-Century Philosophies*, Ed. Constantin V. Boundas (New York: Columbia University Press, 2007) 586.

95 Deleuze and Guattari.

96 de Certeau states, "Sly as a fox and twice as quick: there are countless ways of 'making do'" (1984) 29.

97 Françoise d'Eaubonne. "The Time for Ecofeminism," *Ecology: Key Concepts in Critical Theory*, Ed. Carolyn Merchant, trans. Ruth Hottell (Reprinted Atlantic Highlands, NJ: Humanities, 1994) 174–197.

98 Karen J. Warren. "Feminism and Ecology: Making Connections," *Readings in Ecology and Feminist Theology*, Eds. Mary Heather Mackinnon and Marie McIntyre (Kansas City, KA: Sheed and Ward, 1995).

99 Rose 105.

100 Aldo Leopold. *A Sand County Almanac and Sketches Here and There* (New York: Oxford University Press, 1948).

101 Donna Haraway. *Simians, Cyborgs, and Women: The Reinvention of Nature* (London: Free Association Books, 1991).

102 Rosi Braidotti. *Nomadic Subjects: Embodiment and Sexual Difference in Contemporary Feminist Theory* (New York: Columbia University Press, 1994) 6.

103 Braidotti 144.

104 Mikhail Bahktin. *Rabelais and His World*, trans. Helene Iswolsky (Bloomington, IN: Indiana University Press, 1984).

105 Kristeva 6.

106 Louis Althusser. "Ideology and Ideological State Apparatuses," *Lenin and Philosophy and Other Essays*, Eds. Aradhana Sharma and Akhil Gupta (Malden, MA: Blackwell Publishing, 2006) 86–111.

107 Judith Butler. "Performative Acts and Gender Constitution: An Essay in Phenomenology and Feminist Theory," *The Feminist and Visual Culture Reader*, Ed. Amelia Jones (New York: Routledge, 2003) 392–402.

108 Butler 2003.

5 Hollywood Hills

109 Visit www.concreteanddust.com/#!maps_mobility|c24pc.

110 Visit www.concreteanddust.com/#!hollywood_hills|c20x9.

111 Bonnie Roche. "The Mishkan as Metaphor-form and Anti-form: On the Transformation of Urban Space," *Cross Currents* 52, 2002: 342.

112 D. J. Waldie. *Holy Land: A Suburban Memoir* (New York: St. Martin's Press, 1996) 23.

113 Waldie 23.

114 Sandra Barrera. "Rooms with a View," *Daily News* 27 Mar. 2010: L1–L5.

115 For further discussion see John Berger, *Way of Seeing* (London: BBC and Penguin Books, 1972); Laura Mulvey, "Visual Pleasure and Narrative Cinema," *Screen* 16(3), 1975: 6–18.

116 The storm represents the desire to understand the increasingly transient nature of identity, to cleanse through the muck and grit of Hollywood to make sense of perceived power in beauty and its connection to the plastique. The plastique is a version of beauty that creates a falsity, a heightened sense of lack and desirability. There is a storm coming. And storms always transform the environment.

117 www.trulia.com/.

118 www.trulia.com/.

119 www.trulia.com/.

120 Barrera L1–L5.

121 John W. Robinson. *Trails of the Angeles 100 Hikes in the San Gabriels* (Berkeley, CA: Wilderness Press, 1971) 5.

122 Ted Andrews. *Animal Speak: Spiritual and Magical Powers of Creatures Great and Small* (St. Paul, MN: Llewellyn Publications, 1993).

123 Jennifer Price. "Thirteen Ways of Seeing Nature in LA," *Land of Sun-Shine*, Eds. William Deverell and Greg Hise (Pittsburg, KS: University of Pittsburg Press, 2005) 224.

124 James D. Houstan. *Californians: Searching for the Golden State* (Santa Cruz, CA: Otter B. Books, 1998) xi.

125 Ecofeminists' focus on these essentialist assumptions about women's innate connections to nature prides itself on the ability and duty of women to take care of the environment. For further discussion see: Dorothy Dinnerstein, *The Mermaid and the Minotaur: Sexual Arrangements and Human Malaise* (New York: Harper Collins, 1976); Susan Griffin, *Woman and Nature: The Roaring Inside Her* (New York: Harper & Row, 1978); Ynestra King, "Healing the Wounds: Feminism, Ecology, and the Nature/Culture Dualism," *Healing the Wounds: The Emergence of Ecofeminism*, Ed. Irene Diamond (San Francisco, CA: Sierra Club Books, 1990); Sherilyn MacGregor, *Beyond Mothering Earth: Ecological Citizenship and the Politics of Care* (Vancouver, BC: University of British Columbia Press, 2006); Mary Mellor, *Breaking the Boundaries: Towards a Feminist Green Socialism* (London: Virago Press, 1992); Sara Ruddick, *Maternal Thinking: Toward a Politics of Peace* (New York: Beacon, 1989); Ariel Sallah, *Ecofeminism as Politics: Nature, Marx and the Postmodern* (London: Zed Books, 1997).

126 Clark Davis and David Igler, Eds. *The Human Tradition in California* (Wilmington, DE: SR Books, 2002).

6 Hollywood Hills, Revisited

127 Michael Taussig. *Mimesis and Alterity: A Particular History of the Sense* (New York: Routledge, 1993).

128 Dorrian and Rose 16–17.

129 Rose 89.

130 Vandana Shiva. *Earth Democracy: Justice, Sustainability, and Peace* (Boston, MA: South End Press, 2005) 15.

131 Berger.

132 Bernardo Attias. "The Table Dance: Performing the Commodity Process," *Organization for the Study of Communication, Language and Gender*. Los Angeles, CA, 15–18 October 2009. Karl Marx. *Capital: Volume One*, trans. Ben Fowkes (London: Penguin, 1990).

133 Butler 392.

134 Donna J. Haraway. *Simians, Cyborgs, and Women: The Reinvention of Nature* (London: Free Association Books, 1991) 155.

135 Haraway 1.

136 Haraway 1.

137 Donna J. Haraway. *Modest Witness@Second_Millenium. FemaleMan*(c)*Meets_ OncoMouse_: Feminism and Technoscience* (New York: Routledge, 1997) 503.

138 Ingrid Bartsch, Carolyn DiPalma, and Laura Sells. "Witnessing the Postmodern Jermiad: (Mis)Understanding Donna Haraway's Method of Inquiry," *Configurations* 9(1), 2001: 127–164, p. 138.

139 Jacques Derrida. *Of Grammatology*, trans. Gayatri Chakravorty Spivak (Baltimore, MD: The John Hopkins University Press, 1974) 49.

140 Hans Ulrich Gumbrecht. *Production of Presence: What Meaning Cannot Convey* (Stanford, CA: Stanford University Press, 2004) 110.

141 Peggy Phelan. *Unmarked: The Politics of Performance* (London: Routledge, 1993) 49.

142 Michel Foucault. *Discipline and Punish: The Birth of the Prison*, trans. Alan Sheridan (New York: Vintage Books, 1977) 201.

143 de Certeau.

144 Dean MacCannell. *The Tourist: A New Theory of the Leisure Class* (Berkeley, CA: University of California Press, 1999).

145 Urry.

146 Baudrillard 6.

147 Maria Lugones, *Pilgramages/Peregrinages: Theorizing Coalition Against Multiple Oppressions* (Lanham, MD: Rowan and Littlefield, 2003).

148 Jane Monica Drexler. "Politics Improper: Iris Marion Young, Hannah Arendt, and the Power of Performativity," *Hypatia* 22, 2007: 10.

7 West Hollywood

149 Visit www.concreteanddust.com/#!maps_mobility|c24pc.

150 Visit www.concreteanddust.com/#!west_hollywood|c1huf.

151 Cresswell 2006.

152 www.weho.org/.

8 West Hollywood, Revisited

153 http://avenueswh.com/.

154 Consult the following sources for further information: Judith Butler. *Gender Trouble* (New York: Routledge, 1999); Teresa De Lauretis, *Technologies of Gender: Language, Discourse, Society* (London: Palgrave Milgram, 1989); Michel Foucault, *The History of Sexuality: An Introduction* (London: Penguin Books, 1984); Eve Kosofsky Sedgwick, *Epistemology of the Closet* (Berkeley, CA: University of California Press, 1990).

155 Karen Lovaas, John P. Elia, and Gust A. Yep, Eds. *Shifting Ground(s): Surveying the Contested Terrain of LGBT Studies and Queer Theory* (Binghamton, NY: Harrington Park Press, 2006) 6.

156 David Roman. *Acts of Intervention: Performance, Gay Culture, and AIDS* (Bloomington, IN: Indiana University Press, 1998).

157 William Turner. *A Genealogy of Queer Theory* (Philadelphia, PA: Temple University Press, 2000).

158 Lee Edelman. *No Future: Queer Theory and the Death Drive* (Durham, NC and London: Duke University Press, 2004).

159 Greta Gaard. "Queer by Nature," *Love, West Hollywood: Reflections of Los Angeles* (New York: Alyson Books, 2008) 147.

160 Judith Halberstam. *In a Queer Time and Place* (New York: New York University Press, 2005) 2.

161 Jose Esteban Munoz. *Disidentification: Queers of Color and the Performance of Politics* (Minneapolis, MN: University of Minnesota Press, 1999) 32.

162 Elizabeth Galewski. "Playing Up Being a Woman: Femme Performance and the Potential for Ironic Representation," *Rhetoric and Public Affairs* 11, 2008: 279–302.

163 Steven Angelides. "Historicizing (Bi)Sexuality: A Rejoinder for Gay/Lesbian Studies, Feminism, and Queer Theory" *Shifting Ground(s): Surveying the Contested Terrain of LGBT Studies and Queer Theory*, Eds. Karen Lovaas, John P. Elia, and Gust A. Yep (Binghamton, NY: Harrington Park Press, 2006) 152.

164 M. Jacqui Alexander. *Pedagogies of Crossing. Meditations on Feminism, Sexual Politics, Memory, and the Sacred* (Durham, NC and London: Duke University Press, 2005) 70.

165 William E. Connolly. *Capitalism, Christianity, America Style* (Durham, NC and London: Duke University Press, 2008) 27.

166 Althusser.

167 Annamarie Jagose. *Queer Theory: An Introduction* (New York: New York University Press, 1997).

168 Larry Knopp. "On the Relationship Between Queer and Feminist Geographies," *The Professional Geographer* 59, 2007: 49.

169 Munoz.

9 Topanga Canyon

170 Visit www.concreteanddust.com/#!maps_mobility|c24pc.

171 Visit www.concreteanddust.com/#!topanga|c1qbx.

10 Topanga Canyon, Revisited

172 Paul Rodaway. *Sensuous Geographies: Body, Sense, and Place* (London: Routledge, 1994).

173 Perhaps, this is what Yi-Fu Tuan understands as topophilia or a love of place. For further discussion see Yi-Fu Tuan 1974.

174 G. Pollini. "Elements of a Theory of Place Attachment and Socio-Territorial Belonging," *International Review of Sociology* 15, 2005: 497–515.

175 Harold Proshansky, A. K. Fabian, and R. Kaminoff. "Place-Identity: Physical World Socialization of the Self," *Journal of Environmental Psychology* 3, 1983: 57–83.

176 I. Altman and S. M. Low, Eds. *Place Attachment* (New York: Plenum, 1992).

177 R. Hay. "Sense of a Place in Developmental Context," *Journal of Environmental Psychology* 18, 1998: 5–29.

178 bell hooks. *belonging: a culture of place* (New York: Routledge, 2009) 1.

179 Rodaway 145.

180 Rodaway 31.

181 Rodaway 12.

182 Putnam Tong 249.

183 Chela Sandoval. *A Methodology of the Oppressed* (Minneapolis, MN: University of Minnesota Press, 2000).

184 Sandoval 41.
185 Rodaway 31.
186 John Dewey. *The Public and Its Problems* (Athens, OH: Swallow, 1927).
187 Aimee Marie Carrilo Rowe. "Be Longing: Towards a Feminist Politics of Relation," *Feminist Formations* 17, 2005: 17.
188 Iris Marion Young. "The Ideal of Community and the Politics of Difference," *Feminism/Postmodernism*, Ed. Linda J. Nicholson (New York: Routledge, 1990) 301.
189 Antonio Gramsci. *Selections from Prison Notebooks*, Ed. and trans. Quintin Hoare and Geoffery Smith (New York: International, 1971) 418.
190 Augusto Boal. *Games for Actors and Non-Actors* (New York: Routledge, 1992).
191 Boal 12.

WORKS CITED

Agee, James and Walker Evans. *Let Us Now Praise Famous Men*. Boston, MA: Houghton Mifflin, 1941.

Agnew, John and James S. Duncan, Eds. *The Power of Place: Bringing Together Geographical and Sociological Imaginations*. Boston, MA: Unwin Hyman, 1989.

Alexander, Bryant Keith. "Telling Twisted Tales: Owning Place, Owning Culture in Ethnographic Research." *Opening Acts: Performance in/as Communication and Cultural Studies*, Ed. Judith Hamera. Thousand Oaks, CA: Sage, 2006. 49–74.

Alexander, M. Jacqui. *Pedagogies of Crossing. Meditations on Feminism, Sexual Politics, Memory, and the Sacred*. Durham, NC: Duke University Press, 2005.

Altman, I. and S. M. Low, Eds. *Place Attachment*. New York: Plenum, 1992.

Althusser, Louis. "Ideology and Ideological State Apparatuses." *Lenin and Philosophy and Other Essays*, Eds. Aradhana Sharma and Akhil Gupta. Malden, MA: Blackwell Publishing, 2006. 86–111.

Andrews, Ted. *Animal Speak: Spiritual and Magical Powers of Creatures Great and Small*. St. Paul, MN: Llewellyn Publications, 1993.

Angelides, Steven. "Historicizing (Bi)Sexuality: A Rejoinder for Gay/Lesbian Studies, Feminism, and Queer Theory." *Shifting Ground(s): Surveying the Contested Terrain of LGBT Studies and Queer Theory*, Eds. Karen Lovaas, John P. Elia, and Gust A. Yep. Binghamton, NY: Harrington Park Press, 2006.

Attias, Bernardo. "The Table Dance: Performing the Commodity Process," *Organization for the Study of Communication, Language and Gender*. Los Angeles, CA, October 15–18, 2009.

Bahktin, Mikhail. *Rabelais and His World*, trans. Helene Iswolsky. Bloomington, IN: Indiana University Press, 1984.

Barrera, Sandra. "Rooms with a View," *Daily News,* March 27, 2010: L1–L5.

Barthes, Roland. *The Pleasure of the Text*. New York: Wand and Hill, 1973.

Bartsch, Ingrid, Carolyn DiPalma, and Laura Sells. "Witnessing the Postmodern Jermiad: (Mis)Understanding Donna Haraway's Method of Inquiry," *Configurations* 9,1 (2001): 127–164.

Baudrillard, Jean. *Selected Writings.* Ed. Mark Poster. Stanford, CA: Stanford University Press, 1988.

Berger, John. *Way of Seeing.* London: BBC and Penguin Books, 1972.

Berry, Wendell. *The Unsettling of America.* Berkeley, CA: University of California Press, 1996.

Boal, Augusto. *Games for Actors and Non-Actors.* New York: Routledge, 1992.

Braidotti, Rosi. *Nomadic Subjects: Embodiment and Sexual Difference in Contemporary Feminist Theory.* New York: Columbia University Press, 1994.

Bridge, Gary and Sophie Watson, Eds. *A Companion to the City.* Oxford: Blackwell, 2000.

Brison, Susan J. *Aftermath: Violence and the Remaking of a Self.* Princeton, NJ: University Press, 2003.

Butler, Judith. *Gender Trouble.* New York: Routledge, 1999.

Butler, Judith. "Performative Acts and Gender Constitution: An Essay in Phenomenology and Feminist Theory." *The Feminist and Visual Culture Reader*, Ed. Amelia Jones. New York: Routledge, 2003. 392–402.

Cancienne, Mary Beth and Celeste N. Snowber. "Writing Rhythm: Movement as Method," *Qualitative Inquiry* 9 (2003): 237.

Cohen-Cruz, Jan, Ed. *Radical Street Performance: An International Anthology.* London and New York: Routledge, 1998.

Connolly, William E. *Capitalism, Christianity, America Style.* Durham, NC and London: Duke University Press, 2008.

Conquergood, Dwight. "Performance Studies: Interventions and Radical Research," *The Drama Review* 46 (2002): 145–156.

Corey, Frederick. "Performing Sexualities in an Irish Pub." *Text and Performance Quarterly* 16 (1996): 146–160.

Crawford, Lyall. "Personal Ethnography." *Communication Monographs* 63 (1996): 158–170.

Cresswell, Tim. *In Place/Out of Place: Geography, Ideology and Transgression.* Minneapolis, MN: University of Minnesota Press, 1996.

Cresswell, Tim. *On the Move: Mobility in the Modern Western World.* London: Routledge, 2006.

Davis, Clark and David Igler, Eds. *The Human Tradition in California.* Wilmington, DE: SR Books, 2002.

Dear, Michael and Steven Flusty. "Postmodern Urbanism," *Annals of the Association of American Geographers* 88 (1998): 50–72.

de Certeau, Michel. *The Practice of Everyday Life*, trans. Steven Rendall. Berkeley, CA: University of California Press, 1984.

d'Eaubonne, Françoise. "The Time for Ecofeminism." *Ecology: Key Concepts in Critical Theory*, Ed. Carolyn Merchant, trans. Ruth Hottell. Reprinted Atlantic Highlands, NJ: Humanities, 1994. 174–197.

De Lauretis, Teresa. *Technologies of Gender: Language, Discourse, Society.* London: Palgrave Milgram, 1989.

Deleuze, Gilles and Felix Guattari. *A Thousand Plateaus: Capitalism and Schizphrenia*, trans. Brian Massumi. Minneapolis, MN: University of Minnesota Press, 1987.

Denzin, Norman K. *Interpretive Ethnography: Interpretive Practices for the 21st Century.* New York: Sage, 1997.

—— "Aesthetics and the Practices of Qualitative Inquiry," *Qualitative Inquiry* 6 (2000): 256–265.

Derrida, Jacques. *Of Grammatology*, trans. Gayatri Chakravorty Spivak. Baltimore, MD: The Johns Hopkins University Press, 1974.

Dewey, John. *The Public and Its Problems.* Athens, OH: Swallow Press, 1927.

Dinnerstein, Dorothy. *The Mermaid and the Minotaur: Sexual Arrangements and Human Malaise.* New York: Harper Collins, 1976.

Dorrian, Mark and Gillian Rose. *Deterritorialisations . . . Revisioning Landscapes and Politics.* New York: Black Dog Publishing, 2003.

Drexler, Jane Monica. "Politics Improper: Iris Marion Young, Hannah Arendt, and the Power of Performativity," *Hypatia* 22 (2007): 1–15.

Duncan, James and David Ley, Eds. *Place/Culture/Representation.* London: Routledge, 1993.

Edelman, Lee. *No Future: Queer Theory and the Death Drive.* Durham, NC: Duke University Press, 2004.

Ellis, Carolyn. *The Ethnographic I. A Methodological Novel about Autoethnography.* Thousand Oaks, CA: AltaMira, 2004.

—— "The Other Side of the Fence: Seeing Black and White in a Small Southern Town," *Qualitative Inquiry* 1 (1995): 147–167.

—— and Art Bochner. "Telling and Performing Personal Stories: The Constraints of Choice in Abortion." *Investigating Subjectivity: Research on Lived Experience*, Eds. Carolyn Ellis and Michael Flaherty. Newbury Park, CA: Sage, 1992. 79–101.

Elliot Eisner. *The Arts and the Creation of Mind.* New Haven, CT: Yale University Press, 2002.

—— and Thomas Barone. "Arts-Based Educational Research," *Complementary Methods for Research in Education*, Ed. Richard M. Jaeger, 2nd ed. Washington, DC: American Educational Research Association, 1997: 73–94.

Finley, Susan. "Painting Life Histories," *Journal of Curriculum Theorizing* 17,2 (2001): 13–26.

—— "Arts-Based Inquiry: Performing Revolutionary Pedagogy," *Handbook of Qualitative Inquiry*, Eds. Norman K. Denzin and Yvonne S. Lincoln, 3rd ed. Thousand Oaks, CA: Sage, 2005: 681–694.

—— and J. Gary Knowles. "Researcher as Artist/Artist as Researcher," *Qualitative Inquiry* 1 (1995): 110–142.

Fradkin, Philip, L. *The Seven States of California: A Natural and Human History.* Berkeley, CA: University of California Press, 1997.

Franklin, Adrian. *Tourism: An Introduction.* London: Sage, 2003.

Foucault, Michel. *Discipline and Punish: The Birth of the Prison*, trans. Alan Sheridan. New York: Vintage Books, 1977.

—— *The History of Sexuality: An Introduction.* London: Penguin Books, 1984.

Gaard, Greta. "Queer by Nature," *Love, West Hollywood: Reflections of Los Angeles.* New York: Alyson Books, 2008.

Gale, Ken and Jonathon Wyatt. "Inquiring into Writing," *Qualitative Inquiry* 13 (2006): 796–797.

Galewski, Elizabeth. "Playing Up Being a Woman: Femme Performance and the Potential for Ironic Representation," *Rhetoric and Public Affairs* 11 (2008): 279–302.

Geist Martin, Patricia, Lisa Gates, Liesbeth Wiering, Erika Kirby, Renee Houston, Anne Lilly, and Juan Moreno. "Exemplifying Collaborative Autoethnographic Practice via Shared Stories of Mothering," *Journal of Research Practice* 6,1 (2012): Article M8. Retrieved March 1, 2010, from http://jrp.icaap.org/index.php/jrp/article/view/209/187.

Geertz, Clifford. *The Interpretation of Cultures.* New York: Basic Books, 1973.

Gingrich-Philbrook, Craig. "Autoethnography's Family Values: Easy Access to Compulsory Experiences," *Text and Performance Quarterly* 25 (2005): 297–314.

Goldberg, Natalie. *Writing Down the Bones.* Boston, MA: Shambhala, 1986.

Gramsci, Antonio. *Selections from Prison Notebooks,* Ed. and trans. Quintin Hoare and Geoffery Smith. New York: International, 1971.

Griffin, Susan. *Woman and Nature: The Roaring Inside Her.* New York: Harper & Row, 1978.

Gumbrecht, Hans Ulrich. *Production of Presence: What Meaning Cannot Convey.* Stanford, CA: University Press, 2004.

Halberstam, Judith. *In a Queer Time and Place.* New York: New York University Press, 2005.

Haraway, Donna J. *Simians, Cyborgs, and Women: The Reinvention of Nature.* London: Free Association Books, 1991.

Haraway, Donna J. *Modest_Witness@Second_Millenium. FemaleMan(c)Meets_Onco Mouse_: Feminism and Technoscience.* New York: Routledge, 1997.

Harrington, Susie. "Responsive Design: Integrating the Spirit of Place with the Vision of Home." *The Art of Natural Building: Design, Construction, Resources,* Eds. Joseph F. Kennedy, Michael G. Smith, and Catherine Wanek. Gabriola Island, BC: New Society Press, 2002.

Harvey, David. *The Limits to Capital.* London: Verso, 1999.

—— "Cosmopolitanism and the Banality of Geographical Evils," *Popular Culture* 12,2 (2000): 529–564.

Hay, R. "Sense of Place in Developmental Context," *Journal of Environmental Psychology* 18 (1998): 5–29.

Hayden, Dolores. *The Power of Place: Urban Landscapes as Public History.* Library of Congress, 1997.

hooks, bell. *belonging: a culture of place.* New York: Routledge, 2009.

Houston, James D. *Californians: Searching for the Golden State.* Santa Cruz, CA: Otter, 1998.

Ingram, David B. and John Protevi. "Political philosophy," *Columbian Companion to Twentieth-Century Philosophies,* Ed. Constantin V. Boundas. New York: Columbia University Press, 2007: 570–589.

Irwin, Rita, L. and Alex de Cosson, Eds. *A/r/tography: Rendering Self through Arts-Based Living Inquiry.* Vancouver, BC: Pacific Educational Press, 2004.

Jacobs, Jane. *The Death and Life of Great American Cities.* New York: Vintage, 1961.

Jagose, Annamarie. *Queer Theory: An Introduction.* New York: New York University Press, 1997.

Jameson, Jenna. *How to Make Love Like a Porn Star: A Cautionary Tale.* New York: It Books, 2004.

Jennings, David. *Skin Flick.* Fairfield, CA: 1st Books, 2000.

Keith, Michael. *After the Cosmopolitan? Multicultural Cities and the Future of Racism.* London: Routledge, 2005.

King, Ynestra. "Healing the Wounds: Feminism, Ecology, and the Nature/Culture Dualism," *Healing the Wounds: The Emergence of Ecofeminism*, Ed. Irene Diamond. San Francisco, CA: Sierra Club Books, 1990.

Kingwell, Mark. *Consciousness and the City*. Toronto, ON: Viking Canada, 2008.

Knopp, Larry. "On the Relationship Between Queer and Feminist Geographies," *The Professional Geographer* 59 (2007): 47–55.

Kristeva, Julia. *Desire in Language: A Semiotic Approach to Literature and Art*, trans. Thomas Gora, Alice Jardine, and Leon S. Roudiez. Oxford: Basil Blackwell, 1982.

Lamott, Anne. *Bird by Bird: Some Instructions on Writing and Life*. New York: Anchor Books, 1994.

Leavy, Patricia. *Method Meets Art: Arts-Based Research Practice*. New York: The Guilford Press, 2009.

Lefebvre, Henri. *The Production of Space*, trans. Donald Nicholson-Smith. Cambridge: Blackwell, 1991.

Leopold, Aldo. *A Sand County Almanac, and Sketches Here and There*. New York: Oxford University Press, 1948.

Lovaas, Karen, John P. Elia, and Gust A. Yep, Eds. *Shifting Ground(s): Surveying the Contested Terrain of LGBT Studies and Queer Theory*. Binghamton, NY: Harrington Park Press, 2006.

Lugones, Maria. *Pilgramages/Peregrinages: Theorizing Coalition Against Multiple Oppressions*. Lanham, MD: Rowan and Littlefield, 2003.

MacCannell, Dean. *The Tourist: A New Theory of the Leisure Class*. Berkeley, CA: University of California Press, 1999.

MacGregor, Sherilyn. *Beyond Mothering Earth: Ecological Citizenship and the Politics of Care*. Vancouver, BC: University of British Columbia Press, 2006.

Martin, Biddy and Chandra Talpade Mohanty. "Feminist Politics: What's Home Got to Do with It?" *Feminist Studies/Critical Studies*, Ed. Teresa de Lauretis. Bloomington, IN: Indiana University Press, 1986.

Marx, Karl. *Capital: Volume One*, trans. Ben Fowkes. London: Penguin, 1990.

Massey, Doreen. *Space, Place and Gender*. Minneapolis, MN: University of Minnesota Press, 1994.

McNeil, Legs and Jennifer Osborne. *The Other Hollywood: The Uncensored Oral History of the Porn Film* Industry. New York: It Books, 2005.

Mellor, Mary. *Breaking the Boundaries: Towards a Feminist Green Socialism*. London: Virago Press, 1992.

Mohanty, Chandra Talpade. *Feminism without Borders: Decolonizing Theory, Practicing Solidarity*. Durham, NC: Duke University Press, 2003.

Mullen, Carol, A. "A Self-Fashioned Gallery of Aesthetic Practice," *Qualitative Inquiry* 9 (2003): 165–181.

Mulvey, Laura. "Visual Pleasure and Narrative Cinema," *Screen* 16.3 (1975): 6–18.

Munoz, Jose Esteban. *Disidentification: Queers of Color and the Performance of Politics*. Minneapolis, MN: University of Minnesota Press, 1999.

Olthuis, James. "Otherwise than Violence: Toward a Hermeneutics of Connection," *The Arts, Community and Cultural Democracy*, Eds. Lambert Zuidervaart and Henry Luttifkhuizen. New York: St. Martin's Press, 2000. 137–164.

Patrick, Tera. *Sinner Takes All: A Memoir of Love and Porn*. New York: Gotham, 2009.

Pelias, Ronald. *Writing Performance: Poeticizing the Researchers Body*. Carbondale, IL: SIUC Press, 1999.

Phelan, Peggy. *Unmarked: The Politics of Performance.* London: Routledge, 1993.

Piantanida, Maria, Patricia L. McMahon, and Noreen B. Garman. "Sculpting the Contours of Arts-Based Educational Research within a Discourse Community," *Qualitative Inquiry* 9 (2003): 182–191.

Pink, Sarah. *Doing Visual Ethnography.* London: Sage, 2001.

Pollini, G. "Elements of a Theory of Place Attachment and Socio-Territorial Belonging," *International Review of Sociology* 15 (2005): 497–515.

Price, Jennifer. "Thirteen Ways of Seeing Nature in LA," *Land of Sun-Shine*, Eds. William Deverell and Greg Hise. Pittsburgh, PA: University of Pittsburg Press, 2005. 224.

Proshansky, H. M., A. K. Fabian, and R. Kaminoff. "Place-identity: Physical World Socialization of the Self," *Journal of Environmental Psychology* 3 (1983): 57–83.

Putnam Tong, Rosemarie. *Feminist Thought: A More Comprehensive Introduction.* Boulder, CO: Westview Press, 1998.

Reed-Danahay, Deborah, Ed. *Auto/Ethnography: Rewriting the Self and the Social.* Oxford: Berg Publishers, 1997.

Richardson, Laurel,. "Writing: A Method of Inquiry," *Handbook of Qualitative Research*, Eds. Norman K. Denzin and Yvonna S. Lincoln, 2nd ed. Thousand Oaks, CA: Sage, 2000. 923–948.

—— "Getting Personal: Writing-Stories," *International Journal of Qualitative Studies in Education* 14,1 (2001): 33–38.

Robinson, John W. *Trails of the Angeles 100 Hikes in the San Gabriels.* Berkeley, CA: Wilderness Press, 1971.

Rodaway, Paul. *Sensuous Geographies; Body, Sense and Place.* London: Routledge. 1994.

Roche, Bonnie. "The Mishkan as Metaphor-form and Anti-form: On the Transformation of Urban Space," *Cross Currents* 52 (2002): 342–352.

Roman, David. *Acts of Intervention: Performance, Gay Culture, and AIDS.* Bloomington, IN: Indiana University Press, 1998.

Ronai, Carol Rambo. "Multiple Reflections of Child Sex Abuse: An Argument for a Layered Account," *Journal of Contemporary Ethnography* 23,4 (1995): 395–436.

Rose, Gillian. *Feminism and Geography: The Limits of Geographical Knowledge.* Minneapolis, MN: University of Minnesota Press, 1993.

Rowe, Aimee Marie Carrilo. "Be Longing: Towards a Feminist Politics of Relation." *Feminist Formations* 17 (2005): 1–46.

Ruddick, Sara. *Maternal Thinking: Toward a Politics of Peace.* New York: Beacon, 1989.

Sallah, Ariel. *Ecofeminism as Politics: Nature, Marx and the Postmodern.* London: Zed Books, 1997.

Sandoval, Chela. *A Methodology of the Oppressed.* Minneapolis, MN: University of Minnesota Press, 2000.

San Fernando Valley Economic Research Center, *Report of Findings on the San Fernando Valley Economy.* California State University Northridge, 2007–2008.

Scott-Hoy, Karen. "Form Carries Experience: A Story of the Art and Form of Knowledge." *Qualitative Inquiry* 9 (2003): 268–280.

Schneekloth, Lynda. "The Frontier is Our Home," *Journal of Architectural Education* 49 (1984): 210–225.

Sedgwick, Eve Kosofsky. *Epistemology of the Closet.* Berkeley, CA: University of California Press, 1990.

Shiva, Vandana. *Earth Democracy: Justice, Sustainability, and Peace.* Boston, MA: South End Press, 2005.

Springgay, Stephanie, Rita L. Irwin, and Sylvia Wilson Kind. "A/r/tography as Living Inquiry through Art and Text," *Qualitative Inquiry* 11 (2005): 897–912.

Spry, Tami. "A 'Performative-I' Copresence: Embodying the Ethnographic Turn in Performance and the Performative Turn in Ethnography," *Text and Performance Quarterly* 26 (2006): 711.

Solomon, Steven. *Water: The Epic Struggle for Wealth, Power, and Civilization.* New York: Harper Collins, 2010.

Szerszynski, Bronislaw, Wallance Heim, and Claire Waterton, Eds. *Nature Performed: Environment, Culture and Performance.* Oxford: Blackwell, 2003.

Taussig, Michael. *Mimesis and Alterity: A Particular History of the Senses.* New York: Routledge, 1993.

Tuan, Yi-Fu. *Topophilia: A Study of Environment, Perceptions, Attitudes, and Values.* New York: Columbia University Press, 1974.

—— *Space and Place: The Perspective of Experience.* Minneapolis, MN: University of Minnesota Press, 1977.

Turner, William. *A Genealogy of Queer Theory.* Philadelphia, PA: Temple University Press, 2000.

Turner, Victor. *From Ritual to Theater: The Human Seriousness of Play.* New York: Performing Arts Journal Publications, 1982.

Urry, John. (2002) *The Tourist Gaze*, 2nd ed. London: Sage.

US Census Bureau, *Population Estimates.* Retrieved July 2008, from www.census.gov/popest/counties/CO-EST2009–01.html.

US Department of Housing and Urban Development, *City of Los Angeles Five-Year Consolidated Plan (Program Years 2008–2013).* Retrieved March 2010, from http://cdd.lacity.org/pdfs/conplan0813/2008_ReportGeneral.pdf.

Waldie, D. J. *Holy Land: A Suburban Memoir.* New York: St. Martin's Press, 1996.

Warren, Karen J. "Feminism and Ecology: Making Connections," *Readings in Ecology and Feminist Theology*, Eds. Mary Heather Mackinnon and Marie McIntyre. Kansas City, KS: Sheed and Ward, 1995. 105–123.

Watrin, Rhonda. "Art as Research," *Canadian Review of Art Education* 26 (1999): 92–100.

Wolcott, Harry. "The Ethnographic Autobiography," *Auto/Biography* 12 (2004): 93–106.

Young, Iris Marion. "The Ideal of Community and the Politics of Difference," *Feminism/Postmodernism*, Ed. Linda J. Nicholson. New York: Routledge, 1990. 300–323.

INDEX